"PERVERSE MIND"

"PERVERSE MIND"

Eugene O'Neill's
Struggle with Closure

Barbara Voglino

Madison • Teaneck
Fairleigh Dickinson University Press
London: Associated University Presses

Associated University Presses
440 Forsgate Drive
Cranbury, NJ 08512

Associated University Presses
16 Barter Street
London WC1A 2AH, England

Associated University Presses
P.O. Box 338, Port Credit
Mississauga, Ontario
Canada L5G 4L8

The paper used in this publication meets the requirements of the American National Standard for Permanence of Paper for Printed Library Materials Z39.48-1984.

Library of Congress Cataloging-in-Publication Data

Voglino, Barbara, 1940–
    Perverse mind : Eugene O'Neill's struggle with closure / Barbara Voglino.
        p.   cm.
    Includes bibliographical references and index.
    ISBN 0-8386-3833-3 (alk. paper)
    1. O'Neill, Eugene, 1888–1953—Criticism and interpretation.
    2. American drama—Psychological aspects. 3. Closure (Rhetoric)
    I. Title.
    PS3529.N5Z886   1999
    812'.52—dc21   99-26439
                                                                       CIP

PRINTED IN THE UNITED STATES OF AMERICA

I dedicate this book to James T. Voglino,
my husband of thirty-five years,
who after patiently tolerating O'Neill
as his rival for three years
is finally "gittin' the end o' b'arin' it!"
([Eben] *Desire under the Elms* 3.1.363)

Contents

Preface

"The time has come," the Walrus said,
  "To talk of many things:
Of shoes—and ships—and sealing-wax—
  Of cabbages—and kings— "
                    —*Through the Looking-Glass*

"To approach fiction by way of closure is not . . . at all narrow," Marianna Torgovnick observes in her study of novelistic closure.[1] In drama, also, the examination of closure extends to such wide-ranging subjects as structural patterns, which include peripeteia and circularity; thematic implications and ideas; verbal and gestural devices; character analyses; and even relevant extratextual material concerning the author and his culture.

Because of the scope involved in studying closure, even when concentrated on selected plays from the three-volume output of Eugene O'Neill (which includes fifty plays of varying lengths), I shall attempt to define my subject further in several ways. First, I will be dealing—with the exception of occasional references to the formidable fragment, *More Stately Mansions*—primarily with the completed plays, as they appear in the 1988 three-volume, Library of America edition[2] (which includes *Mansions* ["the unexpurgated edition"]). My study therefore excludes most of the unrealized plays of O'Neill's projected "A Tale of Possessors Self-Dispossessed" cycle, and, for the most part, the various drafts that exist for some plays (eight for *Days without End,* according to Travis Bogard, and five versions of Hickey's exit in *The Iceman Cometh,* according to Judith E. Barlow).[3] Rather I shall attempt to focus upon what O'Neill himself wished to present as finished work. Second, since it is neither necessary nor feasible to examine all fifty plays in order to perceive O'Neill's gradual evolution toward effective closure, I shall be concentrating on nine plays selected for their relevance to closure rather than for their overall quality. Thus I devote a chapter to two of O'Neill's less commendable efforts, *Dynamo* and *Days without End*, while omitting, for example, the far finer *Ah, Wilderness!* and *A Touch of the Poet.* I have also tried to include plays from approximately each decade of O'Neill's

9

thirty-year career as a dramatist (1913–43). While I have not deemed it worthwhile to devote more than brief references to his apprentice work (in which category I include most of his work before *Beyond the Horizon*, although the earlier *Glencairn* plays merit more attention than some of his later plays), I shall be examining three of the more important plays from his early period (*Beyond the Horizon* [1918], *"Anna Christie"* [1920], and *Desire under the Elms* [1924]), three plays from what may be considered his mid period (*Dynamo* [1928], *Mourning Becomes Electra* [1931], and *Days without End* [1933]), and three plays from his late period of undisputed greatness (*The Iceman Cometh* [1940], *Long Day's Journey into Night* [1941], and *A Moon for the Misbegotten* [1943]). Since the late plays offer the finest examples of effective closure, my emphasis will necessarily lie there. A third limitation of my work is that I do not plan to examine closure in scene and act endings per se, but only as they may appear relevant to the definitive closure of the play. Finally, interpretive directorial decisions that may affect closure in individual productions are, except for occasional mention, also beyond my scope. In this study I shall be dealing with closure mainly as it is implied by O'Neill's text.

A few words about my methods seem in order. Analyses of the various plays are presented, for the most part, chronologically, since my subject is the evolution of O'Neill's closure from the early plays to his later dramas. The exception is *Days without End* (1933), which I treat in the same chapter as *Dynamo* (1928), and before *Mourning Becomes Electra* (1931), since O'Neill intended *Dynamo* and *Days without End* to be part of the same trilogy. My textual citations to the plays are designed to enable readers to locate cited passages more easily in different editions of O'Neill's work; they designate act, scene (if applicable), and page numbers. Thus "2.1.317" means "act 2, scene 1, page 317." Also, since dramatic closure, by most contemporary definitions, is a process involving audience or reader participation, I shall be referring frequently to the "viewer" or "reader" in order to assess the potential effect of a particular closure or closural technique upon its recipient.

Acknowledgments

As the seminal inspiration for this project I must credit the profoundly moving presentation of Eugene O'Neill's play *A Moon for the Misbegotten* at the Morosco Theater, New York, in 1974. I believe it was this remarkable performance starring Jason Robards and Colleen Dewhurst that stimulated the avid interest in O'Neill and the structure of drama that I have pursued since that date.

With regard to the outcome of that pursuit, *"Perverse Mind": Eugene O'Neill's Struggle with Closure*, I welcome this opportunity to express my warm personal thanks to Dr. John V. Antush of Fordham University (Rose Hill Campus) for his insightful guidance in the initial development of this work, the earlier version of which was copyrighted by the UMI Company of Ann Arbor, Michigan, as *The Evolution of Closure in the Plays of Eugene O'Neill* by Barbara Voglino in 1998. I also extend my gratitude to John Connell, former head of the Reference Department at the Fordham University Library (Rose Hill Campus), and to the rest of the Reference staff for their untiring assistance to me in my research efforts. Sincere thanks as well to Dr. Margaret Loftus Ranald (Emeritus, Queens College) for the meticulous direction which enabled me to complete this study in its present form, and to Christine Retz, managing editor of Associated University Presses, for her patient technical assistance.

This book might not have been possible without the existence of certain key works: the *Selected Letters of Eugene O'Neill,* edited by Travis Bogard and Jackson R. Bryer; the excellent biographies of the late Louis Sheaffer *(Eugene O'Neill: Son and Playwright* and *Eugene O'Neill: Son and Artist);* Arthur and Barbara Gelb's *O'Neill;* and the useful compilation of production reviews of O'Neill's plays by Jordan Y. Miller *(Eugene O'Neill and the American Critic: A Biographical Checklist),* to name just a few.[1] To the authors or editors of these works, as well as to those responsible for the other critical studies on O'Neill and examinations of closure that I cite, I am deeply indebted.

Copyright holders of O'Neill's work have been most kind in granting me permission to quote from his material. I would like to extend my gratitude to the following:

11

The Berg Collection of English and American Literature, The New York Public Library, Astor, Lenox and Tilden Foundations, for permission to use quotations from Eugene O'Neill's letters to Beatrice Ashe (1914–16).

The Eugene O'Neill Review for permission to use material from Barbara Voglino's article "'Games' the Tyrones Play" (Spring 1992 issue).

Yale University Press for permission to use the quotations from *Long Day's Journey into Night* by Eugene O'Neill (Copyright © 1956 and renewed 1984) published by Yale University Press and reprinted by permission of Yale University Press, and for permission to use the quotation from *More Stately Mansions* by Eugene O'Neill (Copyright © 1988), published by Yale University Press and republished in its unexpurgated form by permission of Yale University Press.

The General Counsel's Office at Yale University for permission to use the quotations from Eugene O'Neill's plays *Long Day's Journey into Night, A Moon for the Misbegotten, The Iceman Cometh,* and from Eugene O'Neill's letters.

PAC Holding S.A. and the Trust u/w/o Shane O'Neill for permission to use the quotations from Eugene O'Neill's plays *Long Day's Journey into Night, A Moon for the Misbegotten, Dynamo, Days without End, Mourning Becomes Electra,* and *The Iceman Cometh* in the United States.

Random House (UK), Ltd., for permission to use extracts from *The Collected Plays of Eugene O'Neill* (including extracts from *Beyond the Horizon, "Anna Christie," Desire under the Elms, Dynamo, Days without End, Mourning Becomes Electra, The Iceman Cometh, Welded, More Stately Mansions, Long Day's Journey into Night,* and *A Moon for the Misbegotten*) by Eugene O'Neill and published by Jonathan Cape throughout the British Commonwealth excluding Canada.

Random House, Inc. (New York)/Alfred A. Knopf, Inc., for permission to use quotations from *Selected Plays of Eugene O'Neill* by Eugene O'Neill, published by Random House, Inc., and reprinted by permission of Random House, Inc., in the U.S. (where applicable), Canada, and the open market in the English language, including quotations from the following plays:

Beyond the Horizon (Copyright © 1920 and renewed 1948 by Eugene O'Neill),
"Anna Christie" (Copyright © 1922 and renewed 1950 by Eugene O'Neill),
Desire under the Elms (Copyright © 1924 and renewed 1952 by Eugene O'Neill),
Mourning Becomes Electra (Copyright © 1931 by Eugene O'Neill and renewed 1959 by
    Carlotta Monterey O'Neill),
The Iceman Cometh (Copyright © 1946 by Eugene O'Neill and renewed 1974 by Carlotta
    Monterey O'Neill),
Days without End (Copyright © 1934 and renewed in 1961),
Dynamo (Copyright © 1929 and renewed 1957), and
Welded (Copyright © 1923 and renewed 1950).

Random House, Inc. (New York)/Alfred A, Knopf, Inc., for permission to use the quotations from *A Moon for the Misbegotten* by Eugene O'Neill (© 1952 by Eugene O'Neill and renewed 1980 by Oona O'Neill Chaplin and Shane O'Neill), published in *The Later Plays of Eugene O'Neill* by Eugene O'Neill and reprinted by permission of Random House, Inc., in the U. S., Canada, and the open market in the English language.

"PERVERSE MIND"

1

O'Neill's Quest
for Closure

Eugene O'Neill (1888–1953) was aware of his inordinate difficulty with endings from his earliest attempts to write plays. With regard to one of his first efforts as a student in George Pierce Baker's playwriting course at Harvard, he wrote Beatrice Ashe in 1915:

> I have the first draft of the scenario for the first three acts completed but am now in a quandary as to how I shall end the daw-gun thing. I have *one ending which delights my soul* but—you know me. . . . *I do want to strive and give it a reasonably contented ending but my perverse mind doesn't seem to want to let me.* [Emphasis added][1]

Although closure has always been problematic for playwrights (Henry J. Schmidt describes endings as "the most often revised component of any play"),[2] O'Neill seems to have recognized his own difficulty with endings to be compounded by a "perverse mind" that wrestled with and often subdued his better artistic judgment. Although the American of Irish descent was eventually to rank among the world's finest dramatists with such plays as *The Iceman Cometh* (1941), *Long Day's Journey into Night* (1942), and *A Moon for the Misbegotten* (1943), the amateurish stabs at closure that characterize most of his novice work have been justly denounced as "unsatisfying."[3] One reason the early endings fail is their almost ubiquitous reliance upon violence. As might be expected of a young writer whose imagination had been nurtured on countless renditions of *The Count of Monte Cristo* (by his actor/father) and ten viewings of Alla Nazimova as Ibsen's Hedda Gabler,[4] an inordinate number of O'Neill's early works culminate in suicide (*Warnings* [1913], *Abortion* [1914]), insanity (*Ile* [1917], *Where the Cross Is Made* [1918]), murder (*The Web* [1913], *Thirst* [1913]), and imminent death from consumption

15

(*The Web* [1913], *Beyond the Horizon* [1918], and *The Straw* [1919]). As Barrett H. Clark noted in 1929, through overuse the violence loses its tragic impact and becomes an all too obvious way of bringing a plot to a stop.[5]

Another reason O'Neill's early play endings have often failed to satisfy viewers is his overexplicitness. The Austrian writer/critic Hugo von Hofmannsthal commented on two of O'Neill's most successful plays to date (1923), *The Emperor Jones* (1920) and *The Hairy Ape* (1921), as being "too direct, too simple, too expected." Hofmannsthal added, "[I]t is a little disappointing to a European with his complex background, to see the arrow strike the target towards which he has watched it speeding all the while."[6] The sophisticated viewer or reader, accustomed to the interminable complexity and unpredictability of—let us say—Henry James, may be bored by the directness and predictability of O'Neill's early plays.[7]

Overexplicit in a different direction—in the sense of being overstated to the point of ludicrousness—are the gushing, melodramatic conclusions that characterize many of the plays of O'Neill's later early period and mid period. In a series of "religious" plays (*The Fountain* [1922], *Welded* [1923], *Lazarus Laughed* [1926], and *Days without End* [1933]), he attempts to dramatize mystical insights and affirmations through what he hailed in "Memoranda on Masks" (1932) as the temple of the theater.[8] The conclusion of *Welded* exemplifies the overwhelming effect of these closures. In the final moments the overpossessive husband, reunited with his wife in a crucifixional embrace (*"they form together one cross"* [3.276]), declares passionately: "I feel like crying out to God for mercy because life lives . . . with you I become a whole, a truth! Life guides me back through the million hundred years to you. It reveals a beginning in unity that I may have faith in the unity of the end!" (3.275–76).[9] Gustav H. Blanke comments on this ending:

> Such a crude affirmation at the end of this unconvincing work arouses the suspicion that it is not the result of experience and personal struggle and searching, but rather the seizing upon illusion of one who is in doubt.[10]

Blanke's insightful comment suggests that O'Neill may have been trying to convince himself with excessive affirmation and exclamation points of what he was, in fact, unable to believe.

If O'Neill's insistence upon strong, affirmative closure during what Edwin A. Engel calls the playwright's "yea-saying" period of the 1920s,[11] and in *Days without End* (1933), was intended to alleviate the personal anxieties that appear reflected in the above plays, he seems to have failed. In *Welded* (1923), a fictionalized account of his own marital difficulties with the independent Agnes Boulton,[12] O'Neill attempts to justify—very likely to

Agnes as well as to himself—his extraordinarily possessive demands on her life by attributing a mystical, religious value to marriage. Unlike Eleanor Cape, the wife in *Welded*, however, Agnes continued to insist upon her individuality. In 1926 O'Neill renewed his acquaintance with Carlotta Monterey, a woman who would be able, to a large extent, to merge her identity with his. In 1929 he divorced Agnes and married Carlotta.

Another attempt to alleviate anxiety on O'Neill's part appears discernible in *Lazarus Laughed* (1926). The title character's bold speeches about the nonexistence of death, in the face of which he laughs, suggest an effort to dispel the specter of death that haunted O'Neill's life as well as his plays. In the past six years his father, mother, and only brother had died in quick succession (in 1920, 1922, and 1923, respectively). Even after *Lazarus Laughed*, however, death remained a prominent subject in O'Neill's plays (*Strange Interlude, Dynamo, Mourning Becomes Electra, Days without End, The Iceman Cometh, A Moon for the Misbegotten*), although his conception of death gradually mellowed, in the later plays, into the less terrible, more to be wished-for release from suffering.

A third dramatic effort that has often been construed as an attempt to alleviate personal anxiety on O'Neill's part—this time regarding his lack of religious belief—is represented by the conclusion of *Days without End* (1933).[13] John Loving, a former Catholic long bereft of belief (like O'Neill), experiences a "leap of faith" and returns to the Church at the end of the play. The play finishes with a series of ecstatic affirmations resembling those of *Welded* and *Lazarus Laughed:* "Love lives forever! Death is dead! . . . Life laughs with God's love again! Life laughs with love!" (4.2.180). When Sophus Keith Winther asked O'Neill if this ending meant he had returned to Catholicism, the playwright's response suggests he may have been indulging in wishful thinking: "I haven't. But I would be a liar if I didn't admit that, for the sake of my soul's peace, I have often wished I could."[14]

If the affirmative closures of the above plays may be interpreted as an effort on O'Neill's part to procure his "soul's peace" (or personal closure), his creative action reflects what Joseph Conrad described as a deeply felt human need: "the desire for finality, for which our hearts yearn with a longing greater than the longing for the loaves and fishes of this earth." Closure, says Murray Krieger, is "an aesthetic need felt by the human imagination." People need fictional patterns with beginnings and endings, asserts Frank Kermode in his classic work, *The Sense of an Ending* (1966), to give meaning and coherence to their lives.[15]

O'Neill's quest for closure actually began long before he wrote his first play. His lifelong search for reassurance from his anxieties appears directly traceable to his mother's morphine addiction.[16] As a young child he suffered from her frequent remoteness and practice of going off alone to indulge her habit.[17] Like her literary counterpart, Mary Tyrone in *Long Day's Journey into Night* (1941), Ella O'Neill's interest in her family must have varied in accordance with the amount of morphine she had taken. At times she must have been unaware of young Eugene's presence.[18]

The sudden discovery of the reason his mother had failed to fulfill his needs did not make his emotional devastation any easier to bear.[19] Many years later, in Simon Harford's accusation of his mother (*More Stately Mansions* [1939]), O'Neill would still describe the shocked anguish of that traumatic moment with passionate immediacy:

> I have never forgotten the anguished sense of being suddenly betrayed, of being wounded and deserted and left alone in a life in which there was no security or faith or love but only danger and suspicion and devouring greed! . . . By God, I hated you then! I wished you dead! I wished I had never been born! (4.2.534 [unexpurgated edition])

Following his shattering "enlightenment," O'Neill, who had already begun questioning his religious upbringing as a result of the inefficacy of his prayers to ameliorate his mother's erratic behavior,[20] proceeded to renounce Catholicism for the rest of his life. In the next few years he also began drinking, gradually developing an alcohol dependency as his older brother, Jamie, had done. Also like Jamie, he became increasingly estranged from his father, whom both sons blamed for their mother's addiction.

Although Ella O'Neill finally recovered from her morphine addiction before her death in 1922,[21] it is evident that O'Neill was still seeking some sort of closure with her memory when he wrote *Long Day's Journey into Night* in 1941. Throughout his career O'Neill had created one fictional autobiographical hero after another who longed for a detached or absent mother: Eben Cabot, Reuben Light, Orin Mannon, John Loving, Simon Harford, and Edmund and Jamie Tyrone—and this is not a complete list. In *More Stately Mansions* (1939), which O'Neill never completed and had intended to destroy, he devised a metaphor for his bereft condition in the fairy tale Simon recalls his mother telling him in his childhood. A young king, dispossessed of his kingdom by a beautiful enchantress, spends his life searching for a certain magic door that, the enchantress has indicated, can lead him back to his lost kingdom. When he finally discovers the door, however, the enchantress intimates she might be deceiving him—that the door might not, in fact, lead to his kingdom but to a worse situation than his present condition of exclusion. Succumbing to fear, the young king, unable to open the door, remains by it until he dies. The harsh ending to this tale had deeply disturbed young Simon, who strongly identified with the exiled king. He, too, had been condemned by his enchantress/mother to wait outside a door—the entrance to the summerhouse that his mother frequented and from which he was excluded. Simon had always begged his mother to provide a happier conclusion to the tale. Now grown to manhood, Simon, in the play's action, tries to improve the ending himself, at least with regard to his own parallel situation of exclusion. He insists to his mother, who has long avoided the summerhouse for fear of madness, that they open the door and enter together. Despite Simon's passionate plea to at last enjoy the security of greater intimacy with his mother, however, the play concludes with Deborah pushing him away and entering the summerhouse alone. Simon, who suffers a concussion as a result of his mother's violent physical rejection, is reduced to a state of childlike dependency upon his wife that lasts many months.

Like Simon Harford, Edmund Tyrone, the fictional counterpart of Eugene O'Neill in the more overtly autobiographical *Long Day's Journey into Night*, is a dispossessed young king waiting for his enchantress/mother to grant him the peace and security she stole from him in his childhood.[22] Like Simon, who implores his mother not to shut the door on him again, but instead allow him to reclaim her love, Edmund begs his mother to quit injecting the morphine that causes her to mentally "shut out" the Tyrone family. The concluding action of the two plays is startlingly similar. In the unfinished *More Stately Mansions* Simon grabs hold of his mother, who, pushing him aside, enters the summerhouse alone to her fantasy world of eighteenth-century romance. In the final scene of *Long Day's Journey into Night*, Edmund, like Simon, grabs hold of his mother, who brushes him aside to deliberately immerse herself in the illusory past induced by her drug. In both plays the rejected sons are unable to follow their fleeing mothers. Simon is reduced to a childlike state as a result, and confuses his wife, Sara, with his mother. Although Edmund's future is not known, his real-life counterpart (O'Neill) required that at least one of his wife Carlotta's many roles in his life be that of a mother.

Like his fictional counterparts Simon and Edmund, O'Neill tried many "doors" before finding his true "kingdom" in the creation of drama. He tried the adventurous life of a gold prospector, but he contracted malaria in Honduras (1910). He tried the life of a seaman (1909–11) and experienced the mystical sense of "belonging" described by Edmund in *Long Day's Journey into Night* (4.811–12); the inadequate sailor's diet caused permanent damage to his teeth. He indulged in prolonged alcoholic binges, escaping reality through "pipe dreams" like the denizens of Harry Hope's saloon, whom he later described in *The Iceman Cometh* (1940). In 1912 he tried the ultimate

closure at Jimmy the Priest's waterfront saloon: he was saved from a deliberate overdose of Veronal by his friends. Like John Loving in *Days without
End* (1933), he sought various psychological and philosophical substitutes
(such as Nietzsche and Freud) for the religion he had abandoned as a youth.
He tried sex—he had a number of female acquaintances, some of whom
were mistresses, and three wives. He tried money—buying or building luxu-
rious estates such as Brook Farm, Spithead, Casa Genotta, and Tao House
with the proceeds from his plays. None of the above seems to have brought
him the satisfaction he craved. He moved from philosophy to philosophy,
woman to woman, house to house—but his anxieties remained.

   "A work of art is always happy," he wrote in 1921; "all else is unhappy."[23]
Upon determining to seek the satisfaction in writing plays that he lacked in
his life, O'Neill finally found a powerful focus for his existence. To accomplish his goal to create drama, he was able to overcome tuberculosis, control his alcoholism,[24] and sublimate his grief over family tragedies. He worked
at a feverish pace—for long hours, sometimes on several plays at a time. He
revised furiously, destroying what he felt unworthy of him and what he was
unable to complete. Thus, owing to increasing illness, he burned or otherwise destroyed most of the work of nearly two decades of his maturity. All
that remains of his projected eleven-play cycle, *A Tale of Possessors Self-Dispossessed,* is one completed play, *A Touch of the Poet* (1939), and two unfinished
works that have survived only by accident: a draft of *More Stately Mansions*
(1939) and a detailed scenario (which includes extensive dialogue) for *The
Calms of Capricorn.*[25]

   Far from providing the relief from anxiety he sought, his work was often a source of torment to him. Despite the conviction that usually sustained him through the completion of a play that his current project was
the "best thing" he had ever done,[26] in 1925 he confessed to a doctor, who
was treating him for alcoholism, that he would become "greatly depressed
after finishing a play because it never turned out to be what he really
wanted."[27] His admitted frustration with the outcome of his plays helps to
explain the alcoholic binges he often indulged in between plays.[28]

   Nevertheless, O'Neill's frustration as an artist appears to have been
almost deliberately self-imposed given the monumental goals he set for himself. What writer, seeking personal and/or commercial success, would attempt such dramatic anomalies as the nearly unproducible *Lazarus Laughed*
(1926) with its huge cast, the "Greek" trilogy *Mourning Becomes Electra* (1931),
another group of three plays seeking to resolve the contemporary spiritual
dilemma (*Myths for the God-forsaken* [uncompleted]), a nine-act play (*Strange
Interlude* [1927]), an eleven-play cycle about the greed of an American
family (*A Tale of Possessors Self-Dispossessed* [uncompleted]), and the lengthy,

repetitious masterpiece *The Iceman Cometh* (1940)? These wide-ranging efforts, which Robert Brustein imputes to O'Neill's "monstrous" ambition,[29] might more accurately be attributed to his romanticization of the unattainable. In 1922 O'Neill told an interviewer:

> Achievement, in the narrow sense of possession, is a stale finale. The dreams that can be completely realized are not worth dreaming. . . . Man wills his own defeat when he pursues the unattainable. But his *struggle* is his success! He is an example of the spiritual significance which life attains when it aims high enough. . . .[30]

O'Neill's emphasis was on effort ("the struggle") rather than completion ("achievement"). Thus, through his efforts to reach extraordinary dramatic goals, he became the struggling hero of his own plot. In O'Neill's view the true champion accepts the challenge of life with all its uncertainties and fights "on to Hercules" (*Days without End* 3.2.158), a goal he sets for himself that can never be reached. Such heroes are rare, however, even in O'Neill's plays. Possibly only Sara Melody Harford (*A Touch of the Poet* [1939] and *More Stately Mansions* [1939]), Edmund Tyrone (*Long Day's Journey into Night* [1941]), and Josie Hogan (*A Moon for the Misbegotten* [1943]) may qualify.

As the preceding examples suggest, O'Neill's romanticization of the unattainable can be strongly linked with the closure of his late plays. As C. W. E. Bigsby has observed, O'Neill's vision of man's glory as lying in the active pursuit of unattainable goals is "a vision which commit[s] the individual to an unending struggle" and logically results in plays that end without any real sense of completion.[31] Throughout O'Neill's career, his plays tend to become increasingly "open" (in the contemporary sense of ambiguous or lacking conclusiveness).[32] The plays of O'Neill's late period of greatness (*A Touch of the Poet, The Iceman Cometh, Long Day's Journey into Night, A Moon for the Misbegotten*) all conclude with marked openness. *A Touch of the Poet* ends with Sara Melody mourning her father's self-divestiture of the very aristocratic pretensions against which she has protested, and preparing to enter a problematic marriage with a man of a higher class. *Long Day's Journey into Night* ends with the Tyrone men drinking to escape the reality of Mary's drug addiction, which appears endless. In *A Moon for the Misbegotten* Jim Tyrone can attain neither a rebirth of joy through Josie's love nor peace from his misery through death. He walks away from the Hogan cottage as he entered it.

A Moon for the Misbegotten (1943) illustrates another aspect of O'Neill's philosophy that contributes to openness in his plays—his belief in eternal recurrence or the circularity of life. Consistent with his admiration for the

German dramatist Gerhart Hauptmann, who maintained, "True drama is basically endless. It is an eternal struggle without result,"[33] O'Neill wrote in 1921, "Life doesn't end. One experience is but the birth of another."[34] Many of O'Neill's dramas seem to illustrate this assertion by "ending" where they began, or completing a circular pattern established early in the play. For example, in *The Emperor Jones* (1920) Brutus Jones enters the Great Forest shortly after the play opens only to emerge from the same point at the end. In *"Anna Christie"* (1920) Anna arrives alone as the play opens and is left alone at the end: her two men ship out on the sea that has claimed many of her ancestors' lives. *All God's Chillun Got Wings* (1923) begins and ends with Ella and Jim playing as children. *The Great God Brown* (1925) begins and ends with families on a pier on a June night. In *Long Day's Journey into Night* (1941) Mary Tyrone, having recently been "cured" of her drug addiction, regresses throughout the "long day" of the play to her former addicted state and immersion in her past. In *Hughie* (1942) Erie Smith reestablishes the relationship with Charles Hughes, the new night clerk of his hotel, that he previously enjoyed with Hughes' deceased predecessor of the same name. In many of the above plays (*Moon, "Anna Christie," All God's Chillun, The Great God Brown,* and *Hughie*) the result of concluding with an apparent return to the beginning is that completion seems indefinitely postponed.[35] The repetition suggests rather a perpetual beginning.

Despite O'Neill's philosophical commitment to circularity and the unending struggle, however, in most of his early and mid-period works, before he has more highly synchronized his technique with his thought, O'Neill seems to attempt closure in the traditional manner of fulfilling the expectation of completeness for his viewer or reader. O'Neill appears to have been torn by the artist's dilemma more recently described by David H. Richter as how to "bring a work to a satisfying conclusion without being false to the boundless nature of human life."[36] Should he, as Henry James advised,[37] commit himself to the job of creating an apparent end (as in many of the early and mid-period plays); or should he conclude his works in the open manner (later adopted by the modernists), which seems more consistent with his professed belief that plays, like life, do not end?

O'Neill seems to have attempted to do both. Possibly in response to the pressure to complete the work satisfactorily without being false, and perhaps also in response to the criticism of overexplicitness, O'Neill's best earlier works end ambiguously, thus inviting the collaboration of the spectator in creating the closure of his choice.[38] As Mary Kay Zettl Myers observes of the more open play endings that have become popular since the modernist breakthrough, the perceptions of the audience become "constitutive as well as interpretive."[39]

O'Neill, like many of the playwrights who were to succeed him, appears to have become increasingly dubious regarding traditional closure as he continued to write. June Schlueter's account of the general metamorphosis of play endings in the twentieth century seems, in fact, to describe O'Neill's thirty-year career:

> [T]he organic end, designed to conclude through resolution, surrenders to the indeterminate or provisional end. A shot in the head [O'Neill's early plays, *Abortion* and *Bread and Butter*] and death by consumption [O'Neill's early plays, *The Web*, *The Straw*, and *Beyond the Horizon*], the predictable *deus ex machina* of the early modern stage, yield to the "perhaps" of Beckett's *Endgame* [O'Neill's late plays, *Long Day's Journey into Night*, *A Moon for the Misbegotten*, and *Hughie*].[40]

Already in response to the critically attacked ending of *"Anna Christie"* (1920), perceived by many audiences as "happy" and condemned by reviewers as a compromise to popular tastes,[41] O'Neill had countered that the play had no ending,[42] but was "merely the comma at the end of a gaudy introductory clause with the body of the sentence still unwritten."[43] Nevertheless, with the exception of *"Anna Christie,"* which ends with uncertainty, he continued to provide fairly traditional closure, although often ambiguous, in his plays up until his late period of greatness.

At least one explanation for the incontrovertible excellence of O'Neill's late plays, which far surpass anything he had previously written, is the greatly improved endings, which, in contrast to the artificially imposed endings of his earlier plays, seem to grow naturally out of the plot and characters. Another important factor contributing to the greatness of the late plays is his choice of subject: he was writing about people he knew. Like the dispossessed young king in Simon Harford's tale *(More Stately Mansions)*, O'Neill finally found the true door to his kingdom as a dramatist in the painful exploration of his own past. Long fearing to open the door fully, O'Neill had actually been writing in various guises about his family all his life. Paradoxically, it was only behind three closed doors, with practically all light excluded (Tao House, California; 1938–44), that O'Neill was at last able to tear open that long-guarded portal and allow his genius to emerge. It is to be hoped that the brilliant result *(The Iceman Cometh, Long Day's Journey into Night, Hughie,* and *A Moon for the Misbegotten)* brought him the personal and artistic satisfaction he had long craved. In his inscription of *Long Day's Journey into Night*, deemed by many his masterpiece, to his third wife, Carlotta, he professed to have attained personal closure at last by facing his dead *"with deep pity and understanding and forgiveness for all the four haunted Tyrones."*

"A work of art is always happy," O'Neill had written in 1921; "all else is unhappy." The Tyrones may not be "happy" in *Long Day's Journey into Night*, but the "work of art" in which O'Neill has forever embodied them certainly is. In the following chapters I shall be examining the intense struggle that preceded the creation of such "happy" (in O'Neill's sense of "artistically superior") "work[s] of art" as *The Iceman Cometh, Long Day's Journey into Night*, and *A Moon or the Misbegotten* during O'Neill's late period of undisputed greatness. More specifically, I shall be describing the evolution of O'Neill's facility with closure over his thirty-year career as a dramatist.

2

Unsettling Ambiguity in
Beyond the Horizon

Beyond the Horizon, completed in 1918, was O'Neill's first full-length drama to be produced (1920) and his first play to be awarded the Pulitzer Prize. Despite contemporary praise for its powerful realism,[1] early reviewers voiced an awareness that the play was flawed. Some objected to its graphic depiction of tuberculosis;[2] others, to what they considered its excessive length. Predictability and overexplicitness were two of the more significant faults pointed out.[3] Early reviewers Alexander Woollcott and Heywood Broun targeted the final scene for its illusion-dispelling effect. Broun attributed the break in the impact of the drama to the lowering of the curtain before the very short final scene, which he argued "compels a wait at a time when tension is seriously impaired."[4] Although Broun's explanation seems feasible enough regarding the reaction of an audience attending a staged production, the wait for a scene change does not account for the similar discomfort experienced by readers. The illusion-dispelling quality noted by Woollcott and Broun seems more likely attributable to the sudden change in tone, matter, and the demand placed upon the audience by the final scene, which raises questions when the audience has been prepared to expect a conclusion. More recent criticism of the play's closure has focused on its ambiguity.

Up until the last scene, however, *Beyond the Horizon*, an explicitly presented, highly predictable drama, is more remarkable for its lack of ambiguity. The play is composed of three acts, each divided into two scenes. Audience expectations regarding closure are set up in the first act. Two brothers, very different in character, exchange destinies. Young Robert Mayo, upon learning that his friend Ruth loves him, renounces his chance to fulfill his lifelong dream of exploring "beyond the horizon" on his uncle's ship. Instead of sailing around the world as he had intended, he remains home to

marry and work the family farm, a job for which he is physically and emotionally unsuited. His brother, Andrew, who loves farmwork and had intended to marry Ruth, good-naturedly takes Robert's place on the three-
year voyage. Before the end of act 1 James Mayo, the father, announces the
theme of the play. He warns Andrew, "You're runnin' against your own
nature, and you're goin' to be a'mighty sorry for it if you do" (1.2.596).

For the next three scenes, the drama rather laboriously depicts the progressive fulfillment of the father's dire prediction—intended for Andrew—
with regard to both brothers. Robert, upon whose plight the play focuses,
has betrayed his poet's awareness of a higher reality by surrendering to his
biological attraction to Ruth. His initial moment of decision results in seem-
ingly endless suffering in the form of poverty, marital unhappiness, and a
recurrence of the tuberculosis that causes his death. By the end of the play
his character has deteriorated as well: he has become jealous and vengeful.
Andrew's punishment for not remaining on the Mayo farm is more subtle.
After the voyage with his uncle he undertakes a huge farming venture in
Argentina and accumulates a large fortune, which he proceeds to lose
through unwise speculation. As might be expected to result from his risk-
fraught lifestyle, his eyes develop a look of *"ruthless cunning"*(3.1.639), and he
becomes inclined to distrust people. Upon returning to the Mayo farm five
years later, he discovers himself bereft of family as well as financial security.
His parents having already died, and his sole sibling dying, Andrew is left
with only his sister-in-law, Ruth, whom the dying Robert has requested he
marry, and whom Andrew has grown to despise.

Thus far the plot has proceeded rather steadily toward its predictable
end, like Hofmannsthal's arrow speeding toward its target.[5] The spectator's
"perception of structure"[6] has led him to anticipate that closure will be
synonymous with the ultimate fulfillment of the father's prophetic warning
to his sons for "runnin' against [their] . . . nature[s]." Another important
structural device that the audience expects to influence closure is the technique of ironic reversal established early in the play with the brothers' exchange of destinies and repeated at significant intervals throughout the
drama. This pattern of reversing the expectations of the characters in *Beyond the Horizon* is, in fact, repeated so consistently as to give away the plot.
As H. G. Kemelman observed (1932), "The complete and perfect frustration of the characters destroys all suspense. The audience knows what is
coming: after the first act, they can predict the rest of the play."[7] For example, at the start of act 2 all the characters have their hopes pinned on
Andrew's imminent return from the voyage. Ruth hopes to renew Andrew's
former romantic interest in her; Robert and his mother expect Andrew to
take charge of the failing farm. Their very eagerness prepares the audience

for the disappointment that will ensue: Andrew sails off for Argentina the next day. A nearly identical situation occurs at the beginning of act 3, when everyone is once again waiting for Andrew's return. Ruth has telegraphed Andrew about Robert's need for medical attention. She and her mother are desperately hoping for financial assistance, since Robert has been too ill to work the farm. Robert, who deludes himself about the gravity of his illness, also hopes to borrow money from his brother so that he and Ruth can move to the city. The audience, recalling the pattern of ironic reversal that has been established in acts 1 and 2, expects a repeat performance of Andrew's first homecoming, which in fact occurs. Andrew arrives at the Mayo farm financially and spiritually broken. The specialist he brings is too late to save Robert's life.

If the play had ended at this highly foreseeable, if somewhat tedious, point, its conclusion would meet both Barbara Herrnstein Smith's require-ment for closure (in poetry) that it result in a cessation of expectations for the audience[8] and June Schlueter's condition that the production of mean-ing be complete.[9] The theme "be true to yourself" has been hammered in relentlessly from start to finish: Robert's self-betrayal has resulted in misery for all concerned. The total sum of his life's efforts is zero—no children, no crops, no happiness, and no literary output (he speculates on his potential for writing). With Robert dying, Ruth exhausted, and Andrew at the nadir of his personal and financial fortunes, nothing more of interest can be ex-pected to occur. The viewer is ready to accept the lamentable end toward which the structure of the play has led.

The viewer is in for a surprise, however. The "perverse mind" of Eu-gene O'Neill would not allow this "reasonably contented ending"[10] for which he has meticulously prepared throughout the drama. The fact is, the very concept of "contentment" appears to have had a derogatory connotation to O'Neill, who in 1921 defined "happiness" as "an intensified feeling of the significant worth of man's being and becoming . . . not a *mere smirking contentment* with one's lot" (emphasis added).[11] In *Beyond the Horizon,* instead of being satisfied with the ending within easy grasp, the playwright demon-strates his preference for the unattainable[12] by introducing Robert's theatri-cally heightened speeches in the final scene. The spectator is startled by the change in tone, which suggests a redemption not supported by the action of the play, and which contrasts strangely with the preceding, naturalistically detailed rendition of poverty and misery. Nor is the spectator prepared for the new interpretive demand placed upon him at this late stage. Unsettled from his comfortably receptive position, he needs to rekindle his imagina-tion, which has been smothered by the play's overexplicitness. He must first decide Robert's intent in bequeathing his wife to his brother (3.1.647). Is the dying Robert acting out of a spirit of forgiveness and comradery? Or is he trying to punish his brother, regarding whom he has exhibited bitter jealousy only a short time earlier in this very scene (3.1.632)? The viewer or reader may also need to make decisions regarding his own eschatology in order to interpret the closure, which O'Neill leaves ambiguous. The dying Robert joyfully purports to have been redeemed through suffering and sacrifice, so that he may resume his earlier-abandoned quest after death. Is the audience to conclude that Robert's self-assessment is correct, or that he dies tragically self-deluded? If the viewer concludes Robert is deluded, as I believe further analysis confirms, the question becomes the nature of Robert's self-delusion. Does the play depict his irrevocable forfeiture, through marrying Ruth instead of sailing "beyond the horizon," of his right to pursue the "quest"? Or is he deluded about the very possibility of undertaking such a quest? Without an understanding of Robert's final condition, the production of meaning that ought to result from the closure[13] is incomplete, leaving closure *en l'air*.

Modern closural theories attest to the prerogative of individuals to assist in creating their own closures for ambiguous works. Interpretation is no longer the mere act of *"construing,"* but "the art of *constructing,"* asserts Stanley Fish.[14] The reader, says Wolfgang Iser, must "[work] things out for himself."[15] According to Henry J. Schmidt the reader's effort to impose closure on an ambiguous work can have the propitious effect of "assuring one of the correctness of one's beliefs and of the fundamental stability of one's social and moral environment."[16]

A number of readers and viewers have chosen to interpret the ambiguous ending affirmatively. Like Robert Mayo, who invents a gratifying fiction to ensure that his suffering not be meaningless, some readers and viewers may deliberately seek "the promise of a morally legible universe"[17] in Robert's poetic last speeches. Thus, even so illustrious a critic as T. S. Eliot, fresh from completing his celebrated religious work, *The Waste Land* (1922), was able to perceive the ending of *Beyond the Horizon* as "magnificent."[18] Similarly, Arthur Hobson Quinn (1927 was impressed by the "exaltation of the spirit"[19] in Robert's dying speech: "I'm happy at last . . . free to wander on and on—eternally! . . . It isn't the end. It's a free beginning—the start of my voyage! I've won . . . the right of release—beyond the horizon!" (3.2.652). Even some very reputable modern critics have taken Robert's final speech literally. Travis Bogard describes Robert's death as "close to a blessing, both a release from pain and a reunification with the element that is rightfully his. . . . he moves through death into the mainstream of continuous life energy. In Edmund Tyrone's words, he has 'dissolved' into the secret."[20]

Still more recently Virginia Floyd has interpreted the final scene as signifying redemption through suffering.[21]

Nevertheless, a consideration of what precedes and succeeds Robert's triumphant dying speech, as well as Robert's character and O'Neill's own comments pertaining to Robert, would seem to preclude the positive readings of the closure that O'Neill's poetic language suggests. In dying, Robert says he has been redeemed through suffering, that he has "won to [his] trip—the right of release—beyond the horizon" through the "sacrifice[s]" he has made (3.2.652). However, nothing in the play indicates any "sacrifice" on Robert's part. If anyone has sacrificed it is Andrew, who surrendered both Ruth and the farm to his brother. But even Andrew's sacrifice was minimal: he later realizes he never loved Ruth, and satisfies his farming instinct on a much larger scale in Argentina. As for Robert, he merely made the wrong choice and was too weak to extricate himself from the consequences. This is not "sin," for which Robert requires "redemption," but mere human frailty. His fidelity to Ruth even after the collapse of their relationship seems less attributable to "sacrifice"—particularly after their little daughter's death—than passivity coupled with illness on his part.

Far from being redeemed through suffering in any significant sense, Robert, as I have indicated, undergoes a deterioration of character as a result of his unhappy marriage and the death of his child. In acts 1 and 2 Robert is gentle and loving until his nagging wife expresses the wish she had married Andrew instead of him. In act 3 the couple's personalities seem to have reversed. Now Ruth wearily ministers to her sick husband's needs, while Robert indulges in vehement name-calling: Ruth is a "fool"; the local doctor is a "damned ignoramus" (3.1.633). Still embittered by Ruth's "defection" of five years ago (her preference for Andrew), Robert jealously accuses his wife (3.2.632), who numbed with despair no longer feels love for anyone, of still waiting for Andrew as she did in act 2. Raging with fever, Robert can scarcely contain his envy of the brother he once loved: "Andy's made a big success of himself. . . . And now he's coming home to let us admire his greatness" (3.1.634).

Although Robert still has lucid moments in which he recognizes his accountability (3.1.635), he deliberately sets himself up as a kind of prophet for the purpose of judging and administering punishment to his brother. Seizing upon Andrew's unfortunate financial history, Robert professes to see a "spiritual significance in [the] picture" of his brother "gambl[ing] in a wheat pit with scraps of paper" (3.2.646-47). Mercilessly attacking Andrew in his most vulnerable area, he continues, "[Y]ou're the deepest-dyed failure of the three [of us], Andy. You've spent eight years running away from yourself [Robert conveniently forgets that it was his action which sent Andrew away]. . . . You used to be a creator when you loved the farm. You and life were in harmonious partnership" (3.1.646–47). Yet Robert is guilty of the same self-betrayal. He, too, has lost his "harmonious partnership" with life, and now it appears, from the change in his character, that he has lost not only the life he might have had, but the very self that once dreamed of that life. After telling Andrew he must "be punished" and will "have to suffer to win back" (3.1.646–47), he makes what on the surface would appear a magnanimous dying gesture were it not for the implications of "punishment" and "suffering" that immediately precede it. He orders Andrew to marry Ruth: "Remember, Andy, Ruth has suffered double her share. . . . Only through contact with suffering, Andy, will you—awaken. Listen. You must marry Ruth—afterwards" (3.1.646–47). The insinuation is that the suffering involved in being wedded to Ruth will "redeem" Andrew in the same manner as it did Robert—destroy what may remain of his character and perhaps cause his death.

The final closure does not bode well for Andrew and Ruth. If Robert had deliberately set out to destroy the possibility of a meaningful relationship between them, he could scarcely have accomplished his goal any more effectively than by commanding them to marry. The closing dialogue of the play, which ought—if anything—to clarify the author's intent, decidedly undercuts an affirmative reading of Robert's death. As Andrew and Ruth face each other across Robert's corpse, Andrew is furious with Ruth for not reassuring Robert she had not meant what she once said about preferring Andrew. Gradually his anger subsides, however, as a result of Ruth's sobs and the memory of Robert's dying wish that they wed. As the play closes, Andrew falters with empty words regarding their future. Ruth, for her part, is too far *"beyond the further troubling of any hope"* (3.2.653) even to care. Although their future relationship is left somewhat open, audience expectations regarding the possibility of happiness for them together have ceased. If they do eventually marry, their union will most likely continue the cycle of misery established in the beginning of the play with Ruth's marriage to Robert.

If Marianna Torgovnick's assertion with regard to the novel that the ending is "the single place where an author most pressingly desires to make his points"[22] may be considered applicable to drama, it is significant that O'Neill finishes the play with this despairing tableau. Albert E. Kalson and Lisa M. Schwerdt conclude, "There is nothing ahead for the dead or the living—only repetition, never change."[23] The hopefulness of Robert's dying speech appears effectively negated by the depiction of misery that succeeds it.

Far from being redeemed through suffering, as some critics have interpreted the closure, Robert is one of O'Neill's many self-deluded characters. He began dreaming by the window as a sickly child in order to forget his pain. Throughout his life he seems to have lived more significantly in dreams and poetry than through his actions. Like Tennyson's Lady of Shalott his perception of reality, or the outside world as it exists objectively, is clouded. He never realizes Ruth loves him until she tells him, nor does he recognize that she has stopped loving him until she tells him. Moreover, even Robert's dream of the quest is but dimly conceived: it is not powerful enough in his mind to compel him to sacrifice in order to achieve it (in the manner in which O'Neill, himself, sacrificed for his goal to create drama). Instead Robert rather lazily attempts to exchange one dream for another: "I think love must have been the secret—the secret that called to me from over the world's rim—the secret beyond every horizon" (1.1.583). In act 3, raging with fever, he is more deluded than ever. Like the sickly child who dreamed by the window to forget his pain, he plans to start a new life in the city: "Life owes us some happiness after what we've been through. *(vehemently)* It must! Otherwise our suffering would be meaningless—and that is unthinkable" (3.1.636). In desperate need of illusion to validate his wasted life, he goes to the window seeking confirmation of his new dream in the rising of the sun. But he is too early; the sun has not risen yet. All he sees is black and gray, which he himself concludes to be "not a very happy augury" (3.1.637). After overhearing the specialist brought in by Andrew confirm his imminent death, Robert quickly grasps at a new dream, one less easily dispelled as illusory. He claims to be continuing his original plan to journey "beyond the horizon," having won through "sacrifice" (3.2.652) the "right of release" (3.2.652), and envisions himself "happy at last" and "free to wander on and on—eternally" (3.2.652). Like Captain Bartlett in another play written the same year, *Where the Cross Is Made* (1918), who dies happy in the belief that his treasure has been restored, Robert Mayo dies as deluded as he has lived.

O'Neill did not admire this young man gifted with a poet's imagination who clipped his wings through lack of character to pursue his goal and, consequently, remained literally and figuratively bound to the soil below. Several years earlier (1914) O'Neill had defined "be[ing] true to one-self and one's highest hope" as the ultimate "good."[24] That same year he had sent Beatrice Ashe an excerpt of writing that had impressed him as valid: "[T]he only way in this world to play for anything you want is to be willing to go after it with all you've got—to be willing to push every last chip to the middle of the table. It don't make a bit of difference what it is: if you get a hand you want, play it!"[25] Robert Mayo was not willing to push that "last chip" to the table, and O'Neill saw him as a moral coward:

a weaker type . . . a man who would have my Norwegian's inborn craving for the sea's unrest, only in him it would be conscious, too conscious, intellectually diluted into a vague, intangible, romantic wanderlust. His powers of resistance, both moral and physical, would also probably be correspondingly watered. He would throw away his instinctive dream and accept the thralldom of the farm for—why almost any nice little poetical craving—the romance of sex, say.[26]

O'Neill himself could have been saddled with a wife and child as a very young man. Out of conscience he married the respectable Kathleen Jenkins, whom he had impregnated, in 1909. Immediately afterward, however, he departed on a series of adventurous voyages, only meeting the son she later bore him (Eugene O'Neill Jr.) one time before he was grown.[27] In *Beyond the Horizon*, written nine years later, the same year as his second marriage to Agnes Boulton, O'Neill may unconsciously have been attempting to justify his desertion of Kathleen as preferable to a life of clipped wings like Robert's.

In one of his more lucid final moments, Robert Mayo condemns himself for his lack of courage regarding the pursuit of his dream. Fleeing his sickbed for the outdoor road, from which he can view his last sunrise, Robert assesses his life:

I couldn't stand it back there in the room. It seemed as if all my life—I'd been cooped in a room. *So I thought I'd try to end as I might have—if I'd had the courage—alone*—in a ditch by the open road—watching the sun rise. (3.2.651, emphasis added)

He then invents an elaborate fiction concerning his death to compensate for his wasted life, thus qualifying him to take his place among the numerous men and women in the O'Neill canon who, unable to face reality, resort to the comfort of dreams. But although O'Neill sympathized with his weaker fellow men who need dreams in order to survive, he did not admire them or depict them as heroes. Robert deludes himself in his final speeches: he never attains that mystical glimpse of the ultimate that he proclaims. As William J. Scheick concludes, "Rob never crosses the threshold, never penetrates in fact, language or dream the mystery beyond the horizon of life."[28] Through his denial of the dream he has progressed to disillusionment, suffering, bitterness, and death, and that is the extent of his journey.

Finally, although the self-deluded nature of Robert's final speeches seems clear upon closer examination, the ultimate nature of Robert's tragedy remains ambiguous. Is Robert to be pitied because, through his own admitted moral cowardice, he has failed to pursue the mystical quest that once beckoned him "beyond the horizon"? Or does Robert's tragedy involve his delusion about the very existence of such a quest in the hostile world of the play? Scheick concludes, "Everything in the play . . . implies the inability of humanity to get beyond the horizon in any sense; . . . such a quest . . . is an illusion characteristic of, perhaps crucial to human life, and defines its radical tragic nature."[29] Although Scheick's argument has merit in consideration of O'Neill's frequent depiction of the human need for "pipe dreams" *(The Iceman Cometh)* in his plays, O'Neill himself appears to have been preoccupied with such a quest. In *Long Day's Journey into Night* (1941), Edmund Tyrone, the fictional counterpart of his youthful self, describes a moment of mystical oneness with the universe when "the veil of things" is drawn back: "For a second you see—and seeing the secret, are the secret. For a second there is meaning!" (4.812). Edmund's narration of his experience at sea suggests that O'Neill's own quest for spiritual significance "beyond the horizon" was not without its occasional rewards (which explains why Robert Mayo's dying speech is so poetically rendered as to convince some viewers or readers of its truth). Furthermore, in 1922 O'Neill expressed his admiration for those who sought to soar through the pursuit of unattainable goals:

> Man wills his own defeat when he pursues the unattainable. But his *struggle* is his success! He is an example of the spiritual significance which life attains when it aims high enough. . . .[30]

As stated earlier, O'Neill's own most ambitious endeavor to reach "beyond the horizon" is represented by his effort to attain extraordinary dramatic goals through writing plays. His choice of the word "*un*attainable" regarding his quest, however, suggests uncertainty on his part. It seems possible that O'Neill's failure to clarify the nature of Robert Mayo's tragedy and thus render the closure more meaningful is the result of the playwright's own qualms regarding the validity of such a quest, given man's limitations and the hostile universe in which he has been placed. Terry Eagleton, who defends the reader's right to construct or write his own "sub-text" for ambiguous or evasive works, maintains that "what [a work] does not say, and how it does not say it, may be as important as what it articulates; what seems absent, marginal, or ambivalent about it may provide a central clue to its meanings."[31] The ambiguous ending of *Beyond the Horizon* may represent O'Neill's own doubts concerning his goal to create significant drama, toward which he was sacrificing and dedicating his life.

In conclusion, ambiguous endings are popular in this age, which favors "openness" in preference to those endings described by William Carlos Williams (with reference to poetry) as clicking shut like the lid of a box.[32] It would seem that the ambiguity ought not to be merely imposed upon the play's closure, however, but ought to proceed naturally from the preceding drama. For closure to be effective in an open-ended work (which includes plays with ambiguous endings), asserts Marianna Torgovnick, the test is "the honesty and the appropriateness of the ending's relationship to beginning and middle."[33] The problem with the ambiguity in *Beyond the Horizon* is that the change in tone and demand upon the audience occurs too suddenly (early critics noted the illusion-dispelling effect of the last scene): the audience is not prepared for openness in such an explicitly presented play. In his later plays O'Neill will make ambiguous closures more integral to the dramas, as in *The Iceman Cometh* (1940), for example, a play filled with mystery and uncertainty from the beginning.

O'Neill will undergo a similar evolution by the later plays concerning his facility to maintain suspense. In contrast to the laborious predictability of Robert's deterioration in *Beyond the Horizon*, in *A Moon for the Misbegotten* (1943) another self-betrayed character, Jim Tyrone, journeys toward his destruction. Yet in this very concentrated drama, which occupies only some eighteen hours (in contrast to the novelistic *Beyond the Horizon*, which is spread out over eight years), O'Neill structures the action so that the audience retains some hope for Jim Tyrone's salvation almost until the end.

3

Feminism versus Fatalism:
Uncertainty as Closure in *"Anna Christie"*

"Anna Christie" (1920), O'Neill's second full-length play to win a Pulitzer Prize, gained him more popular fame than *Beyond the Horizon* (1918). The sentimentalized depiction of the regeneration of a prostitute, with its—as it was generally interpreted—"happy" ending, appealed to contemporary middle-class audiences as Robert Mayo's death from tuberculosis had not. But although the play opened (New York, November 1921) to predominantly favorable reviews, nearly all the critics found fault with what they considered the bogus "happy ending."[1] The consensus of opinion was that the closure had been "tampered with"[2] as a compromise to current tastes.[3] Far from being pleased with the theater audiences' acclaim for what some have considered one of the rare comedies in the O'Neill canon, the playwright was devastated by the ironic realization that the commercial success of the play depended upon the audience "believing just what [he] did not want them to [i.e., the happy ending]."[4] O'Neill insisted that he had intended a much more uncertain closure: "And the sea outside—life—waits. The happy ending is merely the comma at the end of a gaudy introductory clause, with the body of the sentence still unwritten."[5]

It is not surprising that audiences failed to grasp O'Neill's intention in *"Anna Christie,"* since he had considerable difficulty formulating his goal even for himself while writing the play. He shifted his focus several times, which necessitated at least four different title changes (*Chris Christophersen, The Ole Davil, Tides,* and *"Anna Christie"*). He also altered the stoker's name, Anna's occupation, and details of the plot. The ending appears to have been particularly problematic. The first draft *(Chris Christophersen)* concludes with Chris accepting the steamship captain's offer to serve as his bo'sun, an ending that Leslie Eric Comens interprets as a comic resolution—Chris returning to and thereby making his peace with the sea.[6] A somewhat later attempt, *The Ole Davil,* which concludes with the characters laughing at Chris's superstitious fear of the sea, also suggests comedy. *"Anna Christie,"* O'Neill's final version of the play, ends (contrary to early audiences' apparent interpretation of the conclusion as "happy") with uncertainty. Despite his repeated efforts, however, O'Neill apparently never devised a denouement for this play that completely satisfied him.[7] Always considering *"Anna"* one of his greatest failures, O'Neill refused to allow it to be published with his collected plays by Joseph Wood Krutch (1932).

It seems a reasonable conjecture that O'Neill's inability to finish *"Anna Christie"* satisfactorily derived at least partly from his tendency—acknowledged even by himself in the previously cited letter to Beatrice Ashe[8]—to project not one ending, but at least two for each play. In *Beyond the Horizon,* for example, O'Neill's "perverse mind" prepares the audience for Robert's destruction and then suggests the redemptive ending (which perhaps "delight[ed his] soul"), only to immediately undercut the idea of redemption in the final bleak sequence between Andrew and Ruth. In *"Anna Christie"* O'Neill's "double vision" operates somewhat differently: he prepares the viewer for two very different closures throughout.

He begins by setting up audience expectations for the traditional "happy ending." The play opens in a New York waterfront saloon with Anna, destitute and ill, having left her life of prostitution to join the father she has not seen for fifteen years and begin a new existence. Overjoyed to learn of his daughter's coming, Chris Christophersen, the Swedish-American captain of a coal barge, explains to the bartender that the reason he left Anna with her cousins on a Minnesota farm for all those years was to protect her from "dat ole davil, sea," which had claimed many of his ancestors' lives and widowed their spouses. The bartender, winking, suggests, "This girl, now, 'll be marryin' a sailor herself, likely. It's in the blood" (1.964). Chris's irrational fury at the very idea of Anna marrying a sailor suggests the direction the play will take. The wary viewer instantly anticipates that closure will involve just such a union as part of Anna's new life.

The comedic plot suggested early in the play proceeds on schedule toward the expected conclusion. After ten days on Chris's coal barge, Anna, appearing healthy and transformed, expresses her love for the sea and the fog, which she feels has cleansed her. Filled with foreboding by Anna's apparently hereditary attraction to the sea, Chris's unnatural fear is further fueled when his barge rescues some survivors of a wrecked steamship immediately following his protestation to Anna, "No! Dat ole davil sea, she ain't God! (2.982). Among the battered men Chris ushers aboard is Mat Burke, whom "God," in the form of the sea, appears to have brought to the barge explicitly to meet Anna. Alarmed by his daughter's obvious attraction to the rescued stoker, Chris orders her to her cabin, but Anna refuses to obey. Instead, she guides the weakened Burke to her own bed to sleep off his ordeal. As Burke is being led off, he prattles about "marrying [Anna] soon" (2.992), leaving Chris stunned and furious about the trick perpetrated on him by "dat ole davil, sea."

In act 3, a week later in Boston, the triangular wrangling comes to a head. Mat attempts to persuade the old Swede to accept him as a son-in-law, but Chris is violently opposed. The arrival of Anna puts an end to their fighting. Claiming that she loves Mat but cannot marry him, she bids him a sobbing "Good-by" (3.1003). The two men, however, paying her scant heed, continue to battle over possession of her. Infuriated, Anna insists upon her independence from male domination by revealing her sordid past. Devastated, Chris and Mat go ashore to get drunk.

Act 4 opens two nights later with a heavy fog that seems an objective correlative for the condition of the three characters, who, overwhelmed as a result of Anna's confession, are unsure what to do. Anna has gone ashore and purchased a train ticket. However, still hoping that Mat will come back for her, she has found herself unable to use the ticket and has returned to the barge. Chris returns after signing on a ship bound for South Africa the next day, having first arranged that Anna will receive all his pay. Mat straggles in last, violently drunk and bruised from fighting; he begs Anna to assure him her confession was a lie. Refusing to retract what she has told him, Anna once again insists that she has changed and swears she has never actually "loved" any other man. This last oath helps to assuage Mat's ego, and he agrees to marry her. Their "honeymoon" will be brief, however, since by a strange quirk of fate Burke has signed on the same ship as her father and will sail the next day.

The projected comedic closure, Anna's successful attainment of a new life, which involves her marriage to a sailor despite her father's opposition, has been fulfilled. Anna, who arrived at the saloon feeling dirty and hating men, has undergone a significant change. Believing that she has been purged of her past by the sea, she acquires a new sense of identity. She also falls in love and struggles to retain her seafaring suitor despite numerous obstacles (her father's objections, her own past, and Mat's irritating possessiveness). A strong-willed young woman who knows what she wants, Anna appears capable of accomplishing what she sets out to do. The play being a comedy, with Anna as its titular heroine, generic expectations have induced the spectator to expect her to succeed.[9]

Anna, in fact, surpasses the audience's expectations. In affirming her own capacity to structure her life, she makes a surprisingly militant assertion of feminism:

But nobody owns me, see?—'cepting myself. I'll do what I please and no
man, I don't give a hoot who he is, can tell me what to do! I ain't asking
either of you for a living. I can make it myself—one way or other. I'm my
own boss. So put that in your pipe and smoke it! You and your orders!
(3.1007)

She refuses to allow either her father or lover to "own" or direct her, and
she boldly defends her past conduct by equating it with the men's. She tells
Mat, "You been doing the same thing . . . in every port. How're you any
better than I was?" (4.1022). Having asserted her independence from male
domination, and having persuaded Chris and Mat to accept her as the ex-
prostitute that she is, Anna has won—particularly by the standards of 1920
audiences—a huge victory for her sex. When Mat returns to the barge still
wanting her, closure—according to David F. Hult's definition of the process
as an "inner movement in the direction of unity or completeness"[10]—appears imminent and the play is virtually over. Anna's proposition that the
three live happily ever after in the "little house" she will prepare for them
while they are away seems the inevitable—if overworked—comedic conclusion. Early audiences appear to have accepted the "happy ending" proposed by Anna because they unconsciously perceived the structure of the
play to be complete at this point. The "satisfying ending," according to
Murray Krieger, "fulfills internally aroused expectations."[11]

The simple comedic ending, however, was not the closure which
"delight[ed the] soul" of Eugene O'Neill, admirer of Gerhart Hauptmann
("True drama is basically endless").[12] Thus, having allowed his heroine to
achieve an identity and life for herself through her determination and courage, O'Neill's "perverse mind" proceeds to undermine her prospect of happiness in the final sequence. Mat's qualms upon learning that Anna's family was Lutheran, after she has sworn on his crucifix, rivals Chris's distrust
of the sea in its fatalism: "Luthers, is it? . . . Well, I'm damned then surely.
Yerra, what's the difference? 'Tis the will of God, anyway" (4.1026). Immediately following, Chris voices his anxiety over the coincidence of them
sailing on the same ship together ("dat funny vay ole davil do her vorst dirty
tricks" [4.1026]); and Mat, in his final speech of the play, starts to agree
with him: "I'm fearing maybe you have the right of it for once, divil take
you." Although Anna tries to "cut out the gloom" by proposing a toast, the
play closes with Chris's fatalistic pronouncement: "Fog, fog, fog, all bloody
time. You can't see vhere you vas going, no. Only dat ole davil, sea—she
knows!" (4.1027). As the final speech of the play, Chris's words have a powerful impact. The fog suggests the dangers of the voyage to come, and also
their futures, which are ultimately unknowable. The audience is left with

the impression that the sea, which has already devoured generations of Christophersens, may be waiting for Chris and Mat to ship out so she can swallow them up.

If it seems remarkable that early audiences appear to have overlooked the final sequence in their interpretation of the ending, it seems doubly so in consideration of O'Neill's evident preparation for the subversion of his "happy ending" throughout this play. Numerous fatalistic allusions challenge the very possibility of purposeful self-determination such as that demonstrated by Anna. The many references to fog, for example, illustrate man's actual helpless or "befogged" condition of being cast adrift in the expansive universe mirrored by the sea, which may at times be malevolent. In this desperate, somewhat ignoble state, the personae of "Anna Christie" grasp at face-saving illusions that make existence more tolerable. O'Neill, himself, referred to these "pitifully humorous gesture[s] in the direction of happiness" as "symbol[s] of what most of us have to do—at any rate, *do* do—every now and then . . . in order to keep on living."[13]

Chris, for example, cannot bear confronting any situations that might require him to accept responsibility for his actions. He cannot even speak frankly to his mistress, Marthy, about leaving the barge in preparation for Anna, but he has to ask the bartender to think up a lie. Fortunately, the good-natured prostitute volunteers to leave. When Anna tries to convince him of his responsibility for her downfall in act 3, he cannot bear to listen but puts his fingers in his ears, which she must physically remove in order to make him hear. Chris's attempt to stop up his ears is consistent with his deliberate avoidance of truth all his life. He refuses to acknowledge personal responsibility for anything—even his desertion of his wife for the life of a sailor—but uses the sea as a scapegoat for all his shortcomings and misdeeds. Regarding Anna, whom he left with his wife's cousins, Chris excuses his neglect of her by asserting his conviction that she would grow up healthier inland than if exposed to the sea. Preferring his illusion to factual verification, Chris never personally checked on Anna's condition. When Anna surprises him by descending upon him in act 1, Chris, finding unexpected solace for his increasing loneliness, cannot bear to lose her so quickly to Mat. Although he has allowed Anna to grow up bereft of his guidance, he (somewhat deludedly, at this late date) undertakes to play the role of concerned father by discouraging her relationship with the rescued stoker. "Don't you want no one to be nice to me except yourself?" (3.995), she asks perceptively.

Chris is not a bad man, only a weak one. His tenderness toward Anna, whom he never blames for her past, is moving. Furthermore, he does finally acknowledge the error of his ways in act 4: "Ay've been tanking, and Ay guess it vas all my fault—all bad tangs dat happen to you" (4.1014–15). When she responds that no one is to blame ("There ain't nothing to forgive, anyway. It ain't your fault, and it ain't mine, and it ain't [Mat's] neither. We're all poor nuts, and things happen, and we yust get mixed in wrong, that's all" [4.1015]), he eagerly reverts to his favorite illusion: "You say right tank, Anna, py golly! It ain't nobody's fault! *(shaking his fist)* It's dat ole davil, sea!" (4.1015).

Mat Burke is quick to condemn Chris's reliance upon the sea as his personal scapegoat. The stoker tells the old Swede he has "swallowed the anchor" (3.999), which the stoker in the earlier *Chris Christophersen* defines as "whin[ing] and blam[ing] something outside of yourself for your misfortunes . . ." (3.2.881). Nevertheless, Mat relies on a number of comforting illusions himself. From his first meeting with Anna, Mat insists upon fabricating fictions about her. In just a few minutes she proceeds in his fancy from a mermaid rising from the sea, to the captain's mistress, to his sainted daughter with a golden crown upon her head (2.987). After Anna shatters her "halo" by revealing the truth about her past, Mat tries to escape from dealing with the truth by going ashore and becoming drunk. The liquor fails to have the desired effect, however, as does the liquor in the much later play *The Iceman Cometh* (1940) after its imbibers are forced to confront the truth. Unable to accept the destruction of his fantasy even while intoxicated, Mat returns to the barge begging Anna for a lie. He is desperate enough to accept any crumb of comfort she can bestow upon him, even the assurance that she has never actually "loved" any man before him. To give his renewed fantasy more substance, she must swear on the crucifix given him by his dying mother, which he firmly believes has always protected him from harm. The effectiveness of the icon, however, is soon called into question by the fact that Anna is not Catholic. Nevertheless, Mat is eventually able to accept Anna's "naked word" (4.1025), because he has replaced the vision shattered by her revelation with a new illusion about her—not only that it was his powerful influence that changed her, but that he will continue to transform her further and further into the wife of his dreams: "For I've a power of strength in me to lead men the way I want, and women, too, maybe, and I'm thinking *I'd change you to a new woman entirely*, so I'd never know, or you either, what kind of woman you'd been in the past at all" (4.1023, emphasis added). Mat has still not accepted Anna as she is.

Anna, as O'Neill presents her, is also difficult for the audience to accept at times. Perhaps in transforming his heroine from typist in the earlier *Chris Christophersen* to trollop in this play, O'Neill neglected to work out all aspects of her character. Anna's explanation of the reason she started working in a brothel—because she felt "freer" and less confined with her body beneath paying customers than as a "nurse" supervising other people's children—is incomprehensible. To those viewers who are able to construe her intense need for the freedom of self-determination as rendering her descent into prostitution credible, however, Anna appears franker and less given to self-delusion than her father and lover. Nevertheless, she deliberately encourages Chris and Mat in their illusions. She leads the newly rescued and still groggy Mat to believe her a lady: ". . . I must say I don't care for your language. The men I know don't pull that rough stuff when ladies are around" (2.985). Similarly, she encourages her father to trust in her innocence. When Chris makes insinuations about her dates with Mat, she replies with inappropriate outrage:

> Say, listen here, you ain't trying to insinuate that there's something wrong between us, are you? . . . Well, don't you never think it neither if you want me ever to speak to you again. . . . If I ever dreamt you thought that, I'd get the hell out of this barge so quick you couldn't see me for dust. (3.994)

Even her admirable enlightenment of the men regarding her past is performed less to disillusion them than to discourage them from dominating her.[14] No paragon of virtue even after her confession, Anna continues to prevaricate. When Mat returns to the barge two nights later, she shows him the train ticket she has bought and insinuates that she will return to her former occupation the next day if he leaves again (4.1021). She does not tell him that Chris has provided for her financially and she will not need to work, but uses every means at her disposal to provoke Mat into claiming her for his own. What is more, her equivocal tactics succeed.

In her joy at regaining both men's affection, Anna attempts to varnish over any of their lurking fears and gloom with a new illusion—the "big happy family." She proposes to "get a little house somewhere and . . . make a regular place for you two to come back to.—wait and see. And now you drink up and be friends" (4.1025–26). This final illusion of Anna creating a home to which her men may return and live "happily ever after" is the illusion apparently shared by many of the viewers of O'Neill's day, who chose to accept Anna's fabrication as fact.

Nevertheless, the ever-pervasive fog that begins and ends the play seems an overpowering objective correlative for man's frequently befuddled, deluded, and/or drunken condition—his helplessness in the face of destiny, as represented by the sea. Furthermore, the frequent use of the word "fix" by the characters, as they, for the most part, futilely attempt to oppose the fog or take control of their lives, supports Chris's fatalism. Chris tries to "fix" (3.994) Burke so that he cannot marry Anna, first by attacking him with a knife, and then by purchasing a gun (for which, reconsidering, he never buys bullets). Both weapons are, therefore, ineffectual against the stoker. Later in the play Chris refers to "fixing" (4.1014) his salary for his coming voyage upon Anna, so that she will have no need to return to her old trade. Although Chris's intentions are good, he is once again abandoning Anna, which was the reason she became a prostitute in the first place. Money may prove an ineffectual substitute for his love. Mat, without using the actual word "fix," attempts to repair his wounded ego by having Anna swear on the crucifix. However, her oath as a Lutheran only exacerbates his doubts. Even Anna refers to "fix[ing]" their predicament at the end, by accepting the men's voyage together and promising them a home. When Chris voices his premonitions of doom, and Mat starts to support him, Anna attempts to distract them from their anxieties with a gay toast: "Aw say, what's the matter? Cut out the gloom. We're all *fixed* now, ain't we, me and you? . . . Come on! Here's to the sea, no matter what!" (4.1026, emphasis added).

As the play comes to a close, Anna is attempting to will her happy ending into being, as does Maggie Verver at the end of Henry James's novel *The Golden Bowl* (1904). Both women's futures are left "open" at the end of the works. In his preface to *The Portrait of a Lady* James defended his inconclusive endings as a literary necessity: "The whole of anything is never told; you can only take what groups together."[15] Also acknowledging the falseness inherent in the very concept of "closure," O'Neill justified the open ending of *"Anna Christie"* as an attempt to represent continuity: "A naturalistic play is life. Life doesn't end. One experience is but the birth of another. . . ."[16] As O'Neill seems to have anticipated in this statement, however, the audience cannot help speculating on the two women's futures. Endings, as June Schlueter points out, have a natural "afterlife" that prompts sequels.[17] The prospect before Anna may be even less optimistic than that facing Maggie, who will at least have the physical presence of her prince. Anna will be alone again after the men ship out, a condition that disheartened her when she first arrived at the saloon, and that may be even harder to bear now that she has known love. Whether or not her struggle for self-determination and happiness is even worthwhile seems unclear from the text: she may be deluded and a mere pawn of fate. Even if the men return to live out her fantasy of domesticity in her "little house somewhere," there is already a crack in the "golden bowl" of her happiness with Mat's desperate search for a supernatural sanction, which, as Clifford Leech argues, is "indicative of a never fully quenchable suspicion."[18] Furthermore, Mat's intention of "chang[ing]" Anna "to a new woman entirely" (4.1023) conflicts with Anna's new sense of identity and suggests a problematic marriage at best. Finally, there is the very real possibility that the men will not return; as Chris points out, sailors, for one reason or another, often do not. What will become of Anna if Chris's money runs out?

Despite the characters' desperate attempts to "fix" their destinies, images of man's helplessness pervade the play. The bulletless gun that drops from Chris's pocket suggests his castrated or powerless condition. Similarly useless, Mat's crucifix brings him little comfort in the society of ex-Lutherans. Finally, Anna's unused train ticket seems another objectification of the ineffectuality of man's efforts at self-determination. Far from being able to control their respective destinies, Chris, Mat, and Anna must wait for the fog to clear so that they can see what life brings.

Throughout most of the play, however, and most emphatically at closure, Anna's projection of happiness appears to conflict with Chris's forebodings of doom. The audience feels torn between the possibilities of self-determination and the implications of fatalism together in the same play. One idea seems to undermine the other. Anna's assertion of independence and attempt to achieve harmony for the trio seem delusional in the face of the impenetrable fog and vast sea upon which, as Chris reminds the viewer in the closing lines, all their fates will ultimately be determined. Furthermore, Chris's fatalistic pronouncements, which, to some extent, may be dismissed as the self-exonerating fantasies of a gloomy old man, appear nearly equally delusional in consideration of Anna's hard-won "victory" over the men. The sea, as Travis Bogard points out, is not nearly so malevolent as Chris insists. Despite its implication in the deaths of Chris's ancestors and Mat's shipmates, the sea is also responsible for cleansing Anna, bringing Mat to her, and giving her hope for a new life.[19] Thus, Bogard concludes, "It is by no means inevitable that the sea [upon which the trio's future will be determined] will betray trust or that the ending will be tragic."[20] The only certainty about the ending is its uncertainty: "You can't see vhere you vas going" ([Chris] 4.1027).[21]

The inconclusive or "open" ending of *"Anna Christie"* represents one of O'Neill's early efforts to deal with what David H. Richter has more recently described as the perpetual dilemma of the artist: "how . . . to bring a work to a satisfying conclusion without being false to the boundless nature of human life."[22] That the closure of *"Anna Christie"* is not satisfying, however, has been most convincingly demonstrated by its apparently widespread misinterpretation by early audiences, who, despite the numerous indications to the contrary in the text, appear to have "reconstructed" the ending to be "happy." They seem to have been able to accomplish this feat primarily because the production of meaning, which June Schlueter asserts is essential for dramatic closure,[23] is not clear. Uncertain whether the play is about self-determination and the equality of women, about the malevolent powers of an uncaring fate, or even about the exasperating uncertainty of individual destinies, audiences seem to have indulged in the type of creativity described by Wolfgang Iser[24] and have completed the play in the manner of their choice. The reader/viewer, according to Terence Hawkes, can close up and "make coherent virtually anything."[25]

The unsatisfactoriness of the conclusion to *"Anna Christie,"* as acknowledged by many critics and, to some extent, even by O'Neill,[26] in no way indicates that open endings are inadequate per se, however. According to Marianna Torgovnick, open-ended works can also attain effective closure: "The test is the honesty and the appropriateness of the ending's relationship to beginning and middle, not the degree of finality or resolution achieved by the ending."[27] It is in regard to "appropriateness" that the closure of *"Anna Christie"* appears to fail. Unlike *The Golden Bowl*, a serious study of complex characters, *"Anna"* is a comedy featuring, to a large extent, stock comedic characters like Mat Burke, and as such invokes the generic expectation that things will "turn out right" in the end. In strong contrast to the "happy" resolution generally associated with comedy, the "open ending," according to Robert M. Adams, is most suitably used in connection with the somber view that "man is essentially alone with his responsibilities in a complex and divided cosmos."[28] Although O'Neill was basically in accord with this view of man's aloneness, it seems a heavy weight to attach to the personae of this particular play, whom O'Neill himself professed to see as "a bit tragically humorous in their vacillating weakness."[29] The incongruous combination of comic characters and action with cosmic solemnity may well have been responsible for the unintentional laughter provoked in the audience during a recent New York performance of the play.[30] The comedic context of *"Anna Christie"* seems to require a more conclusive ending for the viewer to obtain closural satisfaction.

As the various versions of the play bear witness, however, O'Neill wrestled with finishing *"Anna Christie"* to little avail. Disturbed by audiences' misinterpretation of his final version, he wrote a detailed explanation of his intentions concerning the ending to the *New York Times* (18 December 1921), the very length of which suggests that he had, as he suspected, "failed."[31] What appears to have happened is that, having prepared the play for two different endings, each of which negates the other, O'Neill was unable to end the play without vastly rewriting a piece upon which he had already been working for more than two years. "The devil of it is, I don't see my way out," he confessed to George Jean Nathan.[32] The feeling that it was time to put *"Anna"* aside and move on may have been a major factor in his resorting to inconclusiveness as an ending.

A more personal conflict may also have affected his capacity to complete the play. According to Henry J. Schmidt, "Endings that seem incommensurable with the preceding action may signify a philosophical crisis. . . ."[33] The defense of women's equality is a new theme for O'Neill in "*Anna*," and one not in keeping with the function of servitude generally assigned to the heroines of his plays (Mrs. Roylston in *Servitude* [1914], Nora Melody in *A Touch of the Poet* [1939], Sara Melody Harford in *More Stately Mansions* [1939], Josie Hogan in *A Moon for the Misbegotten* [1943]). The women who do not minister to their men's needs in O'Neill's plays are usually depicted as misguided and made to suffer for their failure (Maud Steele Brown in *Bread and Butter* [1914], Martha Jayson in *The First Man* [1921], Ella Downey Harris in *All God's Chillun Got Wings* [1923], and Mary Tyrone in *Long Day's Journey into Night* [1941]).

During the composition of "*Anna Christie*" O'Neill had married the independent novelist Agnes Boulton, who refused to subordinate her own writing career to his, and whose character may have contributed to his creation of Anna. Although O'Neill had probably admired her self-determining character at first, he may have begun to doubt their compatibility by this point: Agnes apparently failed to satisfy his needs as a wife. In 1926 he began seeing the actress Carlotta Monterey, who, while fully capable of asserting herself (as she did on occasion), was willing to efface herself, to a large degree, in order to serve him in such various functions as mistress, mother, domestic organizer, and secretary. In 1929 O'Neill was finally able to divorce Agnes and marry Carlotta. Although O'Neill respected and was attracted to more overtly self-assertive women like Beatrice Ashe (1914–16), Louise Bryant (1916–17), and Agnes/Anna, he appears to have been more comfortable with a woman like Carlotta (with whom he remained, for the most part, until his death), who could subordinate herself to his needs. Perhaps it was this underlying conflict in his feelings about women that compelled him to undermine his theme of feminine equality in "*Anna Christie*" with the concept of fatalism.

4

"Devout" Admirers of the Sunrise:
Theatricality in *Desire under the Elms*

Desire under the Elms (1924) is considered by many to be among O'Neill's greatest dramatic achievements.[1] Playwright Sidney Howard, O'Neill's contemporary, ranked the powerful impact of *Elms* with that of Shakespeare's *Macbeth*.[2] Louis Sheaffer appraises *Elms* as "one of the author's outstanding works,"[3] and Frederic I. Carpenter alludes to the "full stature"[4] the drama was eventually to attain after its initially tepid reception by the critics.

The premiere of *Desire under the Elms* (Greenwich Village, November 1924) started a controversy. Many of the early reviewers were repelled by what they considered the "hideous characters" and the "sordidness" of the play.[5] The combination of patricidal and oedipal desires, adultery, technical incest, and particularly the infanticide that precipitates the closure appears to have overwhelmed their judgment regarding the solid merits of the play. Heywood Broun was among the few who conceded that the play approached greatness, although he, too, concluded it marred by "theatricality,"[6] which is most apparent in the tumultuous closure. Percy Hammond declared that he had seen "few pictures in a theatre so stark" as the scene in which old Ephraim is confiding his life history to Abbie in their bedroom, while she and Eben are lusting for each other through the walls.[7] The content of the play, in fact, aroused such a furor that it was subjected to a "play jury" in New York (where the result was full acquittal). In Boston and New England productions of *Desire under the Elms* were banned. Nevertheless, despite its initially problematic reception, the play enjoyed a long run and has been revived numerous times on both professional and amateur stages.

Set on a farm in New England in 1850, *Elms* is the shockingly credible drama of family members who have lost their sense of moral direction. As the play opens, Ephraim Cabot's three sons are waiting for his return from a long absence. When the seventy-six-year-old patriarch drives up with a young bride, Ephraim's two older sons, concluding that the new wife will inherit the farm, immediately leave. Their younger half-brother, twenty-five-year-old Eben, who remains to protect his interest in the property, is eventually seduced by his thirty-five-year-old stepmother, who is plotting to become pregnant by Eben in order to present Ephraim with a "son" to inherit the farm. Abbie almost succeeds in carrying out her plan to dispossess Eben. Nine months after their first sexual encounter, she produces a male child whom unsuspecting old Ephraim accepts as his new heir.

Since the characters are, for the most part, unsympathetic, audience interest regarding closure centers around the expectation of punishment. As with *Macbeth*, the viewer watches to see how the characters' various downfalls will be brought about. The snag that develops to thwart Abbie's plan to secure the farm for herself is the unexpected love that arises between her and Eben. When the young man learns from his father that Abbie deliberately conceived the baby in order to supplant him, he is furious and threatens to leave. Desperate to keep him, Abbie smothers the infant to death (not played on stage) to prove her love for Eben supersedes her desire for the farm. Horrified by her murder of his son, Eben calls in the sheriff. Reconsidering afterward, however, he joins Abbie in acknowledging his responsibility for the tragedy. As the play closes, the guilty pair are being led off to prison and possible hanging. The implication of impending punishment provides the anticipated closure to the preceding spectacle of sin.

Of the various evils depicted in the play, one stands out as primal: *Desire under the Elms* is first and foremost a drama about greed and possessiveness. Although physical "desire" plays a large role in fulfilling the implications of the work's title, the "desire" to possess the farm has the broadest relevance, since it applies to every character in the play. Old Ephraim is so attached to the farm, which he has hewn out of the rocky terrain with his backbreaking toil, that he fantasizes burning it down rather than allowing it to pass into the hands of any of his heirs.[8] His older sons, Simeon and Peter, who have labored on the farm all their lives, remained working during their tyrannical father's absence only because of their hard-earned interest in eventually owning the farm. Abbie and Eben, up until the final portion of the play, are virtually obsessed with possessing the farm. Eben wants the farm, which had belonged to his mother, at least partly to dispossess the father who possessed and destroyed (according to Eben) the mother Eben loved. To this end the young man steals his father's hidden money and buys out his brothers' fictional shares, crying jubilantly, "It's Maw's farm agen! It's *my* farm! Them's *my* cows! I'll milk my durn fingers off fur cows o' *mine!*" (1.4.331, emphasis added). Possessive adjectives such as "my" and "mine" are used an inordinate number of times in the play. Just minutes after Eben's

exuberant declaration of ownership, Abbie drives up to the farm with her
new husband:

> ABBIE—Hum! . . . It's purty—purty! I can't b'lieve it's r'ally *mine*.
> CABOT—*(sharply)* Yewr'n? *Mine*! . . . *Our'n*—mebbe! . . .
> ABBIE—A woman's got t' hev a hum!
>
> (1.4.335, emphasis added)

When Abbie enters the house, she exerts her possessiveness over everything: "This be *my* farm—this be *my* hum—this be *my* kitchen" (1.4.339,
emphasis added). She even extends her clutches toward Eben, her new
"son," telling him, ". . . I got t'fight fur what's due me out o' life, if I ever
'spect t'git it" (1.4.339).

Against this background of greed and possessiveness, old Ephraim, with
his constant religious pretensions, emerges as the epitome of hypocrisy.
Simeon bitterly recalls the patriarch's departure from the farm, which resulted in his third marriage: "'I'm ridin' out t' learn God's message t' me in
the spring like the prophets done,' he says. I'll bet right then an' thar he
knew plumb well he was goin' whorin', the stinkin' old hypocrite!" (1.3.330).
Ephraim is not only hypocritical and lecherous, but he is a money-oriented
"slave-driver" who "uses up" people in the name of his God, who he claims
to be "hard." Ephraim appears to have married Eben's mother mainly for
her legal ownership of his farm, and then worked her to death in the same
merciless manner that he made himself and his sons work, hoarding all the
profit from their labors in a secret place for himself. Everyone hates him—
the neighbors, his wife, and even his sons. A powerful man, who at the age
of seventy-six can still tire out the fiddler with his dancing, Ephraim complains that no one has ever understood him (2.2.348); but he, himself, appears to have loved no one but himself. Far from being the God-fearing
Calvinist he feigns to be, he is "a lecher, and a miser," as Frederick Wilkins
points out, lacking "love, humility, understanding, self-awareness: all the
ideals [of the early Puritans]."[9]

Desire under the Elms, as Wilkins has insightfully demonstrated, represents O'Neill's conception of Puritanism gone wrong. The original Puritan
ideals of love and sharing are portrayed as having been corrupted into the
"dying, love-denying, hard and icy heritage" exemplified by Ephraim, to
which Wilkins refers as "puritanism" with a small *p*.[10] The emphasis in 1850
New England, according to O'Neill, is on the accumulation of material
possessions rather than personal virtues such as love. Noting O'Neill's
Diff'rent, *Dynamo*, and *Mourning Becomes Electra*, which are also set in Puritan

New England, Wilkins concludes, "As in every O'Neill play in which Puritanism is dominant, the only hope seems to lie in rejecting it."[11]

In *Desire under the Elms* Eben, in one sense, appears to emerge as that hope: he deliberately rejects the hypocritical brand of religion flaunted by his Bible-spouting father. When Ephraim calls upon the "Lord God o'Hosts" to "smite the undutiful sons with Thy wust cuss" as Simeon and Peter are leaving for California, Eben breaks in violently: "Yew 'n' yewr God! Allus cussin' folks—allus naggin' em! . . . T'hell with yewr God!" (1.4.340). The concept of "sin," which has probably been flung in his face all his life by his father, has become a joke to Eben. He tells his brothers regarding Minnie, the town prostitute: ". . . I don't give a damn how many sins she's sinned afore mine or who she's sinned 'em with, my sin's as purty as any one on 'em!" (1.2.326). Among the numerous adjectives which have been used to describe "sin," Eben's "purty" may well be unique. Eben seems to be using the word "sin" for its shock value—to emphasize his scorn for old Ephraim's preaching.

At least one reason Eben is initially attracted to Abbie is that she is exactly the opposite of his hypocritically puritanical father. Openly acknowledging her carnal desire for him, Abbie does not attach much significance to the Divine: "Vengeance o' God on the hull o' us! What d'we give a durn? I love ye, Eben! God knows I love ye!" (2.3.355). Disregarding formal religion and its commandments against covetousness, adultery, and murder, Abbie and Eben make their own religion of sexual love, to which even its fruit, their beautiful son, must be sacrificed.

Some critics interpret Abbie and Eben's affair as inspirational. Edwin A. Engel, despite his conviction that the closure of the play is unconvincing,[12] sees *Desire under the Elms* as a celebration of "the divinity of nature" and "the triumph of pagan naturalism over indurated religion."[13] In the same vein, Barrett H. Clark interprets Abbie and Eben as having achieved a kind of victory over their puritanical surroundings: "They have drunk deep of life and passion, and they have no regrets. . . . Though they have lived among those whose religion is hateful, they have broken through into the light of day."[14] Of what this "light of day" might possibly consist, however, Clark does not attempt to elaborate.

The viewer may wonder what remains for the adulterous pair after formal religion and Judeo-Christian morality have been discarded. Living only for the glories of the flesh, Abbie and Eben seem little better than animals. Indeed, O'Neill often refers to his personae in animal terms. Old Ephraim, uncomfortable in human society, prefers sleeping with his cows. Hence it is not surprising that his progeny are described as bovine. Eben is frequently referred to as a "calf" (2.4.357 [by Ephraim]) or a "bull" (2.1.341 [by Abbie]). His brothers are described as *"two friendly oxen"* (1.1.321). Abbie, the newcomer in the family, seems to slither like a snake in her famous description of sexual desire, in which the hissing *s* sounds recall Satan in the Garden of Eden:

> (. . . *her body squirms desirously—she murmurs languorously)* Hain't the sun strong an' hot? Ye kin feel it burnin' into the earth—Nature—makin' thin's grow—bigger 'n' bigger—burnin' inside ye— making ye want t'grow—into somethin' else—till ye're jined with it—an' it's your'n—but it owns ye, too—an' makes ye grow bigger like a tree—like them elums—*(She laughs again softly, holding his eyes. He takes a step toward her, compelled against his will.)* Nature'll beat ye, Eben. Ye might's well own up t'it fust's last. (2.1.342, emphasis added)

The "Nature" described by Abbie, which compels man to be joined with it to the extent that it "owns" him and can "beat" the resolutions of his will, seems more sinister than divine.

Furthermore, the result of all this "pagan naturalism" appears to be not so much triumph and illumination, as Engel and Clark maintain, but C. W. E. Bigsby's "moral anarchy."[15] Eben, for example, never repents the deadly hatred of his father he expresses in the opening scene when he hopes aloud that the long-absent patriarch is dead (1.1.321). When he believes Abbie has killed Ephraim at the end of the play, Eben, despite his astonishment, is not angry but glad: "An' serves him right! . . . the old skunk . . ." (3.3.370). Sworn to avenge his mother's death by eventually repossessing what he claims was her farm, Eben has extended his intense rivalry toward his father, even before Abbie's arrival, toward dispossessing the old man sexually as well. Early in the play Eben boasts to his brothers of having repudiated his father's prior claim on Minnie, the town prostitute: "I jest grabbed holt an' tuk her! *(proudly)* Yes, siree! I tuk her. She may've been his'n—an' your'n, too—but she's mine now!" (1.3.328). Simeon's reply at this point gives the wary viewer a clue as to the future direction the play will take. Having just learned that their aged father is bringing home a bride, Simeon speculates to Eben, "Mebbe ye'll try t'make her your'n too?" (1.3.329).

Nor is Eben troubled by the quasi-incestuous nature of his attraction to Abbie. Possessing Abbie is rather clearly Eben's way of not only dispossessing his hated father but possessing the mother he had always desired and has lost. "I'm yer new Maw" (1.4.338), Abbie first introduces herself in seductive tones. Eben initially succumbs to her sexual invitation in the par-

lor in which his dead mother was "laid out" for burial (2.2.352), where both
he and Abbie feel her presence and manage to convince themselves she
approves. In order to facilitate the seduction, Abbie encourages Eben to
recreate his mother for her, so that she can play the role of "mother" more
effectively:

> ABBIE— . . . Tell me about yer Maw, Eben.
> EBEN—They hain't nothin' much. She was kind. She was good.
> ABBIE—. . . I'll be kind an' good t' ye!
> EBEN—Sometimes she used t' sing fur me.
>
> . . . .
> ABBIE— . . . I'll sing fur ye! I'll die fur ye! . . . Don't cry, Eben! I'll take
> yer Maw's place! I'll be everythin' she was t' ye! Let me kiss ye, Eben! . . .
> (2.3.353–54)

Although Abbie is depicted as eventually developing a passion for Eben
that transcends her materialistic desires, in their initial sexual encounter in
the parlor Abbie's primary motivation is not the overpowering physical
attraction between her and Eben, so much as her desire for the farm. Scheming to use Eben's lovemaking as a means of producing an heir for old
Ephraim, she calculatingly manipulates Eben's oedipal feelings in order to
seduce him. Like Eben, she seems almost totally without moral feelings or
values. Neither experiences any guilt concerning their technically incestu-
ous adultery. Eben actually lords it over his father (without confessing his
sexual encounter with his stepmother), as if taking pride and pleasure in a
victory over the old man. Abbie, as she waits for the sheriff Eben has sum-
moned to arrest her, also professes no regrets concerning their lovemaking:
"*(lifting her head as if defying God)* I don't repent that sin! I hain't askin' God t'
fergive that!" (3.4.375). That Abbie is sorry for any of her actions—even
killing the baby—comes as a surprise in view of her almost complete lack of
moral awareness.

Virginia Floyd asserts that the conclusion of *Desire under the Elms* "provides the best illustration in the early plays of O'Neill's statement: 'In all my
plays sin is punished and redemption takes place.'"[16] Edgar F. Racey Jr. also
interprets Eben's salvation as being assured when he is "freed of his desire
for the farm, when he returns to Abbie (and the rope)."[17] In the same vein,
Travis Bogard sees Abbie and Eben as finally "find[ing] redemption in recognition of error and the assumption of responsibility."[18] The justification
for this interpretation of the closure is the repudiation of the initial greed
evinced by the couple, which occurs at the end of the play. Abbie destroys
her claim to the farm when she murders her son, who was to be Ephraim's

new heir; Eben renounces his own claim to the property when he follows Abbie to prison. The couple repent their actions that were motivated by greed (Abbie's deliberate conception of an heir to supplant Eben and Eben's distrust of Abbie's motive for having the child, which results in its death) and accept their punishment.

Nevertheless, the extent to which sin and repentance may be considered the theme of the play appears subject to the moral limitations of its personae. If Abbie and Eben are "redeemed" from greed through their love, which causes them to repent those "sins" committed against it, their "redemption" appears confined to an amelioration of character rather than an indication of any "salvation" in the traditional religious sense. The lovers never repent their other crimes against nature, which include patricidal desires, adultery, and technical incest. Only the evening before Abbie murders the infant, Eben exhibits the same murderous rivalry toward his father that he demonstrated in act 1 eleven months earlier. He protests to Abbie regarding their baby, "I don't like this. I don't like lettin' on what's mine's his'n. I been doin' that all my life. I'm gittin' t' the end o' b'arin' it!" (3.1.363). Abbie, who after killing the baby regrets her action, also demonstrates little change of character: she wishes she had killed the old man instead. Regarding their adultery and technical incest, both Abbie and Eben vehemently declare their lack of contrition at the end of the play (3.4.375).

Furthermore, the couple's repudiation of greed and acknowledgment of guilt for the death of their son, which necessarily occurs very late in the play, seems excessively theatrical. The audience has not been adequately prepared for the radical changes in their characters. That such a calculating woman as Abbie, who marries a man forty-one years her senior to acquire a home and seduces his son to ensure her title to it, could have been swept away by so intense a passion as to murder her baby—a deed planned hours earlier to keep Eben from leaving her—defies credibility at the outset. That shortly afterward this same woman, who, the audience is asked to believe, has exchanged her greed for the farm for her desire to keep Eben, then suddenly renounces the opportunity to continue fulfilling that relationship to which she has sacrificed their son (Eben has asked her to run away with him before the sheriff arrives) for another newly developed obsession—her need for punishment—renders her melodramatic. Neither the calculating seductress nor the woman consumed by passion is recognizable in Abbie who, suddenly developing a conscience, declares, "I got t' take my punishment—t'pay fur my sin" (3.4.375). Equally startling is the change in Eben, who metamorphoses in a matter of minutes from a suspicious lover, ready to abandon his mistress, into a devoted companion who will follow her to the death. As the couple is led off, perhaps to be hanged, they seem inexplicably at peace with their fate. The implication is that confession has unburdened their souls, and that they are content because, despite having apparently lost all, "they are now certain of their love for each other."[19]

If this interpretation of the ending sounds mawkish, the fault is O'Neill's. The Hollywood-type ending, in which the lovers stop to kiss and admire the sunrise *"raptly in attitudes strangely aloof and devout"* (3.4.378) before being led off to jail, violates some of the most basic criteria for closure—Marianna Torgovnick's standard of "honesty" and David H. Richter's assertion that the conclusion, in order to be "satisfying" must not be "false to the boundless nature of human life."[20] The word *"devout,"* used to describe the couple's admiration of the sunrise, is particularly overwhelming with its connotations of a more religious-type redemption than that implied by the text. Perhaps, in completing *Elms*, O'Neill was still under the spell of *The Rime of the Ancient Mariner*, which he had adapted for the stage the year before (1923).[21] In Samuel Taylor Coleridge's long dramatic poem the old Mariner is redeemed from the punitive consequences of his unnatural act (killing the albatross) when he inadvertently admires and blesses the water snakes. The closure of *Desire under the Elms*, a dramatic work almost totally lacking the poetic and spiritual qualities of *The Ancient Mariner*, seems to imply a comparable redemption. Abbie and Eben's brief tribute to the morning sky suggests reunion with the natural world, from which they have been estranged through their greed.

Edwin A. Engel relates the theatrical closure of *Elms* to O'Neill's tendency to resolve conflicts "in denouements of sudden insight into the 'age-old processes of nature,' of mystic ecstasy and throbbing exaltation," which he demonstrates in many of the plays of his "yea-saying years."[22] These incredible closures are easy to spot because whenever O'Neill deliberately tries to impose one of his "resolutions" upon a play, he employs high-sounding, poetic language, as though trying to achieve with elevated language what he has failed to render credible through the structure of the play. Rather than ameliorating his attempts at closure, the poetic language usually only emphasizes its failure. Robert Mayo uses this type of language at the end of *Beyond the Horizon*: "It's a free beginning—the start of my voyage! I've won to my trip—the right of release—beyond the horizon!" (3.2.652). However, Robert is a self-deceived character, and the audience can attribute his elevated speech to delusion. Such an interpretation is not possible in *Desire under the Elms*. Abbie and Eben are calculatingly rational, and the poetic language occurs in O'Neill's stage direction.

As Engel concludes, the ending of *Desire under the Elms* is unconvincing:

> [E]cstatic yea-saying has transformed [the couple's] rapaciousness, cun-
> ning, violence [*sic*] into rapturous and unquestioning devotion. *Burning*
> *with desire, panting like two animals*, Eben and Abbie, once their passion is
> consummated, are converted into self-sacrificing lover and tender, for-
> bearing mistress.[23]

Other critics who find the closure unconvincing include C. W. E. Bigsby
and Ruby Cohn.[24] Clifford Leech observes succinctly, "As Abbie forgets to
be a mother, forgets her wish for a secure mistress-ship of the farm-house,
so Eben forgets his longing for the farm, his memory of his mother's wrong.
And these things were too strong to forget."[25] Robert Bechtold Heilman
similarly objects to the lovers' possibly "too easy serenity at the end."[26] In
support of Heilman's assessment, the lovers do not suffer or struggle with
conflicting feelings as do the characters of O'Neill's more convincing later
plays. After two or three minutes during which Eben furiously admonishes
his weeping mistress for killing their baby, both are reconciled to punishment and at peace in their love.

In conclusion, as a drama about the base passions of animalistic creatures, *Desire under the Elms* is powerful and convincing until the closure, which
the incredulous viewer may feel he is being—in Gerhart Hauptmann's words
regarding artificially imposed endings—"coerced to accept."[27] In order to
psychologically credit the transformation of O'Neill's lovers at the end, the
viewer requires at least some inkling of their capacity for change earlier in
the play. For closure to be satisfying for the audience, according to June
Schlueter, "the determinations of the prestructure" must be working; the
closure is supposed to give "an impression of inevitability."[28] Once again (as
in *Beyond the Horizon*) O'Neill's "perverse mind" seems to have undermined
the dark ending for which he has prepared his audience with a sudden
suggestion of redemption (the ending which, I propose, "delights [his] soul").
As if unable to believe the redemptive endings himself, however, he proceeds to undermine them in turn in the final lines of both plays—in *Horizon*
with the final despairing tableau between Andrew and Ruth, and in *Elms*
with the sheriff's closing lines ("It's a jim-dandy farm, no denyin'. Wished I
owned it!" [3.4.377–78]), which recall the possessiveness that originated
the tragedy.

Despite the foregoing defects, however, the closure of *Desire under the*
Elms is not without merit. The couple admiring the sunrise as "purty"
recalls the opening line of the play in which Eben declared the sunset "purty"
before meeting Abbie. The guilty couple may be hanged, but, as the
rising sun indicates, life will go on. Greed also continues, the sheriff's final
speech suggests. A similar tragedy may be repeated. Nevertheless, Barbara

Herrnstein Smith's requirement that closure "[create] in the reader the expectation of nothing"[29] has been fulfilled for these characters. Egocentric old Ephraim is lonelier than ever. He has neither wife nor heir to his life's work—the farm. Even his pathetic efforts to join Simeon and Peter in California are thwarted: Eben has stolen the money he had planned to use for boat passage. The old patriarch loses all but the land he has cleared and whatever cows he can manage to round up. Too disillusioned to marry a fourth time, for his tyranny and selfishness he reaps the isolation he has sown. As for Abbie and Eben after confessing to the murder, their fate is clear—imprisonment or death. Were it not for their too easy "redemption" of character, which somewhat distorts the focus of the play, the production of meaning that ought to emerge from the closure[30] would be clear: greed, selfishness, and lust lead to isolation, violence, and death.

However, O'Neill does not normally labor to convey messages to his audiences in the manner of George Eliot. If he did, he would not be Eugene O'Neill. As Joseph Wood Krutch pointed out in 1924 regarding O'Neill's work up through *Elms*, his achievement does not lie "in the greatness or in the clarity of his thought," but in his depiction of raw emotional power.[31]

5

Two Failed Thesis Plays:
Dynamo and *Days without End*

O'Neill wrote *Dynamo* (1928) and *Days without End* (1933) as part of what was to have been a trilogy (the third play was never written) tentatively entitled *Myths for the God-forsaken*. His purpose in writing the sequence bordered on the messianic. He professed to be

> dig[ging] at the roots of the sickness of today as I feel it—the death of the old God and the failure of Science and Materialism to give any satisfying new One for the surviving religious instinct to find a meaning for life in, and to comfort its fears of death with.[1]

In the two completed plays the heroes, disillusioned with formal religion, are driven by their irrepressible "surviving religious instinct" to a doomed quest for a substitute God. In *Dynamo* Reuben Light turns to science in the form of electricity in his search for a deity. In *Days without End* John Loving, after twenty-five years of exploring and rejecting one form of belief after another, returns to the Catholic Church of his childhood. In both *Dynamo* and *Days without End*, as in O'Neill's other plays written to illustrate a thesis (*The Fountain* [1922], *Marco Millions* [1924], and *Lazarus Laughed* [1926])—for the most part, the characters are wooden, the dialogue flat, and the endings contrived.

DYNAMO (1928)

Dynamo, an unimportant play, is remarkable mainly for its inconsistency of tone. Closure in this play, according to David F. Hult's definition of closure as an "inner movement in the direction of unity or completeness,"[2] is thus rendered even more problematic than usual. The reader (*Dynamo* and *Days without End* are rarely performed), baffled by the rapid shifts in tone, is unable to determine where the action is heading. The opening scene—depicting the conflict between Reverend Light, the Bible-spouting preacher who is terrified of lightning, and Ramsay Fife, the atheist superintendent of a hydroelectric plant who plays practical jokes—suggests comedy of manners *à la* Molière. The following scene, the romantic confrontation between seventeen-year-old Reuben, the minister's gullible son, and Ada Fife, the sixteen-year-old daughter of the clergyman's sworn enemy, is light comedy of the *Ah, Wilderness!* type. In the same scene, however, Reuben's mother hides behind a hedge and works herself up into a fury watching her son's first attempt to kiss Ada: the play appears to be dwindling into farce.

What follows recalls a scene from an Oscar Wilde comedy. Terrified by the "secret" Ramsay Fife has jestingly entrusted him with (Fife has avowed having murdered a man in his "past," but has actually read this story in the newspaper and is trying to discredit Reuben to his smitten daughter), Reuben confides Fife's "confession" to his mother. Although Reuben's mother has promised to remain silent, Reverend Light, having overheard all in the closet where he has been hiding, suddenly emerges. After beating Reuben and locking him in his room, this ordained "light" of Christian charity to the world rushes off to report his neighbor to the police. Reuben, furious with his father for beating him and with his mother for deceiving him, and believing he has lost all credibility with Ada, renounces the formal religion preached by his father and disappears from home for fifteen months.

When Reuben returns in the second act, he is strangely changed. All he talks about is electricity, to which he jokingly refers as the new God: "Electricity is God now. And we've got to learn to know God, haven't we? Well, that's what I'm after!" (2.1.865). Even before visiting his parents' home, he arranges to secure a job at Fife's power plant, so he can be near the dynamos. Upon subsequently learning of his mother's death, for which the minister cannot resist blaming Reuben's absence, the young man is devastated with grief and guilt. Although he begins having sexual relations with Ada, he actually starts to reject her—unconsciously influenced by his mother's dislike of the girl.

Gradually the play takes on a more somber aspect as Reuben starts to lose his grip on reality. His mental disintegration is particularly evident in his changing attitudes toward electricity. Before leaving home he had asserted the utter neutrality of electricity (in the form of lightning) toward man: "[Electricity] doesn't give a damn about [anyone]" (1.852). Even when he returned fascinated by the dynamos, the idea of worshipping electricity was still a joke to him, something to be burlesqued in the language of his

religious training: "It'll be like bringing my gospel to the heathen . . . let
there be electric light!" (2.1.861). As his mental condition deteriorates, however, Reuben starts to take this new "religion" seriously: he begins to asso-
ciate the huge dynamo, upon which he perceives maternal breasts, with the
beloved mother he has lost. In this deplorable state Reuben ardently defends
the dynamo as an object of worship: "[to Ada] You blasphemous fool you!
Do you dare to deny her [the dynamo]! 'The Fool saith in his heart—'"
(3.1.878). The obvious burlesque of religious fervor indicated by Reuben's
language, which combines his father's preaching with the Old Testament,
suggests a satiric intent on O'Neill's part. However, the reader who fails to
perceive humor in the depiction of serious mental illness is unsure whether
to laugh or cry.

The action now proceeds to become undeniably grave, although the
language and imagery remain burlesque. Believing he has received a message from his mother, Reuben kneels down before the generator (a ridicu-
lous image) and tries to pray to it. Upon receiving no response, he concludes that the dynamo, like his mother when she was alive, wants him to
purify himself of his desire for Ada: "She [the dynamo] wants us to realize
the secret dwells in her! She wants some one man to love her purely and
when she finds him worthy she will love him and give him the secret of
truth and he will become the new savior who will bring happiness and
peace to men! And I'm going to be that savior . . ." (3.1.874). Reuben madly
perceives himself as a sort of modern grail-quester who must attain chastity
to win the approval of his god.

The climax of the play is deadly serious. In what Reuben calls the
"temple" area housing the generator, he kisses Ada, whom he has virtually
stopped seeing, to prove he has overcome his lust. Overcome by passion, he
rapes Ada, thus failing the test. Attempting to perform what O'Neill described in a letter to George Jean Nathan as an "expiatory sacrifice,"[3] Reuben
shoots the girl and electrocutes himself on the dynamo.

The concluding sequence returns the play to farce. Upon discovering
Reuben's electrocuted body, Ada's childlike mother protests to the dynamo:
"What're you singing for? I should think you'd be ashamed! . . . [She pounds
on the generator] You hateful old thing, you!" (3.3.885). The image of this
"tall and stout [woman], weighing well over two hundred" pounds (1.2.829–30)
hitting and scolding the machine as if it were a naughty child seems calcu-
lated to evoke laughter in the audience. At the same time, May Fife's naïve
observation that the dynamo is singing when it should be mourning reiterates O'Neill's solemn conviction that the dynamo, like Reverend Light's
God Who failed to strike blasphemers with lightning on cue, is totally indifferent to man.

Despite O'Neill's opinion that *Dynamo* was "one of the [great] ones"[4] while he was writing it, the plot—particularly the ending—suffers from manipulation to illustrate his avowed thesis regarding the failure of science. Reuben's insanity seems contrived to justify his outrageous conduct (no sane person would kneel down and pray to a generator). Furthermore, O'Neill imposed a catastrophic climax on the play which the comedic context did not call for and could not support.

Although Travis Bogard suggests the ending is unclear as to whether Reuben finds God by "crucifying" himself on the dynamo or whether his death demonstrates the futility of man's search for a substitute God,[5] the tone of the play suggests O'Neill can have intended only the latter. To be sure, Reuben thinks he is being reunited with his Mother/God through death, but the dynamo makes not the slightest response to his prayers, nor does O'Neill anywhere suggest that it can. Reuben is insane, and his and Ada's deaths are the meaningless result of "the failure of Science and Materialism to give any satisfying new [God] for the surviving primitive religious instinct to find a meaning for life in." Reuben's last speech, far from suggesting the heroism that Bogard finds it possible to perceive, can only indicate what O'Neill himself described as a "flight from life to security."[6] As Reuben prepares to electrocute himself on the dynamo, he cries out, "I don't want any miracle, Mother! I don't want to know the truth! I only want you to hide me, Mother! Never let me go from you again! Please, Mother!" (3.3.884). In dying, he is seeking to return to the womb.

The inconsistency of tone that mars *Dynamo* does not occur in the next play of the intended trilogy, *Days without End*, in which Catholicism rather than science inspires the religious fervor of the hero. Despite his intention to explore science as a "myth for the God-forsaken," O'Neill appears to have been unable to conceive of technology as a serious object of worship. On one occasion he whimsically compared the possible solaces of science to a "puppy biscuit":

A general idea-title for the trilogy might be God Is Dead! Long Live— What? with science supplying an answer which to religion-starved primitive instinct is like feeding a puppy biscuit to a lion. Or something like that.[7]

Closure does not exist in this play,[8] since its various elements fail to gel. The reader is dissatisfied with O'Neill's heavy-handed use of the oedipal complex and Reuben's resultant insanity to end the play. The violent deaths are unexpected after the farcical tone of act 1. Mrs. Fife's concluding action (scolding and hitting the dynamo) seems a strangely inappropriate lament

for the young lovers' deaths. Instead of experiencing the gratifying fulfillment of structure and cessation of expectations that usually indicate closure
as a play ends, the reader feels as if he has been buffeted around.

DAYS WITHOUT END (1933)

Days without End, another failed play depicting O'Neill's vision of the contemporary spiritual dilemma, is of considerable interest from the standpoint of closure. Complicating O'Neill's already demonstrated difficulty with
this "most often revised component of any play,"[9] the hero, John Loving,
bears a striking resemblance to his creator. Both are writers, both left the
Catholic Church as teenagers owing to a traumatic family incident,[10] and
both are reported to have since quested for faith in one philosophical system after another.[11] Furthermore, both men have engaged in an extramarital affair (O'Neill with Carlotta while he was married to Agnes), which
caused them to fear for their marriages. The striking biographical similari-
ties may help to explain the extreme difficulty that O'Neill experienced
completing this drama. He worked his way through eight draft versions[12]
and at least six different endings[13] before "finishing" this play in a manner
that satisfied no one, not even himself.

The plot is almost an account of the play's troublesome composition:
the imaginative writer/hero struggles to attain closure in his life, which he
associates with the problematic completion of the autobiographical novel
he is writing. John Loving had succumbed to a secret extramarital encounter because he feared a malevolent Fate might destroy his perfect happiness
with his wife, Elsa. Through that solitary act of infidelity with Lucy, Elsa's
best friend, he planned to neutralize Fate's ominous power of reversal by
shattering Elsa's trust in him and closing off his hopes for happiness once
and for all. Thereby he would have ended the suspense of waiting for Fate
and attained—if nothing else—the peace of closure.

As the play opens, however, John is living in fear of attaining the very
closure he has sought—the destruction of his happy marriage. He is afraid
Lucy will expose his adultery to Elsa, who will surely leave him, since she
left her first husband for infidelity. John is writing a novel about this very
situation, which he plans to narrate to his wife. The advantage of the
fictionalized version is that he can create his own ending, and perhaps
through the novel influence closure in the plot of his life. He is having considerable trouble deciding upon his ending, however. He favors having his
hero confess and be forgiven by his wife, but his demonic alter ego, Loving
(objectified as a character, that can be seen only by John, for the purpose of

dramatizing John's inner conflict), recommends having the wife die of pneumonia (as did John's parents when he was a youth) and the hero commit suicide. Still a third ending is proposed—for John, if not for his hero—by John's newly returned spiritual guardian, Father Baird. The priest is confident that his former ward will return to the Catholic Church he abandoned twenty-five years earlier as a result of his parents' untimely deaths.

From the opening dialogue between John and Loving about possible conclusions for the novel, *Days without End* is concerned with the potentially prescriptive or self-fulfilling power of endings. When Loving suggests his dark ending (death by pneumonia and suicide) for the novel, John, apparently fearing his own imaginative power, responds, "It is dangerous—to call things" (1.114). After Lucy telephones and John's anxiety regarding exposure mounts, Loving capitalizes on John's belief that ending the novel can affect the outcome of his life: "You'd better be prepared for any stupid folly. And better get the end of your novel decided upon, so you can tell your plot—*before it's too late*" (1.117, emphasis added). Too late for what? Loving can only mean that Fate, in the form of Lucy, appears to be closing in with an ending; and John had better select his own (via the novel) before that fast-approaching point when his options will disappear.

When John, convinced that Elsa would never forgive him, finally settles upon and narrates a tragic ending to his novel, that ending seems to have the prescriptive force he has feared. As if mesmerized by the ending John has selected for her fictional counterpart, Elsa, who is still recovering from a severe case of the flu, walks out into the rain and returns ill. When Father Baird assures her she will soon recover, she protests, "But that would spoil John's story, don't you think? That would be very inconsiderate after he's worked out such a convenient end for me" (3.2.165). If Elsa dies, Loving assures John, he will virtually have murdered her with his imagination (4.1.172).

At this point, fortunately for John and his wife (if not for the drama), John's prescriptive hypothesis (along with the play) falls apart. Up until Elsa's illness, John, perhaps driven by the sudden deaths of his parents to take overzealous control of his life, has been writing his own plot. Virtually all the action in this drama so far—excluding the unexpected arrival of Father Baird—has proceeded from deliberate choice on John's part. His affair with Lucy was initiated to cause Elsa, who he assumed would eventually learn of it from her friend, to lose faith in him. From the first, Elsa's knowledge of his betrayal was part of his plan. When he narrates his novel to Elsa and Father Baird, another deliberate action on his part, he is using the novel as a vehicle for confessing. Believing that Lucy has not told Elsa yet, he insists Elsa make the connection between the fictional marriage and their own by asking her to identify with the wife. If Elsa is unable to assure him she would forgive the erring husband, he will at least have the consolation of closure for his plot. When Elsa, knowing the infidelity he has described is his own, refuses to forgive, John's original plan for closure proceeds on schedule. His demonic alter ego, Loving, suggests walking in the rain to the flu-weakened Elsa, and she follows his cue. The plot, which thus far has developed through John's carefully planned direction, ought most naturally to have concluded with John's attainment of the unhappy closure he had initially sought—Elsa's death and his own desolation. However, the playwright appears to have been unwilling to dispose of his fictional counterpart in such a way.

The ending O'Neill finally selected breaks the structural pattern of the play, John's control over his "end."[14] In his novel, the hero goes to the church of his childhood, seeking reunion with his dead wife through God—but unable to believe, either commits suicide or carries on in despair. In O'Neill's play, similarly, when John learns that Elsa's illness is life-threatening, he proceeds—like his hero—to the church. Thereafter, however, the action departs drastically from John's novel. What instead transpires is the "end" John, in his despair, had been unable to imagine—Father Baird's "end": John experiences a miraculous return to the faith. Equally miraculous and beyond John's inept control, his wife, Elsa, forgives him and lives.

Considerable speculation exists whether or not the ending, the hero's return to the faith of his childhood, reflects O'Neill's own desire to return to the Church, an interpretation that O'Neill's reported actions and comments do not render clear. O'Neill is reported to have told Philip Moeller that the play ending may have been wish fulfillment on his part (1 January 1934).[15] However, at the same time O'Neill appears to have been constantly trying to minimize the Catholic element in the play. Furthermore, he refused to make any changes to gain Church approval, insisting that he was not writing about Catholicism so much as the more general experience of faith.[16] Recognizing O'Neill's effort to distance himself from the Church, Edward L. Shaughnessy interprets *Days without End* as the product of a writer "formed in the crucible of Irish Catholicism," who was pursued by Francis Thompson's "hound of heaven" to quest for at least some sort of faith (not necessarily Catholicism) all his life.[17] Also attributing *Days without End* to a "religious impulse" on O'Neill's part, Louis Sheaffer quotes from O'Neill's "Memoranda on Masks" (written in 1932 while he was struggling with *Days*), which calls for the return of theater to its spiritual function as a "Temple."[18] Doris Alexander, however, downplays the interpretation of *Days* as a longing for religious faith on O'Neill's part. Using Carlotta's comment on the play's ending that "it has nothing to do with *Christianity* or *prayer*" but is about Elsa's "great and all-consuming *love* for her husband,"[19] Alexander documents *Days* as one in a series of O'Neill plays (including *Servitude* [1914] and *Welded* [1923]) "about the search for God in romantic love."[20] From the conflicting evidence, Travis Bogard (whose study precedes Alexander's book) concludes, "[I]t is impossible to determine whether O'Neill wrote his series of theological dramas because of some inner quest of his own, or whether he was led to these themes because the departure from realism [in his earlier experimental plays] showed him that they were there to be explored."[21]

Nevertheless, it seems possible that by terminating John's dilemma with a return to Catholicism, O'Neill may have been hoping (the "wishful thinking" he acknowledged to Moeller) that the ending's "prescriptive power" concerning a renewal of faith would carry over to him. Unlike John Loving, however, O'Neill was unable to solve his dilemma by returning to the religion of his boyhood. Nor does he appear to have resolved his painful skepticism elsewhere at this point. His correspondence attests to his continuing anxiety, "[T]he end [of *Days*] hardly means that I have gone back to Catholicism. I haven't. But I would be a liar if I didn't admit that, *for the sake of my soul's peace*, I have often wished I could [emphasis added]."[22]

In view of the foregoing admission, it is scarcely surprising that O'Neill's attempt to write an affirmative ending for his hero, exuding what Doris V. Falk describes as "not only optimism, but faith—a positive solution to the 'sickness of today,'" failed to convince most audiences.[23] If the ending lacks conviction, it is because O'Neill could not believe it himself. Rather, he seems to have seized upon it out of desperation after struggling with six different drafts. "Original endings tend to be more successful than revised ones," which often stand out like "artificial limb[s]," Henry J. Schmidt concludes from his study of German dramas.[24] If ever an ending resembled an "artificial limb," John's sudden reversion to Catholicism does. It comes out of nowhere—breaking the structural pattern of the play—and appears imposed upon the plot.

I am not suggesting that the melodramatic ending spoils an otherwise salvageable play. *Days without End* is unbelievable from the outset. That a man, out of fear of his wife's death, nearly precipitates it, and that his wife, out of respect for the plot that has been written for her fictional counterpart, cooperates in her near destruction—both strain credulity. Elsa's sudden forgiveness of John is also inexplicable, and his miraculous reconciliation with God—considering John's businesslike method—seems to culminate the preposterousness of the drama. He tries to bargain with the Deity, arguing that he (John) forgives God for allowing his parents to die; therefore, God ought to forgive his lapse of faith and save Elsa. Nowhere does John exhibit any significant change in character that would justify his miraculous salvation. He has demonstrated an almost total lack of concern for Elsa's well-being throughout the play; even his prayers for her life seem based on his own need for her love, rather than for her.

Early in act 1 Father Baird says, "The end isn't yet, Jack" (1.121). At the end of the play, the reader still feels "The end isn't yet": closure has not yet been earned. The reader's experience of closure as "gratifying" and "secure," writes June Schlueter, depends upon what has preceded it. "If the determinations of the prestructure" are not working, she continues, "the reader will have the feeling of an arbitrary end, unprepared for, unearned."[25] In *Days without End* John has done nothing to merit his miraculous redemption. Since his "leap of faith" has not been justified or accounted for in any way, what is to prevent him—at some time in the future—from "leaping back"? From torturing Elsa all over again? His declaration of faith in the last lines of the play sounds like unmotivated rant: "Love lives forever! Death is dead! . . . Life laughs with God's love again! Life laughs with love!" (4.2.180). Once again, O'Neill appears to be trying to create through words and exclamation points what he has failed to achieve through the action of the play.

The ending of *Days*, which purports to be affirmative, actually bears a curious resemblance to the catastrophic conclusion of *Dynamo*. In both plays the hero's quest for faith terminates in what may be interpreted as a symbolic return to the womb—Reuben Light to the protection of Mother/Dynamo, with whom he seeks oneness, and John Loving to the open arms of Mother Church. In *Dynamo*, as I have demonstrated, O'Neill appears to have deliberately undercut the significance of his hero's electrocution on the dynamo by concluding the play farcically. In *Days without End*, however, O'Neill can only have intended John's miraculous conversion to be taken literally, since Elsa forgives John and lives.

Nevertheless, O'Neill himself professed dissatisfaction with John's final gesture,[26] which Doris V. Falk reads as a terrified withdrawal from life.[27] Similarly providing a "closure" for the play more consistent with the text than that indicated by O'Neill, Gustav H. Blanke argues that "The leap of faith seems the result of anxiety and comes as the equivalent of an intellectual sacrifice."[28] In the same vein, Lionel Trilling sees John's final action as "the annihilation of the questioning mind": John creeps "into the dark womb of Mother Church and pull[s] the universe in with him."[29]

The structural inadequacy of the ending may not be the only reason it has failed to satisfy readers to the extent that some "rewrite" O'Neill's play, however. Strong closures, among which Wayne C. Booth includes "resounding, unambiguous triumphs,"[30] such as John's "life laugh[ing] with love" speech (4.2.180) that follows the priest's announcement that Elsa has forgiven him and will live, are declining in popularity today. Once again William Carlos Williams's argument that a poem should not be so "closed" as to click shut like the lid of a box[31] appears applicable to modern drama. Twentieth-century audiences appear to have outgrown resolutions that suggest the problems of life are totally soluble. The more sophisticated modern viewer is less concerned with absolute closure than with verisimilitude or fidelity to life.

In conclusion, the entire play, *Days without End*, may be considered an evaluative study of strong closure or the effort to impose a decisive ending upon a plot. John Loving is so obsessed with the need for total closure in his life and work that he appears to exemplify Joseph Conrad's turn-of-the-century (1905) conjecture: "Perhaps the only true desire of mankind . . . is to be set at rest."[32] John is unable to enjoy the happiness at hand (his marriage to Elsa) because of his fear that the joy will not last and consequent anxiety to know the "end." Rather than live in a condition of joy shadowed by constant anxiety due to his overactive imagination, John elects to terminate his happiness at once, thus closing his plot. Any sort of closure, to John, is better than suspense. Even having his beloved wife die is preferable to living in fear of such an event. Perhaps he should die too. Perhaps Loving is right—the only true release from life's tormenting uncertainty is suicide: "[W]hy should you wait for an end [death] you know when it is in your power to grasp that end now!" (4.1.175–76). John's excessive anxiety regarding closure not only disrupts the happiness, but endangers the lives of himself and his wife. Furthermore, he suffers immeasurably from imagining disastrous ends that never materialize.

O'Neill, in the headstrong manner of his hero, John Loving, imposed a strong, artificial ending on *Days* that he later regretted; but it was the last time he would do so in his lengthy career. He appears to have learned from John Loving's unhappy pursuit of closure to practice the passive acceptance of life to which John Keats referred as "Negative Capability"—the capacity of remaining in "uncertainties, mysteries, doubts, without any irritable reaching after fact and reason. . . ."[33] Rather than try to "solve" life by "creating" artificial endings for plays like *Dynamo* and *Days without End*, O'Neill would henceforth allow life to unfold for itself. Never again would he attempt to force closure upon his work. From *Ah, Wilderness!* ([1933], the play he wrote in the midst of his struggles with *Days*), through his late great period, his endings are more open and seem to grow out of the plays.

6

Success at Last:
Closure in *Mourning Becomes Electra*

That *Mourning Becomes Electra* (1931) was highly praised only a few decades ago as one of the major dramatic works of the century[1] seems almost a surprise in view of the significant flaws more recently attributed to the trilogy. C. W. E. Bigsby (1982) has pointed out the "studied Freudianism" and melodramatic Gothic elements ("poison bottles, guns, overheard conversations, revealing documents").[2] Another of Bigsby's valid objections to the trilogy concerns its tone of "hysterical intensity,"[3] which was noted by Edwin A. Engel as early as 1953.[4] But the most universally hailed flaw of *Electra* appears to be its prosaic language. Subject, tone, and action appear to demand poetry or great language, the glaring lack of which is deplored by all the critics, and even by O'Neill.

Even more surprising than the huge contemporary critical success of the trilogy so demonstrably flawed with regard to content, tone, and language is the apparent reason for its success. Jean Chothia's surmise (1979) appears a consensus of opinion: "[T]he high praise the play has received can probably be attributed to the effectiveness of the ending."[5] Before *Electra* nearly all O'Neill's plays had been critically attacked for their melodramatic or ambiguous endings, which—as in the case of *Beyond the Horizon* (1918) and *Desire Under the Elms* (1924)—weaken the total effect of the dramas. In sharp contrast to the plays that precede it, the ending of *Mourning Becomes Electra* has been almost universally praised. Virginia Floyd (1985) hails Lavinia's final action of locking herself in the mansion with the Mannon ghosts as "the supreme gesture of atonement in the canon, more dramatic even than Parritt's leap to his death in *The Iceman Cometh* or any of the other suicides."[6] Chothia, noting the "unexpected integrity" of the final sequence of the trilogy, suggests the play action appears almost to have been "constructed in order to present the ending." She observes that whereas manuscript notes and revisions of earlier plays indicate that O'Neill frequently "had no clear ending in mind when he began writing," O'Neill had noted in his diary before beginning the play (August 1929) that he had "'given [his] Yankee Electra [a] tragic end, worthy of her.'"[7]

Closure in this highly praised ending of the three-play work (*The Homecoming*, *The Hunted*, and *The Haunted*) depends largely on the resolution of two questions posed early in the drama: (1) whether Lavinia (O'Neill's "Electra") will succeed in her goal of escaping the Mannon heritage of repression and guilt and lead a fuller life; and (2) how Lavinia will react when she recognizes her true motive—jealousy rather than justice—for directing the murder of her mother's lover, Adam Brant?

Regarding the first question, Ezra's admonishment of Lavinia at the very start of the trilogy suggests the puritanical repression that has been imposed upon her since her birth in the New England community. "Come! I thought I'd taught you never to cry" (*Homecoming* 3.931), he reproves her for the display of emotion she exhibits at his return from the Civil War. What O'Neill is depicting, as I noted regarding *Desire under the Elms*, is what Frederick Wilkins calls the "rigid, cold code of standardized, repressive behavior" that, over the centuries, has replaced the original ideals of Puritanism. It is this "dying, love-denying, hard and icy heritage" that O'Neill repeatedly explores in his New England plays (*Diff'rent*, *Desire under the Elms*, *Dynamo*, and *Mourning Becomes Electra*). Wilkins concludes that the "only hope" for the characters in these plays seems to lie in rejecting the puritan influence over their lives.[8]

"Repressive behavior," one of the corruptions of Puritanism cited by Wilkins, appears to have originated the family tragedy in *Mourning Becomes Electra*. Mannons were expected to be able to control their feelings. When Adam Brant's father allowed his emotion (love for a lower-class Canadian girl) to control him, he was disinherited by Brant's repressive grandfather. Lavinia's father, Ezra, whose coldness has repelled his wife since their wedding night, returns from the war admitting he finds it difficult to "talk—about feelings" (*Homecoming* 3.937). Although he returns longing to establish a more meaningful relationship with his wife, he is too late. Christine, who is still beautiful at forty, has been having an affair with his long-lost cousin, Adam Brant. She deliberately aggravates Ezra's heart condition, and then administers, instead of his heart medicine, the poison procured for her by Brant.

After Ezra's death his son, Orin, finds it difficult to grieve for his father, the General, whom he remembers as "always like the statue of an eminent dead man" (*Hunted* 3.975). Lavinia, however, fiercely admired the high-ranking father who trained her to devote her life to military values such as "duty," "justice," and protecting the family honor from disgrace. Like her father, Lavinia has become a kind of automaton of authority, issuing so many orders that even her brother, Orin, who loves her, refers to her as a "drill sergeant" (*Hunted* 2.965). Having arrived in time to hear her dying father proclaim Christine his murderer, Lavinia resolves to seek justice for his death. She arranges for Brant, Christine's lover, to be shot by Orin, who has become mentally unstable as a result of serving in the Civil War, and whom she needs to direct. When Christine hears the news, she shoots herself. Lavinia's "justice" is perhaps more complete than she had planned.

Beneath this repressed young woman who dresses severely in black, carries herself with a stiff, wooden, military bearing, and snaps out her words *"like an officer giving orders"* (*Homecoming* 1.897), another Lavinia appears longing to emerge. Jealous of her voluptuous mother, Christine, who dresses in green satin and has won the love of both men Lavinia desires (her father and Brant), Lavinia, who deliberately de-emphasizes her resemblance to her mother, actually longs to be she. After her father's death and Christine's suicide, Lavinia feels freer to begin metamorphosing. During a voyage to the South Sea Islands undertaken with Orin, whose condition has worsened as a result of his beloved mother's suicide, Lavinia experiments with passion and discards her black dress for green (Christine's color), the color of life. Both Orin and her fiancé, Peter, notice how much like her mother she has become. Lavinia has returned from the voyage eager to renounce her heritage of duty and repression and to lead a normal life. "Oh, Peter, hold me close to you!" she cries, embracing him. "I want to feel love! Love is all beautiful!" (*Haunted* 1.2.1024). She wants them to "be married soon" and "have children and love them and teach them to love life so that they can never be possessed by hate and death!" (*Haunted* 1.2.1024).

Orin, however, cannot even conceive of escape. Overwhelmed with guilt regarding his mother's suicide, for which he feels responsible, he insists that Lavinia cannot marry Peter Niles and lead the physically and emotionally richer life she intends but instead must be punished. To this effect he is writing a history of the family transgressions that will expose them both as murderers if disclosed. Increasingly crazed by guilt, Orin demands his sister stop seeing Peter and proposes to her that they live together incestuously. In his next breath, however, he momentarily comes to his senses and exhorts Lavinia to go to the police with him and confess. Suddenly he imagines he hears his mother calling him, and having resolved to seek her forgiveness, replies he will follow her. Lavinia, knowing what will ensue, nearly recalls him, but selfish considerations stop her. She shudders when she hears the pistol shot, but she is convinced her brother's death will free her to begin a new life.

Lavinia's sacrifice of Orin is based on delusion, however. None of the Mannons can escape the dark influence of the family dead upon their descendants. The portrait of Ezra in his judge's robes in the study and the numerous Mannon portraits (which include Abe Mannon, Ezra's father) in the sitting room dominate all the interior scenes of the trilogy. The living Mannons are always addressing the portraits as if they were alive and capable of action. In *The Haunted* Lavinia and Orin believe that the dead actually address them. In act 1 Lavinia defends herself against what she perceives as the accusing stare of the portraits: "Why do you look at me like that? I've done my duty by you! That's finished and forgotten!" (1.1016). In act 2 Orin is convinced he is writing his family history at his father's request (2.1026). In act 3 Orin claims to hear his dead mother calling him when he exits to shoot himself: "You've heard me! You're here in the house now! You're calling me! You're waiting to take me home!" (3.1042). On several occasions the "ghosts" appear to enter the bodies of the living and dominate their personalities. Orin tells Lavinia after their South Sea sojourn, "Can't you see I'm now in Father's place and you're Mother?" (*Haunted* 2.1032). Lavinia has just goaded him to anger in the same words used by her mother to taunt Ezra to the fury that brought on his heart attack in *The Homecoming*. She then cries out penitently, "Oh, Orin, something made me say that to you—against my will—something rose up in me—like an evil spirit!" (*Haunted* 2.1031). The Mannon dead seem to be doing their utmost to ensure that their descendants cannot renounce the grim family heritage but must follow in their footsteps.

After Orin's suicide, Lavinia can find no peace in the Mannon "temple of Hate and Death" (*Haunted* 4.1046). The gardener, Seth, indicates she spends her nights outside on the staircase. Still possessed of the frantic hope that marriage to Peter will enable her to escape the family curse, she fills the house with flowers for his sake. When Peter refuses to marry her on the day of her brother's funeral, she begs him to make love to her in that house: "Our love will drive the dead away! It will shame them back into death!" (*Haunted* 4.1052). At the height of her passionate plea for sexual intimacy, however, Lavinia inadvertently addresses her fiancé as "Adam." Drawing back in horror, she at last recognizes her true motive for killing Brant— jealousy rather than the justice she had believed she was seeking. Acknowledging the hopelessness of fighting off the ghosts ("Always the dead between! It's no good trying any more!" [*Haunted* 4.1052]), she sends Peter away. She resumes the quest for "justice"—ostensibly begun in *The Homecoming* with her resolution to avenge her father's death—by condemning and punishing herself.

With the departure of Peter and her self-incarceration in the mansion, the first question posed by the drama has been answered. Lavinia, forced to confront her complicity in the Mannon guilt, has been defeated in her quest to attain a new life. Having already resumed her black dress and stiff bearing since her brother's suicide, she will not dance in the moonlight like the South Sea natives either literally or figuratively. She will continue to mourn the Mannon dead by keeping their secrets and preventing scandal. After Peter leaves, the gardener appears singing the song "Shenandoah," which he has sung throughout the trilogy until it has become a kind of refrain:

> Oh, Shenandoah, I long to hear you
> A-way, my rolling river,
> Oh, Shenandoah, I can't get near you
> Way-ay, I'm bound away
> Across the wide Missouri.
>
> (*Haunted* 4.1045)

The song takes on a new meaning now. Upon hearing him, Lavinia remarks, "I'm not bound away—not now, Seth. I'm bound here—to the Mannon dead!" (*Haunted* 4.1053). "Bound" in the sense of being "tied" to one's destiny replaces "bound" in the sense of determined to leave. The ghosts have claimed her as one of their own. Accepting her destiny as the last living Mannon and bearer of the family curse, Lavinia orders Hannah to throw out the flowers—symbols of life and happiness—which she has gathered into this house of the dead. She takes a last lingering look at the sunlight while Seth nails up the shutters as she has commanded. Then she marches into the tomblike house, never again to emerge.

Lavinia's quest for freedom, despite the fascinating integration of imagery and allusion (the portraits, the South Sea Islands, the song "Shenandoah," and the flowers), appears to have been doomed from the start. The real dramatic question of the play is how Lavinia will react when she discovers the truth about herself (her passion for Brant and motive for murdering him). Early in *The Homecoming* Brant, who had pretended to be courting Lavinia, speculated on Lavinia's capacity for enduring the truth about herself: "You're a coward, are you, like all Mannons when it comes to facing the truth about themselves?" (1.911). When Lavinia finally confronts the sexual feelings for Brant that caused her to murder him, the audience wonders if she will take her life as did many of her predecessors. Brant's father hanged himself; Christine and Orin shot themselves. Will Lavinia take what O'Neill appears to have considered the easy way out—death[9]— or will she have the courage to face her destiny and live?

The self-recognition or truth-facing scene is a device O'Neill uses in many of his plays to facilitate closure. In *Diff'rent* (1920) fifty-year-old Emma discovers the foolishness of her flirtation with a young man of twenty-three and hangs herself. In *A Touch of the Poet* (1939) Con Melody recognizes the ridiculousness of his aristocratic pretensions and reverts to peasant behavior and speech. In *The Iceman Cometh* (1940) Hickey finally obtains some awareness that his murder of his wife may not have been motivated by love, as he has insisted, and is ready to be punished. In the *Electra* trilogy the audience, perceiving Lavinia's self-deception, anxiously anticipates the self-recognition scene as necessary to the completion of the play. If Lavinia were to remain ignorant of her motive for killing Brant, the dramatic irony evoked by the spectator's superior awareness would serve little purpose. Lavinia must be undeceived for the viewer to obtain closural satisfaction from the end of the play.

Barbara Herrnstein Smith defines closure in poetry as a "modification of structure that makes *stasis*, or the absence of further continuation, the most probable succeeding event."[10] The self-recognition scene of O'Neill's *Electra* trilogy exemplifies a comparable "modification of structure," since as a result of Lavinia's "slip of the tongue" the two major questions posed by the play are answered, and the viewer expects little more. Moreover, in contrast to *Beyond the Horizon* (1918), *Diff'rent* (1920), and *Desire under the Elms* (1924), which rely on death and violence to precipitate the "modification of structure" required for closure, and in contrast to *Days without End* (1933), which employs a deus ex machina–type "leap of faith," O'Neill accomplishes the self-recognition with elegant simplicity in *Electra*. A quite credible slip of the tongue causes Lavinia to see the truth about herself and, acknowledging responsibility for her actions, accept punishment by dismissing Peter and locking herself up in the house.

Some critics have mistakenly attempted to shackle Lavinia's reaction to self-recognition with a more blatantly moral interpretation. Chester Clayton Long, for example, interprets Lavinia's release of Peter Niles as an act of love for him, an "act of grace that unsnarls the progressive chain of crime and punishment within the trilogy . . . and thus ends the chain of twisted relationships and distorted order. . . ."[11] In the same vein, Maya Koreneva suggests Lavinia entombs herself for the purpose of ending the Mannon curse by refusing to reproduce future generations for them to haunt.[12] Although some textual support exists for these readings, a consideration of Lavinia's character—she is a headstrong, opportunistic young woman who permits her only brother to commit suicide so that she can be free of his accusations—renders fanciful any notion of her sacrificing her life out of "moral duty" to "the generations to come."[13] Lavinia sends Peter away (propels him away by lying about her sexual experience in the islands) when she realizes she has never loved him—can never love him—because she still loves Adam Brant, the look-alike substitute for her father, even in death. Peter, whom O'Neill scarcely bothers to characterize, has never meant anything more to Lavinia than a convenient means of escape. She is far too self-centered to allow her concern for anyone (even Orin) to take precedence over her own interests.

The only person Lavinia means to help by sending Peter away and entombing herself in the house is, paradoxically, herself—or more accurately, her self-conceived image of herself.[14] Raised in a puritanical, military household to believe duty, justice, and honor the proper motivations for conduct, Lavinia's self-image has suffered severely from recognizing the truth. Killing Brant was not reprehensible in her mind when she believed she had performed the deed for the "right" reason—to attain justice by avenging her father's death. While still under this delusion, she told Hazel defiantly, "I'm not asking God or anybody for forgiveness. I forgive myself!" (*Haunted* 4.1049). Upon recognizing her true motive for killing Brant to be what she perceives as the less admirable combination of jealousy and passion, she despises her action. Now, instead of defying "God or anybody," she seems to regret the lack of a higher authority from which she might seek punitive measures: "[T]here's no one left to punish me. I'm the last Mannon. I've got to punish myself!" (*Haunted* 4.1053).

Lavinia's statement about "no one left to punish [her]" is not literally true. She might, after all, have gone to the police, as Orin suggested earlier, and as Hickey does in *The Iceman Cometh*. Still the headstrong young woman of *The Homecoming* who insisted on controlling her destiny, she now paradoxically exercises her self-determining powers by choosing to renounce freedom and confine herself in the house. Her vigorous assertion of self-punishment vividly illustrates the passion for justice that has been said to exist even in "the soul of the unjust man."[15] Since sexual passion was the cause of her downfall, she attacks that Achilles' heel full force. Renouncing forever the possibility of a full sexual life—or a productive life of any kind—she locks herself up in the house. Young and filled with the desire for life in abundance, she masochistically relishes the anticipation of years of "self-torture," through which she may eventually restore her self-image by atoning for what she perceives as a sin against herself. No saint to atone for her misdeeds in the manner of Hester Prynne in *The Scarlet Letter*, who dedicates her life to performing charitable acts in the community, or Celia Coplestone in T. S. Eliot's *The Cocktail Party*, who becomes a missionary in a Third World country and undergoes martyrdom, Lavinia can only purify herself the way she has been taught since birth—through repression of all her impulses and desires. "Go in peace, my daughter. / Work out your salvation with diligence," Dr. Reilly directs the penitent Celia in *The Cocktail Party*.[16] Given her self-centered nature, Lavinia does what she can to "work out [her] salvation" to some extent.

Mourning Becomes Electra ends on a note of triumph. Orin has assured the portraits, "You'll find Lavinia Mannon harder to break than me! You'll have to haunt and hound her for a lifetime!" (*Haunted* 3.1041). His prophecy shows promise of being fulfilled as the play closes. Lavinia does not kill herself in the familiar self-abnegating pattern of the other Mannons. Instead she gives orders right to the end. The shutters must be nailed down; the flowers are to be removed. She plans to live in the mansion a very long time. Her strength in accepting what she conceives as her fate looks forward to some of O'Neill's later heroes' acceptance of the inevitable— Edmund Tyrone in *Long Day's Journey into Night*, who laughs hysterically when his father once again switches off the lightbulbs after acknowledging the miserliness that has cost him a career as a great actor; and Josie Hogan in *A Moon for the Misbegotten*, who, upon recognizing Jim Tyrone's unmistakable need for a mother, courageously abandons her seductive efforts and fulfills the role he requires to bring him peace. Jean Chothia has observed of the ending of the trilogy, "Lavinia's spirit flashes out, unbowed. Her self-punishment reveals her as an individual being: it is an act of spirited defiance, an exertion of the human will."[17] Roger Asselineau concurs: "As for Lavinia she remains unbending to the end. Fate does not succeed in crushing her. Though defeated, she preserves her human dignity. Mourning does indeed become Electra."[18] O'Neill himself seems to have accurately assessed his audience's reaction to the conclusion of the trilogy: ". . . I flatter myself I have given my Yankee Electra an end tragically worthy of herself! The end, to me, is the finest and most inevitable thing of the trilogy. She rises to a height there and justifies my faith in her! She is broken and not broken! By her way of yielding to her Mannon fate she overcomes it. She *is* tragic!"[19]

In conclusion, if Lavinia's slip of the tongue is the action that precipitates closure, her consequent self-recognition and administration of punishment may be considered to constitute closure itself. June Schlueter writes,

> [T]he point of stability that marks the ending is often made possible structurally by a character's having reached a particular point: if the consequence of recognition, such recognition precipitates a reversal, which concludes the action and anticipates the end of the play. . . .[20]

In O'Neill's earlier plays the attempt to achieve a reversal through culmination of character often results in an incredible or ambiguous conclusion, as in *Beyond the Horizon* and *Desire under the Elms*. In *Mourning Becomes Electra*

Lavinia's self-incarceration as a result of her self-recognition is totally consistent with her headstrong character. Some ambiguity still remains for the audience regarding the extent to which she blames herself, however. The spectator is convinced she feels guilty about her passion for Brant, but whether or not she regrets the deaths of Brant, Christine, or even Orin, with whom she had a closer relationship, is unclear from the text. In O'Neill's later plays (*A Touch of the Poet*, *The Iceman Cometh*, and *A Moon for the Misbegotten*), the closure attained through "culmination of character" is clearer. Con Melody, having been stripped of his pretensions and put in his place, deliberately regresses to peasant speech and behavior. Larry Slade, after condoning Parritt's suicide, is no longer a spectator of life but recognizes his involvement in spite of himself. Josie Hogan, upon recognizing Jim's maternal need and the hopelessness of her marital aspirations, selflessly abandons her seductive efforts and plays the role he requires. O'Neill's facility with self-recognition and reversal to attain meaningful closure improved in both clarity and credibility over the years.

Another means of enhancing the closure of *Electra*, which I have already noted to some extent in *Beyond the Horizon*, *"Anna Christie,"* and *Desire under the Elms*, is the completion of a circular pattern established at the outset of the play. At the end of the play, as in the beginning, Lavinia, once again stiff and square-shouldered, stands at the top of the steps of the mansion. Once again she is a Mannon. As Egil Törnqvist has noted, her "attempt to break loose from the paternal tradition has failed. She is trapped."[21] D. V. K. Raghavacharyulu points out an even broader pattern of recurrence: "[E]ach section of the trilogy starts with the initial irony of a Mannon attempting a second chance in life, which assumes the nature of a challenge to the authority of their collective destiny."[22] Ezra attempts to regain his wife's love, but is murdered. Christine attempts to fulfill her sexual and emotional needs with a lover, who is also murdered; as a result, she commits suicide. The frustration of Lavinia's attempt to improve her life is intended to conclude even more emphatically.[23] Rejecting suicide as "*escaping punishment*" (emphasis added), she claims, "Living alone here with the dead is a *worse* act of justice than death or prison!" (*Haunted* 4.1053, emphasis added). Her self-imposed torment will last a long time and be more painful than death. Thus the pattern of significant recurrence in this play may be viewed as contributing to closure by a negative progression in the destiny of each Mannon who attempts to begin a new life.

Finally, O'Neill's effective use of pantomime and quiet understatement after the emotional turbulence of the play also enhances closure in the final scene.[24] Lavinia's last look at the sunlight as Seth bangs down the shutters is very poignant: *"She ascends to the portico—and then turns and stands for a while, stiff and square-shouldered, staring into the sunlight with frozen eyes"* (*Haunted* 4.1054). Her turning, entering the mansion, and shutting the door are startlingly final. Lavinia's last words, "Tell Hannah to throw out the flowers" (*Haunted* 4.1054), bear quiet tribute to her grim determination. The flowers, which recall her attempt to attain the freedom she associates with the South Sea Islanders, are useless to a person "bound" to dead ancestors and their repressive code. With the departure of Peter (Lavinia's last chance for freedom) and her self-incarceration in the airless mansion (the shutters are being nailed down), the flowers must be discarded. No physical beauty must distract her from the life of penance she projects for herself. In a sense, they are funeral flowers for the girl who wanted love, children, and life in abundance (*Haunted* 1.2.1024) that Lavinia is "burying" in the mansion.

7

Kaleidoscopic Closure: Multifaceted
Meaning in *The Iceman Cometh*

Although O'Neill completed *The Iceman Cometh* in 1940, he refused to authorize a production of the play until October 1946. His six-year "shelving" of a work that has since been hailed (1968), along with *Long Day's Journey into Night*, as "the most substantial dramatic literature ever composed on this continent"[1] did not originate from any uncertainty regarding the play's merits on O'Neill's part. He considered *Iceman* "one of the best things [he'd] ever done. In some ways, perhaps *the* best."[2] Rather he cited his own ill health and the ominous political situation (the onset of World War II) as his reason for the postponement:

> . . . I have been absolutely sunk by this damned world debacle. The Cycle
> is on the shelf, and God knows if I can ever take it up again because I
> cannot foresee any future in this country or anywhere else to which it
> could spiritually belong. . . .[3]

He finally allowed Theater Guild director Lawrence Langner to produce *Iceman* a year after the war was over, when he felt the mood of general euphoria following the Allied victory had subsided enough for audiences to appreciate the play.[4] Despite Langner's insistence that O'Neill drastically cut the reiterative *Iceman*, O'Neill, protesting that the repetitions were a necessary part of his meaning, cut only about fifteen minutes of dialogue from the production script (and he restored that material in the printed version, which was published simultaneously with the production).

Initial critical reaction to the last new O'Neill play to be produced on Broadway during the playwright's lifetime was somewhat divided.[5] Although many critics failed to esteem the work,[6] a number of them recognized its greatness. More universal appreciation for *The Iceman Cometh* would be at-

tained only after O'Neill's death, when some of the same critics who failed
to recognize the play's merit in 1946 would see its power[7] after viewing the
superior Circle in the Square production (New York, 1956). Nearly all the
reviewers of the original production, however, as Langner had predicted,
agreed that the play, which ran for more than four hours, was excessively
long and repetitious. Some critics defended the play's considerable verbiage.
Richard Watts Jr. of the *New York Post*, for example, argued that editing
might "endanger the magnitude of [the play's] spirit."[8] Taking a different
tack, Dudley Nichols, a personal friend of O'Neill, countered objections to
the play's length by blaming the reviewers: "What is really at fault is our-
selves. We have lost the faculty of sustained attention."[9] Nichols's point merits
consideration. "Sustained attention" to the theme, structure, and closure of
Iceman indicates that the length and repetitiveness of the play, however they
may be construed as diminishing the audience's "pleasure" in viewing a
production of *Iceman*, in fact contribute to the work's dramatic effect rather
than detract from its merit.

The four-act play is set in Harry Hope's bar—its *"two windows . . . so
glazed with grime one cannot see through them"* (1.565)—on the West Side of New
York in the summer of 1912. The characters, who inhabit the rooms above
the dingy saloon, recall the chained prisoners of Plato's *Republic*, whose ob-
structed vision could perceive only shadows or reflections on a cave wall
rather than objects of the world of daylight. In the comforting, womblike
atmosphere of the bar, aided by the mind-blurring effects of alcohol, the
denizens of Hope's haven cling to various illusions that help them escape
from what Frank Kermode designates as the world of *chronos*, or the succession of events in time that is generally regarded as "reality."[10] Harry Hope,
for example, who has not left the building for twenty years, fantasizes about
stepping outside and walking around the ward. Jimmy Tomorrow and many
of the other derelicts nourish pipe dreams about regaining the jobs they
once held.

Despite the play's length and large cast of nineteen characters, unity of
place, action, and even time (approximately forty-two hours) combine to
produce a concentrated effect. The action begins with the long-awaited
arrival of Hickey, a hardware salesman, who comes to celebrate Harry
Hope's birthday every year and remains for a two-week drinking spree.
This year the normally jocular Hickey has changed. Instead of drinking
and carousing with his friends, Hickey tries to "reform" them by inducing
them to relinquish the various pipe dreams that, despite their lack of substance, give focus to the denizens' tenuous existence.

Larry Slade states O'Neill's premise in one of the opening speeches of
the play: "To hell with the truth. . . . the truth has no bearing on anything.

The lie of a pipe dream is what gives life to the whole misbegotten mad lot of us, drunk or sober" (1.569–70). The four-act drama is structured to illustrate this thesis. The basic movement, for most of the denizens of the saloon, is from illusion (a belief or opinion not in accord with the facts [Webster's]) to reality (the outside world, as it exists objectively [Webster's]) and back to illusion. Prompted by Hickey, the denizens leave the protective shelter of the saloon, where they exist in the fairly contented state of illusion, to experience a harsh confrontation with the outside world—such as Hope's abortive walk down the street and Jimmy Tomorrow's attempt to reclaim his newspaper job. The foreseeable result recalls T. S. Eliot's observation in *Murder in the Cathedral* (1935): "Human kind cannot bear very much reality."[11] Having been made to recognize the hopelessness of their situations, the inmates lose even their minimal ability to function and seek to "pass out" through drink. "You look dead" (3.677), Hugo tells Hope as he reenters the bar. Jimmy Tomorrow has even attempted to commit suicide. However, as soon as they find an excuse to resume their pipe dreams—the notion that they had only been humoring their friend Hickey because he was obviously insane—they regain their semblance of life. The play ends with them laughing and singing, vividly illustrating the life-sustaining effect of illusion to which Larry attested at the beginning of the play.

The three most important characters illustrate the reverse implication of this thesis: men bereft of illusions desire that final cessation of consciousness which is death. Parritt, who appears illusionless from the start, jumps off the fire escape to his death. Larry Slade, who is brought to relinquish his cherished illusion that he is detached from humanity, longs for death at the end of the play. Hickey, who fails to maintain his illusion that he murdered his wife out of love, as he has fantasized, tells the police he wants to die in the electric chair.

Eighteen-year-old Don Parritt is condemned from the beginning. He has come to Hope's bar seeking a surrogate father in Larry Slade, who befriended him as a child. Unable to bear his guilt for having informed on his anarchist mother, thus causing her to be incarcerated, perhaps for life, Parritt wants Larry to judge and sentence him. Although the young man and Hickey have committed comparable crimes in that each has betrayed a family member—unlike Hickey, who fantasizes that his bullet through the head has put Evelyn at peace—Parritt sees only too clearly that prison, to his freedom-loving mother, is a punishment worse than death. And whereas Hickey is able to imagine Evelyn forgiving him, Parritt realizes the bitterness his mother will feel toward him the rest of her life. In his confessions to Larry, which occur at several points in the drama, he initially attempts to play down the ugliness of his betrayal, perhaps even to himself, by inventing false motives. Nevertheless, in contrast to Hickey, who really believes he killed Evelyn out of love until he remembers calling her a "bitch" after he shot her, Parritt knows that he "killed" his mother, to whom he may have been oedipally attracted and whose numerous love affairs infuriated him, out of hate. Deprived even of the illusion of repentance (he tells Rocky he wishes all whores were "in jail—or dead" [4.687]), the tortured Parritt is unable to either bear or end his misery. Like Hickey at the end of the play, the youth demands judgment and sentencing from an outside source—not from the court system, as does Hickey, but, ironically, from his wronged mother's ex-lover. He hovers about Larry like a vexatious mosquito, inflicting all his guilty secrets upon his unwilling victim, until Larry, moved to action by Hickey's confession and desire for punishment, directs the fatherless young man to the only solace his death-centered imagination can foresee for him: "Go! Get the hell out of life, God damn you, before I choke it out of you! Go up—!" Parritt receives Larry's sentence *"gratefully,"* relieved at last to be told what to do: *"(His manner is at once transformed. He seems suddenly at peace with himself. He speaks simply and gratefully.)* Thanks, Larry. I just wanted to be sure. I can see now it's the only possible way I can ever get free from her" (4.704). Unable to delude himself concerning his guilt, he makes his way to the fire escape as his only hope of attaining peace.

Although Larry attains a state resembling Parritt's merciless clarity of vision by the end of the play, for Larry that transition involves the discarding of illusions. A shrewd appraiser of his fellow inmates, Larry is singularly blind about himself. He refers to "the lie of a pipe dream" as giving life to "the whole misbegotten mad lot of *us*" (1.569–70, emphasis added) when he describes the inmates to Parritt. Then he suddenly excludes himself from the general humanity implied by "us" and asserts himself to be an exception, one who no longer has any illusions (1.578). The play confirms, however, that Larry has at least two misconceptions about himself. To begin with, he believes he is a mere spectator in the "Grandstand" (1.611), who is no longer involved with his fellow men. He attempts to fend off Parritt: ". . . I have a strong hunch you've come here expecting something of me. I'm warning you, at the start, so there'll be no misunderstanding, that I've nothing left to give, and I want to be left alone, and I'll thank you to keep your life to yourself" (1.581). His second illusion or misconception is that, having no further interest in life, he is waiting for death.

Larry's pose of being a detached spectator in the grandstand of life does not fool anyone in the play but himself. O'Neill's stage directions emphasize Larry's overwhelming compassion for the inmates. Jimmy Tomorrow calls Larry's bluff even before Hickey: "You pretend a bitter, cynic philosophy, but in your heart you are the kindest of men" (1.589). Larry is the only inmate who cares enough about his friends' dreams to attempt even a passive defense against Hickey's crusade. When Hickey, upon arriving, starts to analyze and discomfit Parritt, Larry wards off the attack by changing the subject, "Mind your own business, Hickey. He's nothing to you—or to me, either. . . . Tell us more about how you're going to save us" (1.612). Similarly, when Hickey mocks Hugo's illusion of drinking "vine beneath the villow trees," Larry tells Hickey angrily, "Leave Hugo be! He's rotted ten years in prison for his faith! He's earned his dream! Have you no decency or pity?" (2.628). Larry is not even capable of sending the irritating Parritt away when Rocky proposes to evict him (3.653). Larry knows that the desperate young man has nowhere to go.

If the denizens are aware that Larry's detachment is a fiction, they also joke about his claim to be waiting for death (1.600, 1.604). Everyone knows Larry does not really want to die, or he would have jumped off the fire escape long ago. When Hickey arrives, he dubs Larry "Old Cemetery" (2.626), a nickname that sticks. Hickey's professed goal is to make Larry admit he is "just an old man who is scared of life, but even more scared of dying. So [he's] hanging on to life at any price" (2.629). The hardware drummer eventually succeeds in gaining a mocking admission to that effect from Larry (3.675), although Larry fights against him furiously at first.

Hickey also proposes to unmask Larry's pose of detachment. Calling him the "Old Grandstand Foolosopher" (1.611), he insists Larry accept his responsibility to help Parritt with "the right kind of pity" (2.630)—by which he means actively directing Parritt to end his misery, as Hickey has ended his wife's, through death. Larry's usual form of pity, Hickey notes, too often consists of passively "encouraging some poor guy to go on kidding himself with a lie" (2.629). Resisting Hickey's urgings, Larry rejects Parritt's importunities throughout most of the play. In the end, however, Hickey inadvertently succeeds in unseating Larry from his grandstand position. The salesman's anguished confession finally moves Larry to act—in what he believes are Parritt's best interests—by directing the young man to his death. Upon hearing Parritt's body hit the pavement, Larry can no longer maintain his pose of detachment, that pipe dream having vanished through his act of commitment. Bereft of his favorite illusion and, moreover, burdened with responsibility for the young man's death, Larry now truly longs to die (4.710). Like Hope and the other inmates after relinquishing their pipe dreams, Larry experiences a desire to lose consciousness, a condition from which the more perceptive ex-anarchist cannot recover so easily as his friends. He sits alone by the grimy window staring in front of him as the play ends, oblivious to the *"racket"* (4.711) of the illusion-embracing crowd.

Hickey, the third character to "die" as a result of his disillusionment, descends upon his unsuspecting friends like a God-figure from his imagined position of loftiness—the "peace" that he claims to have attained. Before proceeding to direct Harry's birthday celebration, Hickey addresses the group (mostly men in their fifties and sixties) as "boys and girls" (1.613, 2.644, 2.648) and talks down to them as if they were kindergarten children: "Well! Well!! Well!!! . . . Here I am in the nick of time" (2.626). To the meek denizens of Harry's "No Chance Saloon" (1.577 [Larry]), Hickey's commands are terrifyingly authoritative. Parritt confesses to Larry, "I'm scared of him [Hickey], honest. There's something not human behind his damned grinning and kidding." Larry concurs, "Ah! You feel that, too?" (2.635). As it turns out, there is good reason for their qualms. The brand of peace that Hickey is selling them is called "death."

Like Larry, Hickey is a self-deluded character. He claims to have found peace through facing the truth, but he, too, has pipe dreams. His primary illusion is that he killed his wife, Evelyn, whom he was continually disappointing by his periodic drinking and whoring sprees, because he loved her and wanted never to disappoint her again. Hickey also believes he has attained peace himself by destroying his and Evelyn's illusion that he could reform. What is more, Hickey nourishes the illusion that he has come to bring this hard-won peace to his friends.

Ironically, the very intensity of Hickey's efforts to "save" everyone suggests that he is not "peaceful," but is, in fact, desperate to save himself. In retrospect, Larry's remark regarding Rocky the bartender's attempt to convert everyone into pimps ("It isn't contented enough, if you have to make everyone else a pimp, too" [4.687]) applies with particular aptness to Hickey's reform efforts. Just as Rocky needs to convert the world into pimps to feel more comfortable about his own occupation (Rocky is a pimp), Hickey needs to kill everyone's dreams to validate his peace. In other words, Hickey's own peace of mind depends upon his friends' finding peace through a destruction of illusion comparable to that which he has undergone. When, in fact, the inmates become miserable—when he appears to have destroyed their desire to live along with their dreams—Hickey is devastated. As Larry shrewdly notes, Hickey has "lost his confidence that the peace he's sold us is the real McCoy, and it's made him uneasy about his own" (4.688). Acknowledging his personal failure, Hickey calls the police. Confessing his crime, he now seeks through death in the chair the peace that has eluded him.

Upon recalling the murder, after which he laughed and called his wife a "damned bitch," Hickey momentarily recognizes the horrifying truth— that he must have hated Evelyn when he said that, if not all along. He had grown to resent her continual forgiveness, which caused him to despise

himself. Desperate to protect his pipe dream that his violent deed was motivated by love rather than hate, he protests that he must have been insane
when he called her a "bitch." He begs his friend Harry Hope to corrobo-
rate this. The dream that he loved Evelyn is the most important thing in his
life. He will agree to anything to safeguard that illusion—even attest to
insanity all the time he has been at Hope's bar (although earlier in the play
he assured Larry that he was "too damned sane" [2.630]). When the policemen suggest he is concocting an insanity defense to save himself from
the death penalty, Hickey protests vehemently, "God, you're a dumb dick!
Do you suppose I give a damn about life now? Why, you bonehead, I haven't
got a single damned lying hope or pipe dream left!" (4.703). Hickey has not
succeeded in his efforts to convince himself that he was insane. Bereft of his
most cherished illusion—that he loved Evelyn—Hickey, like Parritt and
Larry at the end of the play, desires loss of consciousness and is ready to die
in the chair.

The question of Hickey's sanity has long troubled critics and audiences.
Reviewers of the first production, including Stark Young and Mary
McCarthy, assumed Hickey was insane.[12] In the play Larry refers to Hickey
as "mad" (2.629, 4.688). However, Larry also refers to Parritt (4.705) and
"the whole misbegotten . . . lot of us" (1.570) as "mad." Parritt, who seems
a kind of weak shadow of Hickey, and who interprets Hickey's conflict with
Evelyn as representative of his own quarrel with his mother, unhesitatingly
refers to Hickey's insanity excuse as a "bluff" (4.704). More recent critics
appear, for the most part, in agreement that Hickey is deluding himself
about being insane.[13] Judith Barlow's 1985 study of the various revisions of
Iceman reveals a significant reduction in the number of references to insanity in the final version of the play. She concludes that O'Neill wished to
steer his audience away from the conclusion that Hickey was insane, at
least before his last moments on stage.[14]

Hickey's final moments are ambiguous in the text. He has been desperately pleading, in at least three different speeches, for Hope and the others
to accept the explanation that he was insane when he told his murdered
wife, "Well, you know what you can do with your pipe dream now, you
damned bitch!" (4.700). He exhorts them, "Boys, you're all my old pals!
You've known old Hickey for years! You know I'd never—*(His eyes fix on
Hope.)* You've known me longer than anyone, Harry. You know I must have
been insane, don't you, Governor?" Hope responds with unconcealed eagerness, as the implications of Hickey's claim begin to dawn on him: ". . . Insane?
You mean—You really went insane? *(At the tone of his voice, all the group at the
tables by him start and stare at him as if they caught his thought. Then they all look at
Hickey eagerly, too.)*"

Hickey, unaware of the reason for their renewed interest in him, once again pleads insanity: "Yes! Or I couldn't have laughed! I couldn't have said that to her! . . . ([*As the policemen arrest him*] *to Hope—pleadingly*) You know I couldn't say that to Evelyn, don't you, Harry—unless—." Hope seizes upon Hickey's excuse as a means of rejecting the confrontations with "truth" that he and his cronies have experienced: "And you've been crazy ever since? Everything you've said and done here—."

Suddenly realizing what Hope is thinking, Hickey starts to reprimand the saloon-keeper in his former condescending tone: "Now, Governor! Up to your old tricks, eh? I see what you're driving at, but I can't let you get away with—." However, as Hope's face hardens and he looks away, Hickey, desperate to validate his pipe dream that he loved Evelyn, makes the concession Hope requires of him: "Yes, Harry, of course, I've been out of my mind ever since! All the time I've been here! You saw I was insane, didn't you?" (4.700–702). Hickey yields to Hope's suggestion that he has been "crazy ever since"—an explanation that would permit the inmates to resume their former illusions and regain their liveliness—not so much for his friends' peace of mind, as Thomas Adler contends[15] and as the recent (1998) London production appears to have interpreted the play,[16] as for his own. Hickey's concession is a trade-off.[17] He agrees to let Hope and the group resume their illusions if, in return, they will agree to affirm his.

Unsettling ambiguities remain, however, such as Hickey's explanation to the policemen of his reason for wanting to die in the chair:

([*W*]*ith a strange mad earnestness*) Oh, I want to go, Officer [to face punishment]. I can hardly wait now. I should have phoned you from the house right afterwards. It was a waste of time coming here. I've got to explain to Evelyn. But I know she's forgiven me. She knows I was insane. You've got me all wrong, Officer. I want to go to the Chair. (4.702–3)

O'Neill's description of Hickey's *"strange mad earnestness"* is bewildering to the spectator who has concluded that Hickey is deluding himself about his mental instability. Does O'Neill mean that, from the start of the play, Hickey has been legally "insane"—that is, either unable to "tell right from wrong" or subject to "an impulse he could not resist"[18]—and is therefore not responsible for Evelyn's death? Such an interpretation would diminish the play.[19] A more satisfactory explanation is that the stress of confronting his hatred for Evelyn—even momentarily, before attempting to retreat back into illusion—has finally driven Hickey over the brink. The desperation with which he has been pleading for his friends to accept his excuse of temporary insanity indicates his own dissatisfaction with that explanation.

He needs their acceptance to bolster his own. However, despite the concession he has made to win the inmates' approval, his anxiety is unalleviated:
his mind starts to fragment from the stress.

Until Hickey's speech (one of his last) about wanting to go to the chair
so that he can explain everything to Evelyn, Hickey, although deluded, has
seemed rational. In this speech, however, his powers of reasoning appear to
be straying. There is a desperate breathlessness in the short, choppy sen-
tences, as if he can hardly mouth the words quickly enough. His plan to
meet Evelyn in the afterlife and be forgiven again, thus reinitiating the very
cycle of injury and forgiveness that led him to murder her, is chilling. He
seems in the process of becoming as mad as he claims to have been when he
called his wife a "bitch." In his following speech (his next-to-last in the
play), only a second or two later, however, he once again sounds rational.
He bewails his new vision of his hatred for Evelyn: "Do you suppose I give
a damn about life now? Why, you bonehead, I haven't got a single damned
lying hope or pipe dream left!" (4.703). Bereft of the illusion that he loved
Evelyn, Hickey is ready to die in the chair. Just seconds later, however, in his
agonized closing speech before being led off by the policemen, Hickey is
once again fighting for his illusion with his insanity excuse:

> All I want you to see is I was out of my mind afterwards, when I laughed
> at her! I was a raving rotten lunatic or I couldn't have said—Why, Evelyn
> was the only thing on God's earth I ever loved! I'd have killed myself
> before I'd ever have hurt her! (4.703)

Thus, the audience is confronted with three different Hickeys in his three
consecutive last speeches: a mentally unstable person babbling about dying
and meeting his wife, a clear-sighted man tortured by the merciless truth
that confronts him, and a dreamer struggling to hold on to his most cherished illusion at any price. The composite picture that emerges from these
kaleidoscopic shifts of personality is that of a man teetering on the edge of
insanity. Like Orin Mannon in the final play of the *Electra* trilogy (*Haunted*
3.1041–42), who, in quick successive speeches at first proposes to his sister
that they live together incestuously, then begs her to go to the police with
him and confess, and immediately following responds to the deceased mother
he imagines he hears calling him—Hickey appears to be bobbing in and
out of sanity at the end of the play.

The provocative closure of *The Iceman Cometh* is particularly fine. Practically everything in the play leads toward its awesome conclusion, thus
fulfilling David F. Hult's definition of closure as an "inner movement in the
direction of unity or completeness."[20] Despite the paucity of physical action

in *Iceman*, "movement" occurs throughout the play in the answering of several enigmas or key questions that are posed early in the drama. The most important question is how to resolve the philosophical conflict between Hickey, who insists that men face reality (the objective world outside the saloon), and Larry, who contends people cannot bear too much reality, but need dreams. A second enigma, which is important in building suspense (and thus holding the reader/viewer's attention throughout the four and a half hour play), is the nature of the cause of Hickey's radical change from a fun-loving drinker into a merciless reformer. A third question involves Larry, whose "detachment" is clearly delusional. When Larry declares himself to be free of pipe dreams, the viewer, employing that "anticipation of retrospection" described by Peter Brooks as "our chief tool in making sense of narrative,"[21] immediately anticipates that Larry will be undeceived in the end. The audience suspects that Parritt's demands on Larry will play a role in unseating the ex-anarchist from his grandstand, and wonders how commitment will affect him.

The play gradually moves toward answering—and yet not answering—these initially proposed questions, thus demonstrating closure as a "process"[22] that occurs throughout the play. The answering of the first question, concerning the relative importance of objective reality and illusion (to which the entire play is devoted), concludes with the inmates' return to the illusions that give focus to their lives. Their return results in two distinct closural signals to the audience: "a modification of structure that makes *stasis*, or the absence of further continuation, the most probable succeeding event,"[23] and a production of meaning[24]—men need dreams in order to survive. The denizens' joyful cacophony of songs in the final moments of the play represents what John Gerlach calls "natural termination" or closure: when a character or characters attain bliss, even if that bliss is ironic or the result of self-delusion,[25] as in the case of the inmates, whose illusions show little promise of ever being fulfilled.

The question of what has transformed Hickey is probed by the inmates in acts 2, 3, and 4. Hickey only gradually reveals the answer, once again demonstrating the way "endings are built into beginnings and middles."[26] At the close of act 2 the inmates note that Hickey has not told his usual joke about his wife and the iceman. Has his wife finally run off with the iceman? Hickey replies to their speculations that his wife is dead, but he does not say how or why at this time. In act 3 the inmates wonder about the cause of Evelyn's death. Maybe she committed suicide because of Hickey's continual failure to reform. In response Hickey, adding still more information about the event that has changed him, reveals that Evelyn was killed by a bullet through the head. Once again he omits a significant detail—the perpetrator of the deed, which is revealed in the final act. As act 4 opens, Rocky is already speculating that it was Hickey who "croaked his wife" (4.683). Hickey's ten-page confession confirms Rocky's guess, but the motive Hickey gives—that he killed his wife out of love—comes as a jolt to everyone, including the audience. Even more startling is Hickey's momentary realization (which he immediately denies) that he hated Evelyn. The would-be dream-killer cannot face psychological truth any more courageously than his friends.

The third dramatic question, regarding Larry's pose of detachment, is resolved after Hickey is led away by the police. Larry, apparently in response to Hickey's anguish, is finally moved to leave his grandstand and attempt to help Parritt, who has just made a disclosure that parallels Hickey's. Larry's action on behalf of Parritt is another "modification" of structure that, like the inmates' return to their pipe dreams, indicates closure. As the inmates celebrate their renewal of "hope" with song, laughter, and drink, Larry sits alone facing the window. Before helping Parritt the "old . . . Foolosopher" (1.611), as Hickey has dubbed Larry, had only feigned isolation. Now, like Plato's unchained philosopher—who, after seeing the light, returned to the cave to help his fellow prisoners, only to be rejected by them—Larry's act of commitment has more truly isolated him from the group.

With the fulfillment of structure through the resolution of the dramatic questions, the audience is left with a feeling of completeness, or what Barbara Herrnstein Smith asserts with regard to poetry, the "expectation of nothing" further to occur.[27] The production of meaning, which June Schlueter asserts is necessary for dramatic closure, is also complete. Furthermore, as Marianna Torgovnick asserts with regard to novelistic closure,[28] the ending reveals the essence of the action with particular clarity. The man of vision must try to help the masses of men, for whom life is so terrifying that they must retreat from it through alcohol and dreams merely in order to survive.

The drunken Hugo vividly voices the general fear and misery: "Please, for Gott's sake! [Buy me a drink.] I am not trunk enough! I cannot sleep! Life is a crazy monkey-face! Always there is blood beneath the villow trees! I hate it and I am afraid!" (3.680). If Hugo's cry of despair sounds familiar, the narrator of T. S. Eliot's *The Waste Land* (1922) preceded him with a similar description of thirst, anxiety, and discomfort:

> If there were only water amongst the rock
> Dead mountain mouth of carious teeth that
>   cannot spit
> Here one can neither stand nor lie nor sit. . . .[29]

Hugo's words also look forward in time to Estragon's expression of hopelessness in Samuel Beckett's *Waiting for Godot* (1954), "What'll we do what'll
we do?" (2.46).[30] Estragon's companion, Vladimir, does not want to hear
his private nightmares about being beaten in a ditch every night (1.11).
People are together, but they are really alone. The denizens of Hope's saloon do not really help one another in any significant way. For example,
nobody offers to accompany the terrified saloon-keeper, who has befriended
many of them financially, on his formidable "walk around the ward." Even
Hickey, who professes to be their "savior," responds negatively to Harry's
pitiful request that he come: "No, Harry. Can't be done. You've got to keep
a date with yourself alone" (3.673).

The only consolation the inmates obtain from being together, other
than a sense of "shared situation,"[31] is reinforcement of their respective
pipe dreams. When Hickey causes them to discard their illusions about
themselves, they cannot perform even this supportive function. If they must
be undeceived about themselves, so must everyone else. For example, when
Rocky, as Hickey has urged him, finally acknowledges himself as a "pimp"
in act 3, he offends his hustlers by insisting they are "whores." He also
denounces Hope's excuse—that he was nearly hit by an automobile—for
hastily returning from his long-contemplated walk: "Automobile, hell! Who
d'yuh tink yuh're kiddin'? Dey wasn' no automobile! Yuh just quit cold!"
(3.676). In act 4 after Hickey's confession, however, when Rocky has re-
embraced his illusion that he is a bartender and not a "pimp," he assures
Pearl and Margie that they are "tarts" and not "whores" (4.709). He similarly permits Hope his delusion about the car: "De automobile, Boss? Sure,
I seen it! Just missed yuh! I thought yuh was a goner" (4.706).

Isolation rather than comradery characterizes the existence of the inmates who share drinks and dreams in Harry's saloon. For example, Larry
repeatedly rejects Parritt, upon whose desperate plea ("Don't go, Larry!
You've got to help me!" [3.666]) he literally turns his back. References to
locked doors suggest Larry is not the only "detached" character. If Larry
locks his door against the intrusions of Hickey and Parritt (3.652), Mosher
and McGloin, who have been friends for at least two decades, also deliberately lock each other out (3.667). The image of locked doors, which represents the "locked" or isolated condition of the individual residents, is enhanced
by another relevant image—the unwanted "keys" that pile up as the denizens prepare to leave Harry's haven and return to the world. In some ways
the multiplication of keys seems a forerunner of the proliferation of objects
that characterizes many of the absurd dramas that start to emerge in the
next decade. However, unlike the innumerable chairs in Eugène Ionesco's
The Chairs (1952) or the innocuous toasters in Sam Shepard's *True West* (1981),

the keys seem an important symbol in this drama about locked doors. Toward the end of *The Waste Land* the narrator mentions a key that turned in
the locked door once and once only,[32] implying an opportunity for salvation that has been rejected by modern man. In Eliot's work the key for
reclaiming life in the spiritually dead world of the poem consists of breaking out of one's imprisoned ego and becoming involved with others: "*Datta:
What have we given?*" Eliot's message, which he feels "mad" even proposing to his contemporaries, is "Give, sympathize, control" ("*Datta. Dayadhvam.
Damyata*"). In *The Iceman Cometh* Larry's final action on behalf of Parritt,
although regrettable in its outcome, suggests a similarly positive message:
the price of intellectual superiority is responsibility. As Plato insisted in his
Republic, the man of vision is obligated to try to help the masses. He cannot
"linger" in the light by himself, but must "go down again among those
bondsmen" in the cave and impart whatever benefit he can.[33] If there is any
"key" or hope for saving the world, it must lie in commitment and involvement, whatever the cost—a message that had contemporary political over-
tones at the close of 1939[34] (when O'Neill was completing *Iceman*) as well.

Finally, given O'Neill's vision of the condition of general humanity (for
which the womblike existence of the denizens may be considered a metaphor), the great length and repetitive nature of the play, rather than detracting from its overall merit as numerous critics have contended, actually
contribute to its dramatic impact. O'Neill does not merely disclose the world
of the lower depths; he submerses the audience in it. The reader/viewer
does not just observe life in Harry Hope's bar; he experiences it. A world in
which the possibility of meaningful action or communication is so dubious
that people must invent fictions about themselves to pass the time—in which
people must imbibe alcohol to induce loss of consciousness—is not all that
interesting an existence. O'Neill uses the uncommon length and repetitious
nature of his play, and its paucity of physical action, to induce in his audience a weariness comparable to that which his personae are experiencing.
If the reader/viewer becomes restless, such appears the intention of O'Neill's
art, which, in effect, forewarns the audience against deteriorating into such
a state. During a rehearsal for *Waiting for Godot*, which has often been compared to *Iceman*, Samuel Beckett is reported to have expressed the intention
of "boring" his audience.[35] That O'Neill also meant for the performance
time to pass slowly for the viewer is suggested by his insistence on his repetitions as necessary. When confronted with the fact that he had made the
same point eighteen times, O'Neill is reported by Langner to have replied
quietly, "I *intended* it to be repeated eighteen times!"[36]

In addition to its effectiveness in recreating the desperate ennui of the

denizens for the audience, much of the repetition serves a meaningful, poetic function as well. John Orr has noted, "[T]he strength of the play is
cumulative like a musical symphony. The restatement and recurrence are
progressive. Taken together action and dialogue have an almost operatic
impact upon the eye and ear."[37] One such "recurrence" is the concept of
"waiting," which is repeated in various ways throughout the play: the denizens waiting for Hickey at the beginning, Larry waiting for the sound of
Parritt's body to hit the pavement in act 4, and Larry waiting for death at
the end. Another such "recurrence" consists of repeated references to deaths
and funerals, which help prepare the viewer for the play's terrible, triple-
"death" conclusion. A third impressive repetitive effect concerns the word
"happy," with which Hickey concludes acts 1, 2, and 3. Since the salesman's
actions on behalf of his friends cause them to be anything but "happy," his
use of that word in connection with the denizens emphasizes his ironic
misconceptions regarding that state.

One of the most effective repetitions in *Iceman* is Hugo's drunken rendition of Psalm 137 ("The days grow hot, O Babylon! 'Tis cool beneath thy
villow trees!" [1.583]), which punctuates the play as a kind of refrain. Hugo's
psalm variations, which sometimes include "blood" under the willow trees,
universalize the condition of the inmates by relating them historically to the
condition of the Hebrews in the psalm, who have been requested to sing
and entertain their cruel Babylonian captors. The Hebrews, however, re-
late having hung their harps on the trees. Apparently refusing to forget
their woes through art, they insist upon remembering their beloved Jerusalem, which was pillaged by their captors. In vivid contrast to the courage of
the Hebrews, the exiles of Harry Hope's haven, who are enslaved by their
own pipe dreams and alcohol dependency, sing in a deliberate effort to
forget the world of *"kairos,"* or time "charged with meaning derived from its
relation [to the beginning and] to the end,"[38] from which they have retreated. However, as Jean Chothia notes, the denizens may deliberately
push the "blood" sometimes depicted beneath the willows out of their minds
and "deafen themselves by pounding their glasses and chanting together,
''Tis cool beneath thy willow trees!,' but the echo, 'If I forget thee, O Jerusalem,' [a line from the psalm not recalled by Hugo or the inmates] persists in
the ears of the audience."[39] Chothia's point is the vivid contrast between
the enslaved Jews, who refused to sing for their captors because they identified with the pillaged Jerusalem, and the inmates, who, lacking any such
identification or purposeful connection with events in time as "remembering Jerusalem" signifies, seek forgetfulness and a blurring of their identities
through drunken merriment. Their final chant in unison, which has been

prepared for by two earlier such group chants in the text (2.649, 4.689), suggests that in the prevarication of their discordant "art" there may be "coolness" or relief from pain, but the price is self-betrayal.

The noisy celebration with which the play closes contrasts ironically to the various "deaths" that occur (Parritt, Hickey, and Larry). In recognition of the inmates' apparent revival from their trancelike state at the end, Virginia Floyd concludes that the tone of *Iceman* is "not one of despair but of hope. . . . O'Neill's ultimate message is life rather than death."[40]—But life at what price? the audience may object. On what plane? Drunk or deluded? The denizens' final merriment—a self-induced, narcotized state in which they instantly forget the misery of their friend Hickey, who has just been led off, fail to acknowledge the thud of Parritt's body hitting the ground, and are able to ignore their friend Larry's pain (only Harry Hope tries to make Larry join them)—is an ironic commentary on what is considered "happiness" in this world.

O'Neill may have been fond of his deluded inmates, many of whom represent derelicts he had known at Jimmy-the-Priest's waterfront saloon in his youth. He may even have found the atmosphere of Harry Hope's saloon soothing: he periodically sought peace in such places himself throughout much of his career. However, it is difficult to believe that he found the inmates' condition "hope[ful]" (Floyd) or believed they had attained "happiness" (in the sense of having great pleasure or joy [Webster's]). In 1942 O'Neill indicated that the denizens' "defensive pipe dreams" were pitiable and tragic.[41] When O'Neill described the atmosphere at Harry's as one of "deep inner contentment,"[42] he was speaking ironically. His spokesman in the play, Larry Slade, similarly asserts the denizens' "contentment":

> I've never known more *contented* men. It isn't often that men attain the true
> goal of their heart's desire. The same applies to Harry himself and his two
> cronies at the far table. He's so *satisfied* with life he's never set foot out of
> this place since his wife died twenty years ago. He has no need of the
> outside world at all. (1.584, emphasis added)

Larry's tribute to a man so "satisfied with life" that he has remained inside a building for twenty years is tongue-in-cheek. What kind of "life" could possibly exist in such a circumscribed condition?

The fact is, "contentment" has long been a suspect word in O'Neill's vocabulary. In an early letter to Beatrice Ashe (1915), he confessed his dissatisfaction with "reasonably *contented*" endings (emphasis added).[43] Six years later he sharply disparaged the notion of "contentment" by defining "happiness" as "an intensified feeling of the significant worth of man's being and becoming . . . not a mere smirking *contentment* with one's lot" (emphasis added).[44] In *The Iceman Cometh* (1940), nearly two decades later, "contentment" is what Hickey professes to be promoting through his insidious destruction of the inmates' dreams. Hickey says he wants to "save the poor guy, and make him *contented* with what he is, and quit battling himself, and find peace for the rest of his life" (2.629, emphasis added). O'Neill saw the "contentment" of the inmates as a static condition that adversely affected their potential productiveness. Although O'Neill, at fifty-one, was far more disillusioned than the young man who had romanticized the pursuit of "the unattainable" (1922),[45] he had not yet succumbed to believing the "contentment" of alcohol-induced pipe dreams the hope of mankind. If he had, *The Iceman Cometh* would never have been written. O'Neill could have curled up with a bottle somewhere and withdrawn from the world. Although he appreciated the solace to be found in Hope's haven, he was aware that it was a form of "death," a diminution of man's capacity for significant life.

In conclusion, the meaning of *Iceman* appears to shift with kaleidoscopic swiftness at the end of the play. The quick jumps in focus cause the viewer to examine the play from different angles, with often contradictory results. In my discussion of O'Neill's earlier plays (*Beyond the Horizon* [1918], *"Anna Christie"* [1920], and *Desire under the Elms* [1924]), I cited the ambiguities surrounding closure as a significant flaw. This is not so in *Iceman*: ambiguity, mystery, and multifaceted vision are intrinsic to the play. Hickey's conduct and motives are enigmatic throughout. Many plot details remain undisclosed as well, such as the reason for Parritt's betrayal of his mother and the cause of Larry's flight from involvement to the grandstand. In *Iceman* the meaning of the play is enhanced by its shifting, kaleidoscopic nature like the beauty of a many-sided gem.

For the viewer attempting to interpret the work, *Iceman* is the type of modern text described by Stanley Fish as requiring of its audience "constructing" rather than "construing."[46] Like the narrator in Henry James's story "The Figure in the Carpet" (1896), the viewer must struggle to "create" closure by deriving meaning from the ambiguous work. Three different views of Hickey emerge from his last three speeches before exiting from the play. Similarly, the inmates' concluding return to illusion can be variously viewed as hopeful, tragically ignorant, or deliberately cruel. Larry is another puzzle. Whether his movement toward involvement, which seems admirable, even if involuntary on his part, is, in fact, worthwhile seems questionable given its results: a young man jumps to his death, and an old man is weighed down by more guilt. Yet Larry is the hero of the play—the only character (except the misguided Hickey) who exhibits concern for his fellow inmates, the only one who—however reluctant—attains any significant vision at the end.

Unlike Larry Slade, who bewails his ability to "[look] with pity at the two sides of everything" (4.710), O'Neill, who was similarly gifted, displays his multiplicity of vision in the closure of this drama. The kaleidoscopic method of portraying Hickey's "end," by which I mean that he is revealed to the viewer from three different angles or perspectives (madman, realist, and dreamer) so that the spectator's view of him is not stable, but shifts like the bits of colored glass in a kaleidoscope that has been turned, is continued in the remaining closure of the play. Unlike the concentration on Mary Tyrone at the end of *Long Day's Journey into Night*, or on Josie Hogan at the end of *A Moon for the Misbegotten*, the focus of the conclusion of *Iceman* keeps shifting with cinematic swiftness. At the opening of act 4 Larry, Parritt, and Hugo are sitting together at a table by the window on the left side of the stage. After his lengthy confession and the final speeches that reveal erratic shifts in his personality, Hickey is led away (4.703). Next the focus is on Parritt and Slade, who, in a quick but dramatic exchange of dialogue, conclude with Slade directing Parritt offstage to his death (4.704–5). The viewer, perceiving that Slade has finally recognized his responsibility toward mankind, may tentatively approve. After all, what option existed for Parritt? Once more the focus shifts to the inmates in the process of resuming their illusions (4.705–10). Slade's opening argument that men need dreams in order to survive appears confirmed by the inmates' renewed good spirits. If their dreams are foolish and unproductive, the inmates themselves seem harmless enough. Why should they be made to suffer disillusionment, as Hickey has insisted? Perhaps life on their minimal level is the extent of their capabilities in this world. During this time Hugo, who has noticed that Larry is listening for something and has been questioning him, leaves Larry alone and joins the rest of the group (4.708). In another quick shift the audience observes Larry's reaction to the sound of Parritt's body hitting the ground (4.710). The "old . . . Foolosopher" gasps, shudders, and hides his face—revealing the emotional price commitment has cost him. In his final speech of the drama he mourns the boy's death: "Poor devil! *(A long-forgotten faith returns to him for a moment and he mumbles)* God rest his soul in peace." Suddenly another alternative occurs to the viewer. If Larry could only have loved the fatherless boy, or even extended the concern for him that he does at this moment . . . Larry's reference, in his final speech, to "looking with pity at the two sides of everything" suggests he, also, may have too late perceived a more positive way of helping Parritt. His feeling of failure ("I'll never be a success in the grandstand—or anywhere else!") increases his longing for death. Now the kaleidoscope hurries back to the inmates. Their joyous celebration (4.710–11) suddenly seems cruel immediately following young Parritt's death. The final shift of focus is on Larry's misery as he stares out the window.

The image of Larry staring out the window at the end of the play suggests the condition of the artist trying to make sense of life. Like Larry, who devoted thirty years of his life to the anarchist movement only to become disillusioned by men's greed ("I saw that men didn't want to be saved from themselves, for that would mean they'd have to give up greed and they'll never pay that price for liberty" [1.570]); O'Neill, in 1940, had spent nearly thirty years trying to "save" humanity through his writing. Regarding his projected eleven-play cycle on the subject of American greed, upon which he had already labored for seven or eight years, he was now deeply disillusioned: "The cycle is on the shelf, and God knows if I can ever take it up again because I cannot foresee any future in this country or anywhere else to which it could spiritually belong. . . ."[47] Like Larry, who attempts to retreat to the grandstand, O'Neill saw the absurdity of trying to change people. But just as Larry is unable to ignore Parritt, O'Neill was compelled to continue to write. Gone, however, are the wildly romantic settings (*The Fountain* [1922], *Marco Millions* [1924], *Mourning Becomes Electra*) and the ecstatic messianic conclusions. In his disillusionment, O'Neill could only write what he saw. However, this powerfully felt, unembellished vision, acquired at great personal cost to the playwright, which informs the subjects of all his late plays (*A Touch of the Poet, The Iceman Cometh, Long Day's Journey into Night,* and *A Moon for the Misbegotten*), makes them indisputable masterpieces. Ironically, at the very point when O'Neill appears to have given up attempting to solve the world's problems (as in *The Fountain* [1922], *Welded* [1923], *Lazarus Laughed* [1926], *Dynamo,* and *Days without End*), he appears to have "solve[d]" the artistic dilemma of "bring[ing] the work to a satisfying conclusion without being false to the boundless nature of human life."[48] The honesty and integrity of O'Neill's late plays, which do not impose any artificial endings on the audience but merely present various implications and leave it to the viewer to draw conclusions, represent a high point in the evolution of O'Neill's closural technique.

O'Neill himself paid this play his highest tribute by claiming it to have been

the most satisfying work of all, up to that date—[it was finished before *Long Day's Journey into Night* and *A Moon for the Misbegotten,* O'Neill's other late masterpieces, were written] . . . because it leaves me with no feeling that I fell down on the job in one way or another, that it should be much

better, that I failed to realize my highest hope for it. For me at least, *The
Iceman Cometh* is all I wanted it to be— . . . and *is* fine drama.[49]

Coming from O'Neill, who as a young playwright had experienced such
dissatisfaction upon finishing a work that its completion often precipitated
binges of drunkenness, this statement suggests that with *Iceman* he had at
last attained through his writing the personal satisfaction that he had, by
this point, despaired of finding.

8

Long Day's Journey into Night:
The Question of Blame

High praise from even critics generally hostile to O'Neill's plays[1] appears to confirm *Long Day's Journey into Night* (1941) as "the true summit of his career"[2] and, in accordance with Edwin A. Engel's judgment of nearly two decades ago, very possibly one of the "two [along with *The Iceman Cometh*] best American plays ever written."[3] O'Neill himself believed *Long Day's Journey* was "the best" play he had ever written.[4] Although the chief strength of *Long Day's Journey* appears to be its complex and credible characterization,[5] the manner in which O'Neill attains closure has also received acclaim. In 1964 Robert Brustein hailed the fourth and last act of *Long Day's Journey* as "among the most powerful scenes in all dramatic literature."[6] More recently (1988), Normand Berlin has speculated that in the final sequence of *Long Day's Journey* "we approach what is perhaps the most effective curtain in American drama. . . ."[7] A careful study of the play's closure will elucidate these superlatives.

On a first reading the stage action of *Long Day's Journey* appears a simple unfolding of the inevitable. As the play opens, at breakfast in the summer of 1912, twenty-three-year-old Edmund is already seriously ill, and his father, James Tyrone Sr., and older brother, thirty-three-year-old Jamie, are afraid that concern for his health may cause his mother, Mary, whom they have been solicitously watching, to relapse into the morphine addiction from which she is recovering. The family's continual bickering and game playing to avoid facing the facts of Edmund's as yet undiagnosed consumption and Mary's precarious condition bode ill for all concerned. Tyrone blames a malevolent fate:

> It's damnable *luck* Edmund should be sick right now. It couldn't have come at a worse time for him. *(He adds, unable to conceal an almost furtive uneasiness)*

Or for your mother. It's damnable she should have this to upset her, just
when she needs peace and freedom from worry. . . . (1.734, emphasis
added)

Tyrone's speech, which occurs early in the play, suggests that a fatal con-
spiracy may have been set in motion to destroy this family, against which
their struggles are likely to prove of little avail.

As the first act progresses, Mary's condition—which is the crux of this
play—steadily deteriorates. Jamie and Edmund have heard her moving
around in the spare room the past night—a site that has always been linked
with her drug-taking. When confronted with her activity by Edmund, Mary
angrily uses what she calls the family's "constant suspicion" (1.740) to justify her subsequent relapse. Having apparently succeeded in fighting off
her craving for morphine the previous night,[8] she has already ominously
directed Tyrone and Jamie outside to trim the hedge "before the fog [both
atmospheric and drug-induced] comes back. . . . Because I know it will"
(1.736). Now, after Edmund's inquiry about the spare room, she goads him
with the accusation of distrusting her into allowing her to retire upstairs
alone (1.742). The result is that as early as before lunch the maid, Cathleen,
delivers an alarming report: Mary has been "lying down in the spare room
with her eyes wide open" (2.744). When she comes down for lunch (2.747),
Jamie immediately recognizes her peculiar detachment and bright eyes as
characteristic of drug use.

The prognosis for Mary from the opening curtain is increasing sub-
mersion in the illusory world of drugs. By the close of act 2, when Mary
(who is still rational enough to feel some concern for her family) warns
Edmund to avoid alcohol because of his illness, Edmund responds by proph-
esying the end of the play: "Anyway, by tonight, what will you care?" (2.770).
By act 3 Mary has retreated from her family into memories of her wedding
costume. So absorbed is she by duchesse lace and orange blossoms that she
forgets to ask Edmund the result of his anxiously awaited visit to the doctor
that afternoon. Edmund has to intrude upon her immersion in the past to
inform her, unasked, that he has been diagnosed as consumptive and needs
to enter a sanatorium. Mary's further estrangement from her family through
the use of morphine seems by far the most probable outcome of this "long
day."

Wherein lies the power of this very foreseeable ending? How can it
affect the reader/viewer so profoundly when there is no climax or turning
point? No surprise? The answer seems vital to an understanding of closure
in the less traditionally-structured modern dramas. J. Yellowlees Douglas
(1994), in his discussion of interactive fiction and certain modernist novels

in which the end is apparent early in the work, maintains that "we do not discover closure in the 'ending' of the story. . . . Instead, we find closure in the way in which the narrative gradually confirms our conjectures."[9] In other words, as we read we speculate on the total picture underlying the action, which our further reading will either validate or negate. Closural satisfaction, then, in works such as Ford's *The Good Soldier*, in which the "end" is revealed early—and by extension in works such as *Long Day's Journey* in which the end is clearly foreseeable—depends less on the perception of the actual "end" of the action (what happens) than on the process by which that "end" comes about (how and why it happens), upon which the reader or viewer has been conjecturing. Douglas explains further:

> Our sense of arriving at closure is satisfied when we manage to *resolve narrative tensions* and to minimize ambiguities, to *explain* puzzles, and to *incorporate* as many of the narrative elements as possible into a coherent pattern—preferably one for which we have *a script gleaned from either life experience* or encounters with other narratives. [Emphasis added].[10]

"Resolve narrative tensions . . . explain . . . incorporate"—the reader is expected to work to create meaning out of nontraditional texts. According to Stanley Fish (1980), "Interpretation is not the art of construing but the art of *constructing*" (emphasis added).[11] Furthermore, the story the reader constructs promises to be intensely personal ("one for which we have a script gleaned from either life experience or encounters with other narratives"). June Schlueter (1995) refers to the individual product of the reader's creation ("the readerly text") as that "peculiar misreading that the reader inescapably produces by viewing the writerly text through personal and cultural lenses."[12] Schlueter and her predecessor, Wolfgang Iser, whom she cites, are referring to all texts as subject to personal interpretation. How much more so, then, in a relatively plotless drama such as *Long Day's Journey*, peopled by ambivalent characters who require interpretation, can closure be expected to vary in accordance with the personal experience of each viewer.

Interpretation of *Long Day's Journey* is vastly enriched by re-viewing or rereading the play, at which time the audience is able to view the action from the standpoint of what Frank Kermode designates as "*kairos*."[13] Knowing what has preceded and will follow the breakfast scene, for example, the re-viewer is able to "escape from [mere] chronicity"[14] or the succession of events in time portrayed in the scene and perceive what is happening with greater depth. Recognizing the circle of fear and anxiety that Mary's continual regressions to morphine have caused her family, the re-viewer sympathizes with their game playing. He also perceives the irony in Tyrone's early speech about "luck": the family head habitually declines any responsibility that might entail a commitment to action, but characteristically uses "luck" or its equivalent as a scapegoat the way Chris Christophersen ("Anna Christie") uses "dat ole davil, sea." The re-viewer of Long Day's Journey, then, is in a much more favorable position to begin Douglas's process of "resolv[ing] narrative tensions" from the opening scene of the play.

Assignation of blame is the "narrative tension" or "ambiguity" most likely to plague the audience regarding Long Day's Journey. Who is responsible for the plight of the Tyrone family? Or is James Tyrone Sr. right? Do they just have bad luck? As Egil Törnqvist points out, Long Day's Journey into Night begins exploring aspects of blame and responsibility early in act 1 with Edmund's humorous anecdote about the quarrel between Harker, the Standard Oil millionaire, and Shaughnessy, Tyrone's tenant, who keeps pigs.[15] In some mysterious manner the fence separating the two neighbors broke down, and Shaughnessy's pigs enjoyed a free wallow in the millionaire's ice pond. Despite Edmund's narration of the mutual accusations of the two men, the audience never learns who (or what) broke the fence. In a manner reminiscent of the blind lashing out at each other attributed to Harker and Shaughnessy, which functions as a parodic prologue, the battling Tyrones are continually blaming one another throughout the drama. The viewer, who follows their accusations bewilderedly,[16] is also thrown into the judgmental position of seeking the scapegoat. According to Alvin Kernan this effort on the part of the reader or viewer to comprehend the responsibility of the characters in a play, insofar as it expands his experience with people and life, is one of the legitimate interests in studying drama.[17]

It is no easy task to assign blame among the Tyrones. O'Neill, writing a painfully personal play about his own family, made a heroic effort to be impartial and to disclose both the relevant character flaws and redeeming features of each member of his family. The resulting ambivalence challenges the viewer's imagination to find the "culprit." Edmund (O'Neill's stand-in for himself), to be sure, is exempt from this inquest—unless being born may be considered a crime. His brother shares in the family guilt, however. It was Jamie who entered the infant Eugene's room and gave the baby the measles that caused his death, thus setting in motion the cycle of guilt and pain that contributed to Jamie's own deterioration and to Mary's addiction to morphine following Edmund's birth. Now thirty-three, Jamie is an acknowledged alcoholic whose only work appears to be the bit acting parts his father procures for him. In addition to bitterly disappointing his parents by wasting the promise of his early youth in dissipation, Jamie's destructive influence as a role model for his younger brother may be partly responsible for Edmund's development of tuberculosis.

With regard to Jamie's culpability, however, O'Neill also defends the brother he hero-worshipped in his youth and still loved. As I conclude in my "Games" article (1992),[18] it is not surprising that Jamie—saddled at the age of six[19] with responsibility for his infant brother's death, and further maimed apparently during his impressionable adolescence by the sight of his mother giving herself a morphine injection[20]—became a behavior problem in school[21] and eventually succumbed to a dissipated life. As the scapegoat for Edmund's illness as well as Eugene's death, Jamie is denounced by both parents as an irretrievable ne'er-do-well. His recitation from Rossetti ("'Look in my face. My name is Might-Have-Been; / I am also called No More, Too Late, Farewell'" [4.822]) emerges like a choked cry for help. But instead of offering Jamie his love as a lifeline to pull him out of his despair, Tyrone merely tosses more dirt on his son's grave: "I am well aware of that," he says in response to Jamie's recitation, "and God knows I don't want to look at it" (4.822). Tyrone has buried all hope for Jamie long ago. Yet Jamie (who even drunk seems to know what he is saying) takes a great risk in act 4 by warning Edmund, who appears to be his sole intimate human contact, against his destructive influence. Fearing that alcohol may kill his consumptive brother, Jamie attempts to withhold the bottle from him: "Maybe no one else gives a damn if you die, but I do. My kid brother. I love your guts, Kid. Everything else is gone. You're all I've got left. . . . So no booze for you, if I can help it" (4.814). When Jamie, despite the *"genuine sincerity"* (4.814) of his effort, fails to prevent Edmund from imitating his drinking habits, he is driven to take another tack. He confesses the sibling rivalry that has caused him to hate and attempt to destroy Edmund (at the same time that he loves him). He is, in effect, warning his brother against being influenced by or ever trusting him again. In so doing, Jamie proves he loves Edmund more than he "hates" him, and that his intentions are basically good. Instead of being a mere perpetrator of the family's difficulties, Jamie appears also one of its victims.

A more likely candidate for responsibility is James Tyrone Sr., who raised his genetically susceptible sons with teaspoonfuls of whiskey to quiet their stomachaches and nightmares (3.782), and who continues to dole out whiskey to his alcohol-dependent adult sons. Despite his expensive liquor habits, Tyrone claims to be headed for the poorhouse. Although he actually possesses property valued at a quarter of a million dollars (a fortune in 1912), he continually turns off lightbulbs to avoid making the electric company rich. Mary blames her morphine addiction on Tyrone's penuriousness. She claims that when she was in pain after Edmund's birth, her husband called in the "cheap" (2.2.757) hotel doctor who first gave her the drug. Tyrone, for his part, tells Edmund that the doctor had been recommended to him by the proprietor of the hotel as having a "good reputation" (4.802). Edmund, however, has bitter evidence that his father values money above health. Both he and Jamie blame Tyrone for planning to send Edmund to the state sanatorium[22] rather than to a private hospital, where, they are convinced, he would receive better care. Tyrone attempts to acquit himself of this charge as well: "The state has the money to make a better place than any private sanatorium. And why shouldn't I take advantage of it? . . . I'm a property owner. I help to support it. I'm taxed to death" (4.805). Despite Tyrone's protestations, however, the audience, who sees him so anxious about burning lightbulbs that his sons trip and fall coming home in the dark, suspects that his insurmountable penuriousness[23] must undoubtedly have influenced his decisions concerning the medical treatment of both Mary and Edmund.

In Tyrone's defense, however, O'Neill makes it known that Tyrone, who had to quit school at the age of ten to support his family, was ignorant of the possible transmission of a susceptibility to alcoholism. He had been brought up in the Irish tradition of believing whiskey a health booster and a sign of manliness. The Irish maid, Cathleen, suggests this attitude when she excuses Tyrone's drinking: "Well, it's a good man's failing. I wouldn't give a trauneen for a teetotaler. They've no high spirits" (3.774). Furthermore, Tyrone is not always penurious. He claims to have wasted a small fortune on Jamie's education and thousands more on "cures" for Mary. On this "long day" he surprises Edmund with a ten-dollar bill for car fare to the doctor's office instead of the dollar Edmund had requested (2.2.767). At times Tyrone's miserliness appears only exaggerated thrift. His defense of Hardy as a no-frills doctor who charges a dollar when the others in town with fancy offices charge five (1.730) seems plausible enough. As for turning out lightbulbs, Tyrone's background of dire poverty in his youth explains all. People who have known such circumstances tend to be exceedingly careful with money all their lives. Finally, when confronted with his miserliness and its possible adverse effect on Edmund's chances for recovery, Tyrone is persuaded to allow his son some choice regarding the facility he will enter for treatment.[24]

Tyrone's share of blame for the family's troubles, as I have noted in my "Games" article,[25] seems to lie less in what he has done than in what he has not done. He does not ransack the spare room to confiscate Mary's supply of morphine; he does not attempt to reach some sort of understanding with the local druggist; nor does he deny Mary the use of the car to procure drugs. Hamlet-like, Tyrone seems uncertain if he is even responsible for controlling his destiny. He appears desirous of believing in man's power over his fate: he cites Cassius's words to "dear Brutus" in *Julius Caesar* (4.810) and claims to believe in the power of prayer and "the one true faith of the Catholic Church" (2.2.759). But when he is not attempting to prove a point to his sons, he refers to "luck" (1.734, 4.810) and to Mary's addiction as a "curse" from which she perhaps "can't escape" (1.735). Tyrone's uncertainty regarding his responsibility keeps him from taking any action to remedy the situation. In his confusion, he just sits and waits: "We've lived with this before and now we must again. There's no help for it" (2.2.759). If the terrifying memory of Mary's suicide attempt to some degree prohibits drastic measures regarding Mary's drug supply, Tyrone could at least follow Mary up to the spare room and make an effort to stop her. What is missing is the type of vigorous confrontation that occurs between Tyrone and Edmund in act 4. Only once he hugs her to him and cries, "Dear Mary! For the love of God, for my sake and the boys' sake and your own, won't you stop now?" (2.2.764). But he surrenders all too easily. Tyrone has given up hope of saving his wife as early as before lunch: "Never mind. It's no use now" (2.1.754). When Mary clings to him after the midday meal out of fear or loneliness (a sign that she may really want help), Tyrone leaves her as abruptly as he can.

Although Tyrone's passivity is a contributing factor, Mary seems the most reprehensible Tyrone. It is she who repeatedly takes the morphine and deserts the family who need her, even after undergoing "cures" that have supposedly reduced her addictive cravings. As the play opens, she has already been home from the hospital and ostensibly drug-free for two months. Although her initial addiction appears to have been accidental—the result of a bungling doctor and insufficient knowledge about drug use, Mary's reasons for continuing to seek the solaces of morphine seem more deeply rooted. Ella O'Neill (the real-life prototype for Mary) appears to have been suffering from depression when her third son (Eugene) was born.[26] This condition, which made her more susceptible to the reality-blurring effect of morphine,[27] was not alleviated by bearing a child to replace the infant who had died. William Martin states that many recovering drug addicts eventually become readdicted "because they have not solved the problems that first led them to drugs."[28] Although, in the play, Mary tells her maid she takes the drug for the arthritis in her hands, the real "pain" Mary seeks to relieve appears to be her childish incapacity to face harsh realities such as Edmund's consumption and a married life that has failed to live up to her rather grand expectations. A chronic complainer, she is satisfied with nothing and whines about everything: "I've always hated this town and everyone in it. . . . I've never wanted to live here in the first place, but your father liked it and insisted on building this house, and I've had to come here every summer. . . . I've never felt it was my home. It was wrong from the start" (1.738). The servants are stupid, the chauffeur is only a garage mechanic, etc., etc.; the list goes on. Mary never considers herself fortunate to have a summerhouse, a second-hand automobile (in 1912 when few people owned cars), and a cook, maid, and chauffeur. Instead, she constantly blames Tyrone for failing to provide for her properly as a husband. When Tyrone is late coming in to lunch, she commits the unpardonable sin of blaming him, in the presence of their sons, for marrying her. He should have remained a bachelor, she tells him: "Then nothing would ever have happened" (2.1.752–53). Translation: she would never have taken morphine because no sons would have been born to die, become alcoholic, or grow sick. Such speeches as the foregoing reveal Mary in the very unsympathetic role of nagging wife.

In Mary's defense, however, O'Neill reveals the source of her discontent—the doting father who lavished his quite ordinary means upon fulfilling her every wish. Mary cites her own mother, who said of her, "You've spoiled that girl so, I pity her husband if she ever marries. She'll expect him to give her the moon. She'll never make a good wife" (3.784). The irony is that Mary does not recognize the truth of her mother's prediction. Mary continues, "Poor mother! . . . But she was mistaken, wasn't she, James? I haven't been such a bad wife, have I?" Tyrone's reply is excruciatingly poignant: "*(huskily, trying to force a smile)* I'm not complaining, Mary" (3.784). He still loves Mary and wants to avoid hurting her feelings. However, Mary is not only a "bad wife," her addictive behavior is ruining all their lives. Her rather abject plea for reassurance concerning the acceptability of her performance only confirms the extent of her drug-induced dissociation.

A similar dissociation from fact dominates Mary's memories of the past. By positioning Tyrone's more accurate account of Mary's background in act 4, shortly before the final sequence when Mary returns mentally and emotionally to her girlhood, O'Neill assures his audience that Mary's memories are not to be trusted. For example, Mary, complaining of her loneliness, recalls her many friends at the convent. However, nowhere in her detailed recollections does she ever cite a single name or activity involving a friend. Those who she claims "cut" her after the scandal of Tyrone's former mistress suing him appear to have been mere "acquaintances" rather than friends. The truth, which Mary does not seem to recognize, is that she was always a loner. Her father's favorite and the nuns' pet, she reveled in such solitary activities as practicing the piano and praying to the Blessed Virgin.

In her present married state with the needs of her husband and adult sons still pressing upon her, Mary yearns for the solitude she knew as a girl.

Torn between the human need for companionship and her own personal need for more time alone, she is constantly either leaving her family, as she leaves Edmund after breakfast to go take a "nap," or sending her family away from her, as in the scene after breakfast when she practically pushes Tyrone and Jamie outside to trim the hedge. To justify her antisocial behavior, she denounces Tyrone for being miserly, Jamie for drinking and whoring, and even Edmund for being sick at the wrong time. Edmund, however, is not fooled by her accusations and excuses: he observes the deliberateness of her self-narcotization:

> The hardest thing to take is the blank wall she builds around her. Or it's more like a bank of fog in which she hides and loses herself. Deliberately, that's the hell of it! You know something in her does it deliberately—to get beyond our reach, to be rid of us, to forget we're alive! It's as if, in spite of loving us, she hated us! (4.801)

Ruefully perceiving the implications of Mary's addiction, Edmund suffers.

Nevertheless, it is difficult to condemn Mary for trying to escape reality with morphine when her men seek a comparable oblivion through whiskey. On this particular "long day" they begin drinking earlier than usual, as soon as they suspect Mary has resumed her drug habit, which occurs just before lunch. By late night Tyrone is so *"drunk"* (4.792) he can barely see the solitaire cards; Edmund, who promised to avoid alcohol once his tuberculosis was confirmed, is still drinking; and Jamie returns home drunk but unable to pass out. Also like Mary, who acknowledges her desire to hide in a fog of morphine (3.773), Edmund loves fog: "where truth is untrue and life can hide from itself. . . . Who wants to see life as it is, if they can help it?" (4.796). Edmund's comment reiterates the theme of *The Iceman Cometh* that people cannot bear too much reality. On one occasion when Edmund claims to have been "stone cold sober" and "had stopped to think too long" (4.807), he, as his grandfather Tyrone appears to have done before him,[29] tried the ultimate escape—suicide.

If none of the Tyrones can bear life and all seek to withdraw from it, perhaps Mary's retreat into the fog of morphine is less reprehensible and even necessary. Maybe the problem is not the individual Tyrones but life itself. In many ways the Tyrones appear trapped by forces beyond their control. Heredity plays a large role in this entrapment. Both Jamie's susceptibility to alcoholism and Edmund's illness appear genetically traceable to Mary's father, who died of alcohol-related tuberculosis. Similarly, Edmund's suicide attempt appears to find an antecedent in the probable suicide of Tyrone's father. The personal past of each character presents another powerful form of entrapment. Mary seems to be speaking for O'Neill when she declares the inescapability of the past: "The past is the present, isn't it? It's the future, too" (2.2.765).

Mary's conception of time as *"kairos,"* or a dimension lacking in chronicity,[30] seems drug-induced, however. According to Kermode, "Under certain drugs the 'specious present' is indefinitely lengthened."[31] Nevertheless, both Tyrone and Mary are forever haunted by the death of their infant, Eugene, some twenty-five years earlier. Tyrone, in an innocent display of love for his wife, had wanted her to accompany him on one of his acting tours. Mary, like countless young mothers who enjoy traveling with their husbands, had left the children with her mother, in whose care they ought to have been safe. Unfortunately, this quite blameless action led to Eugene's death, for which the parents have never been able to stop blaming themselves. Tyrone's guilt concerning Eugene (which he never acknowledges) was compounded by his selection of the physician who treated Mary with morphine following Edmund's birth, thus commencing her addiction. This greater guilt, however, was perhaps mitigated by his belief that the doctor, who had been recommended to him, was competent. Mary's guilt concerning Eugene became keener first from "daring"—as a result of her husband's urging and contrary to her own wishes (2.2.766)—to have another child (Edmund) to replace the infant for whose death she falsely considered herself responsible, and finally because of the subsequent addiction, and series of readdictions, which caused her to abandon her family for morphine. Thus her initially "false" guilt (Eugene's death) may have triggered her "real" guilt (the abandonment of her family), by making her more vulnerable to the amnesic, mood-elevating effect of morphine.

Jamie's guilt is comparable to Mary's in that his initial guilt (regarding Eugene's death) appears insubstantial in consideration of his youth (he was only six when he entered the infant's room with the measles). Jamie appears to have been condemned too harshly for going near the baby, despite the fact that he had been warned to stay away. Although Jamie continued to exhibit promise during his youth and, in fact, performed well through prep school, it seems likely that the double trauma of feeling responsible for Eugene's death and coming upon his mother in the act of injecting herself with morphine eventually contributed to his more reprehensible action of deliberate self-destruction through alcohol and whores. As he grew to hate himself for wasting his life, Jamie allowed his "real" guilt to intensify: he attempted to destroy his more promising younger brother, Edmund, as well, by influencing him to follow in his dissipation.

Even Edmund is part of this family cycle of guilt, which begins quite innocently. Edmund is in no way responsible for the pain following his birth that resulted in Mary's addiction. Nevertheless, he cannot help feeling guilty. In fact, the burden of culpability, however unmerited on Edmund's part, seems to have triggered a pattern of self-destruction in him comparable to Jamie's. Edmund, like his brother, is literally drinking himself to death. Also like Jamie (and like his mother with morphine), he finds it difficult to quit. However, although all three are physically endangered by their addictions, in Edmund's case the death sentence is visible on his lungs: if he does not succeed in controlling his drinking, he will die of consumption. Hopefully, the gifted young Edmund will reclaim his life.

Critical opinion is divided upon how much responsibility the characters bear for shaping their destinies. Although Judith E. Barlow and Chester Clayton Long argue that the Tyrones make choices that are important in shaping their destinies, William Jennings Adams contends O'Neill's characters "meet their various dooms without real guilt," since they do not make any crucial decisions that influence their fate.[32] O'Neill does not settle the question of responsibility for the audience in *Long Day's Journey*.[33] By his own admission, he both blames and vindicates each character in turn: "At the final curtain, there they still are, trapped within each other by the past, *each guilty and at the same time innocent*, scorning, loving, pitying each other, understanding and yet not understanding at all, forgiving but still doomed never to be able to forget" (emphasis added).[34]

Nevertheless, an examination of the closure in *Long Day's Journey* indicates O'Neill directing the audience away from the assignation of blame and toward compassion for his tormented family. Although they exercise some choices that adversely affect their lives (such as Tyrone's selection of a spoiled young convent girl for a wife), they in many ways cannot help being what they are. An examination of the fourth act reveals the three candidates for blame virtually exonerated. Jamie, as I have demonstrated, takes a real risk in attempting to save Edmund from himself. Through the courage of his confession he confirms his personal worth at the same time he appears to be undermining it.

Tyrone, in the last act, is not only exculpated from the compulsive penuriousness acquired as a result of his impoverished boyhood, but attains something of a heroic status as well. His narration (confirmed by Mary in 3.787) of working in a machine shop at the age of ten, to support the large family deserted by his father, is moving. What makes his recitation even more poignant to the audience is the realization that Tyrone, at age sixty-five, is still almost totally responsible for the support of his wife, two adult sons, and their household ménage. Tyrone, as if to negate his father's betrayal, does not desert the whining wife whose addiction disrupts their lives. Nor does he turn his derelict son, Jamie, out of the house to fend for himself. Tyrone is there till the end, bitter though it promises to be.

That leaves Mary, who is moving around upstairs during the fourth act. The men, who hear and periodically refer to her motion, dread her coming downstairs. Tyrone has already warned she will be a "like a mad ghost before the night's over" (3.790). The audience awaits Mary's reappearance as the necessary completion to the play. When she makes her startling entrance holding the wedding dress she has dug out of the attic, Mary—her hair braided, dressed in blue like the Blessed Virgin, of whom she prattles girlishly—is the picture of innocence betrayed. She is so far removed from reality that the viewer can no more blame her than her watching family can touch her as she passes beyond their reach at the end of the play. In her almost totally oblivious state, Mary appears less responsible and more sympathetic to the audience.[35] Nevertheless, even Mary cannot completely escape the truth. With the closing words of the play she is back in her present misery[36] recalling the love for James Tyrone that made her "so happy for a time" (4.828). Escape is at best only temporary, O'Neill suggests. The human condition is to live in suffering and keep trying to forget.

Closure is enhanced in this emotional rendition of a situation that does not "end," but continues on indefinitely,[37] by the numerous allusions to terminal conditions[38] and words designating completion in act 4. It is, to begin with, "night"—the finish of the "long day" described in the play's title. Tyrone's references to the poorhouse as "the end of the road" (4.794) and "the final curtain" (4.794) all suggest the play is coming to a close. Edmund actually uses the word "closes" in his quote from Dowson: "Our path emerges for a while, then closes / Within a dream" (4.795). Jamie speculates on Edmund's "funeral" (4.815) and mourns the irretrievable loss of his mother: "All over—finished now—not a hope!" (4.817). Shortly before Mary's entrance and the final sequence, Edmund tells Jamie, "You're the limit! At the Last Judgment, you'll be around telling everyone it's in the bag" (4.820). Finally, when Mary appears, Tyrone refers to her condition in a manner that emphasizes the culminating nature of this particular day:[39] "It's the damned poison. But I've never known her to drown herself in it as deep as this" (4.827). As the play comes to a close, Mary, despite her stricken family's efforts to stop her, is more powerfully narcotized than ever. There seems little hope that she (unlike her real-life prototype, Ella O'Neill, who eventually conquered her addiction)[40] will ever recover.

Another technique O'Neill employs to facilitate his audience's perception of closure in Long Day's Journey is his masterful use of visual and aural impressions, which complement the dialogue of the play to create what Jean Chothia hails as "poetry of theatre."[41] As the fourth act opens, Tyrone is sitting alone playing cards in the dark, except for the reading lamp that illuminates his solitaire game. The foghorn can be heard at regular intervals, along with the warning bells from the yachts at anchor nearby. As the act progresses, lightbulbs are turned on and off with a rhythm that, to some degree, parallels the Tyrones' attempts to both face and avoid reality. For example, after mock-heroically braving the poorhouse by turning on three of the five bulbs in the chandelier, Tyrone proceeds to confess the excessive regard for money that, he is convinced, cost him a great acting career: "What the hell was it I wanted to buy, I wonder, that was worth——" (4.810). In almost the next breath, however, he is turning off the lightbulbs again, concealing his concern for his mounting electric bill with the excuse that the light hurts his eyes.[42] An even more intense illumination of the chandelier succeeds Jamie's astonishing confession of his love/hate for Edmund: *"Suddenly all five bulbs of the chandelier in the front parlor are turned on from a wall switch, and a moment later someone starts playing the piano in there—the opening of one of Chopin's simpler waltzes. . ."* (4.823). Following this dramatic blaze of light and sound, Mary appears with her wedding dress, the picture of *"girlish innocence"* (4.823). A new voice is heard in the final sequence of the play: she speaks the language and has the thoughts of a young girl.

The visual technique most important to closure in *Long Day's Journey* is O'Neill's astonishingly effective use of pantomime. In my treatment of *Mourning Becomes Electra* I noted the significance of Lavinia's closing of the door as the shutters were being nailed in terminating the trilogy. Pantomime in the more sophisticated *Long Day's Journey* involves a more complex series of movements. First there is the moving transfer of the wedding gown from Mary to Tyrone's protective arms: unable to save Mary, at least he can save her beloved gown. Mary's subsequent movements are described by Normand Berlin as contributing to "the most effective curtain in American drama." The drugged woman's actions are so orchestrated that she comes "close to each of her loved ones only to move away from them physically, mirroring her leave-taking into the past."[43] The grief-stricken men are unable to penetrate her self-induced trance. Edmund, behind whom Mary passes last, comes closest. He grabs her arm desperately: "Mama! It isn't a summer cold! I've got consumption!" (4.826). For a second *"he seems to have broken through to her,"* because *"she trembles and her expression becomes terrified."* Then she is far away again. She murmurs, "You must not try to touch me. You must not try to hold me. It isn't right, when I am hoping to be a nun." Edmund drops her arm. There is no hope of reclaiming her. To drown their common sorrow they pour another round of drinks and raise their glasses. Before they can share that drink, however, Mary begins speaking and they lower their glasses, forgetting them. The irony of Mary's closing speech is overwhelming: ". . . I knew she [the Blessed Virgin] heard my prayer and would always love me and see no harm ever came to me as long as I never lost my faith in her" (4.828). The fifty-four-year-old woman, who speaks the last lines of the play in a young girl's voice, no longer prays, because she does not believe the Blessed Virgin would listen to the words of a "lying dope fiend" (3.779). Like modern man (as O'Neill depicts him), she is cut off from her traditional faith and has come to great harm.

As the play closes, the men, who were anxiously watching Mary for signs of drug use at the opening of the play, are again watching her—numbed with despair that the nightmare has recurred. Henry J. Schmidt cites the closing action (or lack of action) as an example of "modern drama's dystopian tableaus":[44] *"(She stares before her in a sad dream. Tyrone stirs in his chair. Edmund and Jamie remain motionless)"* (4.828). C. W. E. Bigsby compares the "silence and immobility" of this final picture to the closure of a Beckett play.[45]

The final impact of the play is loss. Tyrone's acting talent, once praised by Edwin Booth; Jamie's youth and early promise; Edmund's health; the thousands of dollars spent to rehabilitate Mary—all gone, wasted, lost in most cases beyond retrieval. "What did I come here to find?" Mary murmurs poignantly. "It's terrible how absent-minded I've become. I'm always dreaming and forgetting" (4.825). The image of Mary fumbling about, searching for some indefinable necessity she feels she has lost, haunts the play as a metaphor for the human condition. Mary can no longer remember what she "miss[es] terribly" (4.826) and feels she desperately needs. The loss is unspecified and general. There are the obvious losses pertaining to her sons—the death of the infant Eugene, for which she feels guilty; the possible death of Edmund (tuberculosis was often fatal in 1912); and the wasted life of Jamie. Mary tells Tyrone, "I'm afraid Jamie has been lost to us for a long time, dear" (3.780). Mary herself represents a great loss to her family as she moves beyond their reach in the final sequence. Time-related losses also pervade the play. Mary mourns the loss of her reddish-brown hair (1.728) and the slender, flexible fingers that once danced across the piano keys. She claims to have lost her "true self" (2.1.749)—by which she seems to mean the innocent young convent girl who wanted to become a nun before meeting Tyrone. In the last words of the play, Mary also seems to mourn the loss of that first ecstasy of love, when she was "so happy for a time" (4.828).

What seems to confirm the Tyrones' losses as irretrievable (except regarding Edmund, who may regain his health at the sanatorium) is that none of the characters exhibit any behavioral changes that affect the family's overall situation during the course of the play. Robert Bechtold Heilman describes the manner in which the "periodic notes of tragic self-recognition" exhibited by the various Tyrones fail to materialize into a change of behavior. Mary's brief insight into herself as a "lying dope fiend" does not stimulate her to quit morphine. Jamie's awareness of the analogy between his compulsive drinking and Mary's drug addiction does not help him combat his alcoholism. Even Tyrone's fourth-act recognition of the excessive regard for money that cost him his career as a Shakespearean actor does not ameliorate his compulsive thrift. Heilman concludes, "[A]t no time is there a painfully earned self-knowledge which then becomes a determinant of action and a molder of personality."[46] Laurin Roland Porter sees some hope in "the Tyrones' willingness to at last confess their own guilt instead of merely accusing one another," but notes that the confessions in *Long Day's Journey* are not efficacious, since the characters fail to "see their lost ideals as potentially destructive. . . . they aren't so much seeking absolution as they are sharing their disappointment."[47] Whether or not the Tyrones are even capable of change seems unclear from the play.[48]

Some critics have seen a positive significance in the relationships between the men. Certainly in act 4 when Tyrone drops part of his protective mask and reveals the greed that undermined his acting career to Edmund, there is a movement toward greater intimacy. Edmund indicates that the bond between them has been strengthened: "I'm glad you've told me this, Papa. I know you a lot better now" (4.810). Steven F. Bloom, however, argues against "an optimistic interpretation of this play based on new love and understanding that enters into the relationships between Edmund and his father and brother." He notes that although "alliances have shifted somewhat . . . it is certainly not clear that these are permanent realignments; given the nature of this family, in fact, that seems highly unlikely." Instead Bloom sees significance in the fact that "the last drink of the play eludes them."[49] They raise their glasses together as if in mutual commiseration at the sight of Mary's deteriorated condition, but, as she starts to speak in a young girl's voice, they slowly lower their glasses, each lost in his own grief. The Tyrones, despite their love and concern for each other, are not united in mutual support: what they share is despair.

In many ways *Long Day's Journey* (1941) seems a forerunner of absurd drama. The Tyrones' lonely house, surrounded by fog, on the outskirts of a harbor town seems a precursor of the isolated, water-surrounded settings of Eugène Ionesco's *The Chairs* (1951) or Samuel Beckett's *Endgame* (1957). Mary's ambivalence regarding her loneliness foreshadows that of Estragon in Beckett's *Waiting for Godot* (1954). "Don't touch me! Don't question me! Don't speak to me! Stay with me!" cries Estragon to his only friend, Vladimir.[50]

Mary is always either sending her family away (to trim the hedge, to go to the doctor) or leaving them (physically, by going upstairs to lie down, or psychologically by taking morphine). Yet she says she feels lonely. Uncertain whether she desires her family's presence or not, Mary whispers to herself after the men leave in act 2:

> It's so lonely here. *(Then her face hardens into bitter self-contempt.)* You're lying to yourself again. You wanted to get rid of them. Their contempt and disgust aren't pleasant company. You're glad they're gone. *(She gives a little despairing laugh.)* Then Mother of God, why do I feel so lonely? (2.2.771)

An examination of Mary's talk with Cathleen, the maid with whom she attempts to converse (3.773), helps to explain Mary's confusion regarding her family's presence. Companionship is not always effective in relieving the loneliness of individuals imprisoned within their own egos. Communication may border upon impossibility, as the two women's dialogue bears witness. While Mary repeatedly complains about the fog ("That foghorn! Isn't it awful, Cathleen? . . . Last night it drove me crazy. I lay awake worrying until I couldn't stand it any more" [3.772–73]) and her domestic problems with Tyrone, Cathleen keeps responding with comments about the chauffeur, who habitually pinches her ("He can't keep his dirty hands to himself. Give him half a chance and he's pinching me on the leg or you-know-where . . ."). Mary, in her drugged state, is really engaging in a monologue, and, to a lesser extent, so is Cathleen. Occasionally their monologues intersect, but, in fact, neither finds the sympathetic listener she seeks. The two women's isolated speeches in different directions approach the discordant dialogue of Ionesco's *The Bald Soprano* or Beckett's *Waiting for Godot*.

Finally, also like *Godot*, to which O'Neill's play has frequently been compared, *Long Day's Journey*, the action of which is mostly interior and psychological, lacks significant physical action. Normand Berlin observes of both dramas: "Waiting is the play's non-activity, with Mary waiting for her morphine to begin working its soothing magic, with the three Tyrone men playing a waiting game, hoping that Mary did not return to her habit but finally recognizing how hopeless hope really is."[51] In both *Godot* and *Long Day's Journey*, the characters play games to pass the time that weighs heavily on their hands. Vladimir and Estragon play word games and imitate the tree; the Tyrones, in addition to the various games they play to avoid facing the facts of Edmund's consumption and Mary's addiction, play the card games solitaire and casino.

Images of existential man alone in a dark world and stumbling to find his way pervade the play. The picture of Tyrone[52] alone and drunk, playing solitaire in the spotlighted darkness, wasting the talent once praised by Edwin Booth on the various domestic problems that beset him, seems to fit Albert Camus's description of the absurd condition: neither man nor the universe is the singular cause of the absurd, but "it is born of their confrontation."[53] The images of Mary searching for some unrecallable object she has lost, and of both Edmund and Jamie, in separate entrances, stumbling in the darkness of the unlit hallway—all seem potential metaphors for the precarious condition of man alone in an—at best—indifferent universe.

In such a world man can scarcely be blamed for the way his life turns out. Imperfect as the Tyrones may be, they are not evil: in their hearts they love one another and wish each other well. They are ordinary human beings like the viewer's own family, like the viewer himself. They do not deserve their lot. In recognizing the at least partial exoneration from responsibility implied through this closure, the viewer can breathe a sigh of relief: he, too, may be innocent of much of the blame for his life.

Perhaps the best way to endure existence in a world such as this play depicts is to imitate Edmund's example of stoic acceptance. Edmund's *"strained, ironical laughter"* (4.810) when his father once again turns out the lightbulbs (just seconds after regretting his miserliness) prefigures the conduct described by Martin Esslin (1962) as the goal of the absurd dramatists. The theater of the absurd, according to Esslin, attempts to free man from the illusions that are likely to cause him disappointment in life and tries to make him "come to terms with the world in which he lives." For "the dignity of man," Esslin continues, "lies in his ability to face reality in all its senselessness; to accept it freely, without fear, without illusions—and to laugh at it."[54] Edmund, the stand-in for O'Neill in this personal family drama, laughs at his father's inability to change because that is the clear-sighted younger man's only recourse for survival: he must accept life as it is. Through his heroic confrontation with truth, this member of a family who continually seek to escape the truth (through alcohol, drugs, or pretend games) may be able to break out of their circle of entrapment and begin to live, for the first time, on his own. O'Neill does not attempt to impose any artificial hopes upon the ending, as was his practice in such earlier plays as *Beyond the Horizon* (1918), *The Straw* (1919), *Welded* (1923), *Desire under the Elms* (1924), and *Days without End* (1933), but in *Long Day's Journey into Night* (1941) the possibility is there. The younger and, consequently, probably more malleable Edmund has learned much about his father and brother in act 4. The hope that he will be able to avoid their mistakes renders the closure less bleak.

9

"Hopeless Hope": Suspense in
A Moon for the Misbegotten

A Moon for the Misbegotten (1943), the last play O'Neill completed for the stage, pursues the life of Jamie Tyrone, or "Jim" as he is called in this sequel to *Long Day's Journey into Night*, eleven years later in 1923. Although *Moon* has seldom been produced on the stage, probably owing to the difficulty of casting the role of Josie Hogan, who is supposed to be *"so oversize for a woman that she is almost a freak—five feet eleven in her stockings and weigh[ing] around one hundred and eighty"* (1.857), earlier dismissals of the play as melodramatic[1] appear to have been silenced by the overwhelming success of the 1974 Broadway production. Reviewer Clive Barnes hailed *Moon* as "one of the great plays of the 20th century";[2] Walter Kerr declared the play "possibly O'Neill's best."[3] Playgoers themselves accorded Colleen Dewhurst and Jason Robards standing ovations for their moving performances in the leading roles.

A Moon for the Misbegotten has also received high praise from a variety of critics, including John Henry Raleigh, D. V. K. Raghavacharyulu, and Timo Tiusanen. Louis Sheaffer rates *Moon* "one of the author's superior achievements"; and the Gelbs pronounce this drama "among O'Neill's greatest, rich in Irish humor and enormously moving in its brutal tragedy."[4]

Much of the critical commentary focuses upon the play's uneven tone, which Frederic I. Carpenter describes as "alternat[ing] between pigsty comedy and serious tragedy."[5] Unlike the tonal incongruity of such earlier O'Neill plays as *Beyond the Horizon* (1918) and *Dynamo* (1928), which was construed to be a defect, the mingling of tones in *Moon*, as well as in other late O'Neill works, has been hailed. In contrast to the distracting ambiguity of Robert Mayo's poetically exuberant speech at the end of *Beyond the Horizon*, and to the unwarranted whimsicality of Mrs. Fife's pounding on the dynamo after the young lovers' tragic deaths in *Dynamo*, the skillful blending of comedy and tragedy in *Moon* has been credited with being "richly Irish in its mixture of lusty humor and bone-deep sadness,"[6] with achieving "a personal kind of poetry through elements of grotesqueness and irony,"[7] and with thereby averting melodrama.[8] Far from detracting from the effectiveness of this drama as in the earlier plays, O'Neill's technique of combining various tones shows evidence of having evolved by the late plays to produce masterpieces perhaps comparable only to Shakespeare in their richness of scope.

Criticism of *A Moon for the Misbegotten* has also been directed toward its length and structure. Travis Bogard and Suzanne Flèche-Salgues find the play long;[9] Flèche-Salgues suggests it needs condensation. Louis Sheaffer, however, while conceding that the drama is "too long for the story it tells," excuses its meandering on the grounds that *Moon* "builds to an overwhelming climax."[10] Similarly defending the tortuous structure of the play on the basis of its cumulative emotional power, Allan Lewis writes:

> As in all the posthumous plays,[11] the exposition is strained, the relationships painfully constructed, the pulling back and forth repetitive, but the total effect is like an avalanche that gathers momentum slowly, then crushes everything before it.[12]

The avalanche analogy, which suggests the very essence of drama, is a particularly apt description of the emotional power of *Moon*. As Lewis suggests, the unhurried development of the play may well be responsible. In earlier works such as *Welded* (1923), *The Great God Brown* (1925), and even *Mourning Becomes Electra* (1931), the viewer is plunged into complex emotional relationships for which he is psychologically unprepared, creating a sense of unreality and a feeling of remoteness from the characters. In contrast, *Moon*, as Nicola Chiaromonte observes, gives "such an impression of probability that we lose all sense that it is a play."[13] The character of Jim Tyrone is, in fact, so finely drawn that the viewer almost feels as if he were inside his skin. O'Neill's technique of developing his plot and characters more slowly, as in *Moon*, represents an evolution in his facility for creating greater audience involvement: the viewer more fully apprehends the world of the play.

The plot of *A Moon for the Misbegotten*, although simple, is complicated by schemes, masks, and deep-rooted psychological needs. As the curtain rises, Josie Hogan is helping her younger brother Mike escape—as she has helped his two older brothers before him—from their father's "tyranny" on the Connecticut pig farm which the family leases from Jim Tyrone. In parting, the irritatingly priggish Mike admonishes his sister for her vaunted promiscuity with half the men in the neighborhood. He also speculates that she and their father are plotting to trap their alcoholic landlord, who will soon claim an inheritance, into marrying her. Josie, who loves Jim Tyrone,

is indignant at Mike's suggestion. When she relates it to her father, Phil
Hogan, he secretly applauds the idea for uniting the two lovers. Josie, however, declares she would no more ever attempt to trick Jim than she could
imagine a situation in which Jim would betray them. Phil responds that
their alcoholic landlord might, in a moment of drunkenness, sell their farm—
which he has promised to sell them at a fixed low price—to a higher bidder.
In such an unlikely event, Josie assures her father, she would be with him
"in any scheme [against Jim] . . . no matter how dirty" (1.873).

Even as she speaks, Jim appears announcing the imminent arrival of
their neighbor, Harder, the Standard Oil millionaire, who, furious with the
Hogans for allowing their pigs to wallow in his ice pond, has offered Jim a
small fortune for the Hogan farm just to be rid of them. As Harder ap-
proaches, Josie hides Jim in her bedroom, so that he can secretly witness
the riotous scene which ensues without incurring blame from Harder. The
fun-loving Hogans verbally annihilate the straightlaced millionaire, who is
forced to flee. Concerned about Jim's emaciated appearance, Josie urges
him to eat lunch with them: "Promise me you'll eat something, Jim. You've
got to eat. You can't go on the way you are, drinking and never eating,
hardly. You're killing yourself" (1.891). Jim's reply foreshadows the outcome of their projected date to "spoon in the moonlight" (1.883) that
evening: "That's right. Mother me, Josie, I love it" (1.891).

In act 2 Josie, forlornly dressed in her Sunday best, is waiting in the
moonlight for her "beau," who is already two hours late. Phil returns from
the inn, where he has been drinking with Tyrone. Phil pretends to be very
drunk but is actually scheming to unite the pair, who obviously care for
each other. He convinces Josie that Jim has promised to sell Harder their
farm. Angered by Jim's failure to appear for their "date," Josie fails to see
through her father's trick and agrees to lure Jim to her bed before witnesses, which her father will supply. Phil is counting on Jim's honor to marry
Josie afterwards, for both men have seen through Josie's mask of promiscuity and realize that she is actually a virgin. Josie, however, who even in
anger cannot imagine tricking Jim into marrying her, plans to demand only
that Jim keep his promise to sell them the farm. Phil, realizing the seduction will be difficult for his inexperienced daughter, suggests she use whiskey to facilitate her plot.

Act 3 is the crux of the play, the "romantic" confrontation between
Josie and Jim. Normally a teetotaler, Josie serves Jim glass after glass of
genuine "bonded Bourbon," a rarity since Prohibition, and proceeds to
shock Jim by following her father's advice and attempting to drink along
with him. At one point Jim literally knocks the drink out of her hand, telling
her he has spent too many nights with drunken whores; he wants tonight to

be different. Despite his kisses and protestations of love, however, Josie is wary of believing him, until she learns Jim had only been joking about selling Harder their farm and realizes her father has tricked her. Now responding in earnest to Jim's demonstrations of affection, Josie attempts to lead him to her bed. At this point Jim's whole manner changes. In a strange, apparently hallucinatory state he treats her like a whore, and she pulls away in shock. Returning to his senses, Jim protests she should not have acted like a whore trying to lead him to bed; what he wanted from her was different. Heavy with disappointment, he starts to leave.

Suddenly recognizing what Jim has really come for—not an adult romance but motherly love—Josie recalls him. Abandoning her seductive efforts, she cradles his head on her large maternal breasts. Safe in the bosom he has enthusiastically admired, Jim confesses the source of the torment that is destroying him—his outrageous behavior on the train carrying his mother's body back East for burial, when he slept with a piglike whore every night. Overcoming her initial shock, Josie forgives him in his mother's name as well as her own. Jim, temporarily relieved of his burden of guilt, falls asleep on her breast in the moonlight.

Act 4 takes place the following dawn, when Phil arrives (without witnesses) to find Josie still holding Jim. Exhausted, she accuses Phil of scheming to obtain Jim's inheritance. Threatening to leave her father, she sends him into the house. Then she awakens Jim to see the beauty of the dawn, now realizing that he is lost to her but hoping he will at least remember the past night and the peace he felt in her arms. However, although Jim awakes more at peace with himself than usual—and what is most remarkable, without the need of a drink!—he recalls nothing about the previous evening until he tastes the bonded Bourbon they shared. Suddenly remembering all, he is once again overwhelmed with shame and guilt. He tries to exit hastily, but once again Josie recalls him. Before leaving, he acknowledges his appreciation of the beauty of the night and her love. As he walks away, never to return, Josie silently blesses him, wishing him the speedy death he so fervently desires. The implication is that every footstep brings Jim closer to the grave.

If Josie's efforts to save Jim through her love have resulted in failure (as virtually all the convincing male-female relationships in O'Neill's plays, to a large degree, fail [*Beyond the Horizon*, *The First Man*, *All God's Chillun Got Wings*, *Desire under the Elms*, *Mourning Becomes Electra*, *A Touch of the Poet*, and *Long Day's Journey into Night*]), the reason is obvious—the insurmountable difference in their respective needs. Josie requires a husband (or at least a lover), and Jim a mother. A young woman in her sexual prime who is *"all woman"* with *"no mannish quality about her"* (1.857), Josie is still a virgin at twenty-eight and likely to remain so, despite her physical need and evident capacity for love. Encouraged by Jim's kindness, she has allowed herself to fantasize about becoming his wife and curing him of drinking (1.871). Jim has no such fantasies, however. His most fervent desire is to join his deceased mother through death. Already dead to most of his former pleasures, such as playing the horses, what Jim seeks from Josie is not sex, which he associates with prostitutes and which has come to disgust him, but the understanding and forgiveness that his mother would grant him were she still alive to hear his sins.

In *Long Day's Journey into Night* a somewhat younger Jim describes an incident, apparently from his impressionable adolescence, which may have affected his ability to respond sexually to women like Josie. He recalls discovering his mother in the act of giving herself a morphine injection: "Christ, I'd never dreamed before that any women but whores took dope!" (4.818). Deeply disturbed by the incident, which confused "pure" women with whores in his youthful mind,[14] the middle-aged Jim shows evidence in both plays of having dedicated himself to keeping the two categories of women as separate as possible. Even when, desperate for the consolations of a mother figure, "Jamie" escorted the portly prostitute, Fat Violet, "upstairs," as he relates doing in *Long Day's Journey into Night*, he appears to have attempted to maintain the distinction between mother figures and sexual partners. He reports being "ready for a weep on any old womanly bosom" and having "no dishonorable intentions, whatever" (4.816). In *A Moon for the Misbegotten*, when Josie invites him to make love to her, she violates the "virgin/mother" role in which he has cast her. Apparently receiving the sort of jolt he experienced upon discovering that his mother was a drug addict, he behaves erratically. When Josie protests that he is treating her like a whore, he replies without thinking, "Why did you have to act like one, asking me to come to bed?" (3.926).

Although Jim, upon reflection, is sensitive enough to recognize the validity of Josie's sexual need, he defends his rejection of her as a lover on the basis of his unworthiness: "[I]f I could give you happiness—" (3.926). He does not want to "poison" her, he says, as he has poisoned others: "Believe me, Kid, when I poison them, they stay poisoned!" (3.926). No doubt Jim believes what he is saying—that he is acting out of consideration for Josie, but this is not the primary reason he cannot make love to her. As a rule Jim is incapable of subscribing to illusions. He is, in fact, so intent upon ripping off masks that the ugly truths he exposes destroy his will to live. In this unique instance, however, Jim appears self-deceived—and not without cause. The real reason he cannot go to bed with Josie, aside from his inhibiting virgin/whore complex, is his unacknowledged oedipal attachment to his deceased mother, which was the reason he felt such intense rivalry toward his father all his life. A middle-aged son who must retaliate upon his mother for dying by consorting with harlots and returning to alcoholism has never outgrown his dependency upon that parent. Jim confesses,

> It was as if I wanted revenge—because I'd been left alone—because I knew I was lost, without any hope left—that all I could do would be drink myself to death, because no one was left who could help me. (3.931–32)

Like a little boy he whines, "If I could tell her it was because I missed her so much and couldn't forgive her for leaving me" (3.932). Jim's behavior with the "blonde pig" on the train appears to have been a repeat of a pattern established in the past. Sex with prostitutes may have been his usual way of retaliating against the "beautiful" and beloved mother whom he was forbidden to touch. The repeated substitution may have further impaired Jim's sexuality: "nice" girls like Josie remind him of his mother, and he cannot touch them because of the old taboo.

O'Neill indicates in at least several places (3.916) that Jim is physically attracted to Josie (as he probably was to his mother). He *"grabs her in his arms—with genuine passion"* (3.913) only to stop just as suddenly: "Nix. Let's cut it out" (3.913). Not with Mama. He does not realize he is teasing Josie. Misunderstanding his reticence, she attempts to win him to her bed: ". . . I am a virgin. . . . And now you'll never—and I want you to—now more than ever—because I love you more than ever, after what's happened— . . . Come. Come with me. *(She gets to her feet, pulling at his arm— . . .)"* (3.924).

Jim, for his part, is unable to touch her unless he first convinces himself Josie is not Mama but the whore. His behavior when she tries to lead him to her bed is a vivid example of the way he playacts to fool himself. His face and voice undergo a strange metamorphosis. *"He looks at her now with a sneering cynical lust"* and speaks thickly as if he were suddenly drunk: "I know what you want, Bright Eyes. . . . *(He kisses her roughly.)* Come on, Baby Doll, let's hit the hay. *(He pushes her back in the doorway)"* (3.925). Jim appears to be trying to stimulate himself to perform the function of a lover by convincing himself Josie is a whore.

When Josie pulls back in horror, he acknowledges his own confusion regarding his action: "What the hell? Was I trying to rape you, Josie? Forget it. I'm drunk—not responsible. . . . Nuts! Cut out the faking. I knew what I was doing. *(slowly, staring before him)* But it's funny. I *was* seeing things. That's the truth, Josie. For a moment I thought you were that blonde pig— . . ." (3.925). Whatever his motivation, he does not need the whores tonight. That was the reason that he knocked the glass of Bourbon out of Josie's hand. The sight of her drinking had reminded him of "that fat blonde pig on the train" (3.917). Tonight he needs Mama in her normal capacity as listener and comforter, not the sexual intimacy Josie has offered him. Disappointed with the outcome of their moonlight encounter, Jim turns to leave: "I came here asking for love—just for this one night, because I thought you loved me. *(dully)* Nuts. To hell with it" (3.926). At last understanding Jim's need, Josie runs after him: *"She gives him a hug and kisses him. There is passion in her kiss but it is a tender, protective* **maternal** *passion, to which he responds with an instant grateful yielding"* (3.927, emphasis added). Tyrone replies simply, "Thanks Josie. You're beautiful. I love you. I knew you'd understand" (3.927).

Finally, it is Jim's failure to comprehend his sexual problem that prevents him from attaining an adult relationship with Josie. He is so enmeshed in his own anguish that he cannot help her by fulfilling her need. He turns away from lovemaking with the excuse: "There's always the aftermath that poisons you. *I* don't want you to be poisoned—. . . . And *I* don't want to be poisoned *myself*—not again—not with you. *(He pauses—slowly)* There have been too many nights [for Jim, not for Josie]—and dawns. This must be different. *I* want— *(His voice trails off into silence)*" (3.916, emphasis added). The predominance of *I*'s in Jim's speech tells the story.

As Jim's efforts to explain bear witness, not only sexual but even verbal communication is difficult for this pair who reach out to each other in the moonlight. They wear protective masks, the exact opposite of what they are, to protect their fragile egos from hurt. Josie pretends to have slept with half the men in the neighborhood, because she fears her large body, to which she continually refers in a deprecating manner ("a big ugly hulk like me" [2.903], "my big ugly paw" [3.921]), is undesirable. Jim assumes the mask of the hardened cynic, who must debunk even moonlight and *"an exceptionally beautiful sunrise"* (4.942), to disguise the supersensitivity to pain and guilt that causes him to seek oblivion through alcohol and death. Each sees through the other's mask as they attempt to establish contact with each other. Jim knows Josie is a virgin and a teetotaler. Out of respect for her mask, however, he greets her with an ironic allusion to the notoriety in which she takes pride: "[H]ow's my Virgin Queen of Ireland?" (1.877). Josie knows why Jim pretends to debunk everything; his motivation is similar to her own. She tells her father, "[Jim] only acts like he's hard and shameless to get back at life when it's tormenting him—and who doesn't?" (1.872). Nevertheless, despite their mutual awareness and even acceptance of each other's masks, they become irritated with the pretenses that make it difficult for them to really talk to each other. Becoming satiated with Josie's coarse allusions to her sexual experiences and his Broadway "tarts," Jim protests, "For God's sake, cut out that kind of talk, Josie! It sounds like hell" (1.878). Over and over again, he begs her, "Just be yourself" (2.910). Similarly, Josie, despite her understanding of Jim's need to joke cynically about everything, becomes irritated when Jim pretends he is going to sell their farm to Harder: "Will you shut up your rotten Broadway blather!" (1.890). Their continuous dissimulation isolates them from their own feelings as well as from each other. Jim, for example, whose loverlike speech and actions encourage Josie's seductive efforts, apparently never realizes that he has no intention of going to bed with her.

A Moon for the Misbegotten, as its title implies, is a play about alienation. Josie is physically alienated from normal relationships with men. Her great size and strength *("She is more powerful than any but an exceptionally strong man"* [1.857]) cause men to feel threatened by her. The mask of a wanton that she assumes alienates her still further—from her priggish brother and even, to a certain extent, from her father and Jim, who are often unsure how to respond to her pretense. Jim, the black sheep of the Tyrone family, was alienated from his now-deceased father, who possessed the mother Jim adored. A social outcast as well, his classical education and fine clothes are incongruous with his "whore and barkeep" friends, as Phil points out (1.875). Alienated even from his Irish ancestry by dint of his education, Jim has to *"imitate"* (1.875) Phil's brogue.[15]

In a larger sense, the trio in the Hogan shanty are alienated from the world. Ironically, it is not the literal "pig-keepers," Phil and Josie Hogan, who are "pig-like," but the rest of the greedy, money-oriented society that we glimpse from the play. Jim Tyrone constantly refers to prostitutes, who render sex in exchange for money, as "pigs." Phil Hogan refers to the Harders, his millionaire neighbors, as "pigs" with their "snoot[s] in the air" (1.881). He compares his own "ambitious American-born pigs" (1.881), which do not miss any opportunities to wallow in Harder's ice pond, to American capitalists like Harder, who are motivated by greed. The references to prostitutes and to the Harders are practically the only allusions to the world outside that appear in the play. In such a materialistic society, it seems rather a virtue that the main characters are "misbegotten" or "different" from their money-worshipping neighbors. A unique quality shared by both Jim Tyrone and the Hogans is generosity. Instead of losing his soul in the struggle for economic advancement, Phil, who subsists on the meager result of his pig-keeping labors and pretends to be stingy with his liquor, would actually give away his shirt (3.918 [Jim]). Jim himself has promised to sell the farm to the Hogans at a price below its market value and far below the magnificent sum offered by Harder: money is less important to Jim than the Hogans' friendship. Josie's generosity of heart needs little comment:

she forgoes her own sexual and emotional needs to fulfill Jim's need for a mother confessor in the moonlight.

Through the manner in which O'Neill's last play distinguishes between the very human trio in the cottage and the "pigs" without, *A Moon for the Misbegotten* may be considered a predecessor for Eugène Ionesco's *Rhinoceros* (1960). In the absurd drama, which begins innocently enough, the whole human race gradually metamorphoses into rhinoceroses except for the hero and his girl. When Daisy, too, defects to the horned creatures, Berenger remains the last human on earth. The audience is left fearing that Berenger may not be able to hold out very long—a fact that seems terribly important to the continuation of life as we know it.

In *A Moon for the Misbegotten*, also, it seems crucial that this couple, so alienated from the rest of society by their sensitivity and values, marry and propagate the earth with their kind. It is important to Josie, who requires a husband to fulfill her naturally loving, maternal nature; it is important to her father, who is concerned about his daughter's happiness and who thinks of Jim as a son; it is vital to Jim, particularly, as undoubtedly his sole remaining chance for survival. Furthermore, O'Neill appears to have selected the two people on earth best qualified to help each other. If anyone could nurture Jim back to health and give him a zest for living, it is Josie, with her great physical and emotional strength, her boundless vitality, and her huge heart. Similarly, if anyone could draw Josie out of the virginity in which she may be imprisoned (Jim indicates that she has dated some of the rough neighborhood men and rejected their advances [3.923–24]), it is Jim, a natural gentleman who rises in her presence (1.877), Jim, who sees through her mask of coarseness and appreciates her worth. The outcome of their encounter is more than a sexual tease. For viewers who can ignore the biographical fact that the real-life prototype for Jim Tyrone drank himself to death, the extremely high stakes increase the suspense. The future of much of what remains commendable about human existence—mutual respect, the capacity for deep feeling, and the commitment to values—seems to depend upon this union. If Charlotte Brontë had had a hand in writing the end, Josie would certainly have nursed Jim back to health, as the heroine of *Jane Eyre* did Edward Rochester. Instead, however, the conclusion of *A Moon for the Misbegotten* is subject to the terrible realism of the late Eugene O'Neill. Throughout the play O'Neill has depicted Jim Tyrone as a "dead" man, too far gone physically and emotionally for salvation. Furthermore, O'Neill is writing the story of his own brother, who, in fact, died the year after his mother in 1923, the year depicted in this play.

Nevertheless, in a sense the "great miracle" (4.936) to which Josie sardonically refers really takes place. Josie's compassionate response to Jim's need is a miracle of love and self-sacrifice. Her brief moment of insight into Jim's need causes her to completely reverse her seductive behavior. Putting aside her own disappointed fantasies, she concentrates all her maternal capacities into helping Jim: "I'm sorry I was so stupid and didn't see—But I see now, and you'll find I have all the love you need" (3.927). The inspiring realization of the human potential for unselfishness, as represented by Josie, makes the closure less sad.

Josie's effort, however, is more commendable than its result. Jim departs, to be sure, none the worse for their night together. There is even some indication that he obtains a measure of peace, although, as usual, he feels compelled to undermine it: "It's hard to describe how I feel. It's a new one on me. Sort of at peace with myself and this lousy life—as if all my sins had been forgiven—*(He becomes self-conscious—cynically)* Nuts with that sin bunk, but you know what I mean" (4.942). Similarly ambiguous is his response to the beautiful sunrise: "Don't spoil this dawn! . . . God seems to be putting on quite a display. I like Belasco better. Rise of curtain, Act-Four stuff. (. . . *quickly and angrily*) God damn it! Why do I have to pull that lousy stuff?" (4.942). Like John Loving in *Days without End*, Jim has a demon inside him that quickly negates any positive sentiments on his part. More convincing than Jim's muddled speeches is the fact that he awakes with no desire for a drink. With his recollection through the bonded Bourbon, however, all his guilt and self-loathing appear to return. Josie may have forgiven him in her name and in the name of his mother; all humanity might forgive him; but he cannot forgive himself. Jim's only hope for peace, of which he has had a refreshing foretaste in Josie's arms, is the grave.

Although the change in Jim is barely acknowledgeable, Josie emerges from "their night" a stronger person. She has faced the fact of Jim's hopelessness and survived. Rather than blaming Jim for disappointing her romantic expectations, she bravely acknowledges her own failure to recognize the obvious. She, herself, had described Jim in his initial approach to the Hogan cottage as "a dead man walking slow behind his own coffin" (1.874). She tells her father,

> He did nothing to bring me sorrow. It was my mistake. I thought there was still hope. I didn't know he'd died already—that it was a damned soul coming to me in the moonlight, to confess and be forgiven and find peace for a night—. . . . (4.937)

Furthermore, she takes solace in the new pride she has acquired through the act of giving. She has told Jim, "I'm proud you came to me as the one in the world you know loves you enough to understand and forgive—" (3.933).

Like Nora Melody in *A Touch of the Poet* (1939), and her early predecessor, Mrs. Roylston in *Servitude* (1914), who take pride in their unselfish devotion to their egotistical husbands, the source of Josie's new pride is her ministration to Jim's need. It appears unlikely that she will require her old wanton facade any longer. She has an identity now; she has gained confidence in her own intrinsic worth.

Human, nevertheless, Josie desires some small acknowledgment of her efforts on Jim's behalf—his recollection of the beauty of the night and the brief respite from torment he found in her arms. The final tension of the play concerns his remembrance of the night, which Josie at first encourages, until, realizing the suffering remembering would cause him, she urges him to leave quickly. This is Josie's final magnificence—her ability to sacrifice even that bit of satisfaction for herself to help the man she loves. Nevertheless, O'Neill, perhaps a little in love with his heroine himself, grants her desire. Suddenly recalling the events of the preceding night through the taste of the Bourbon, Jim pays tribute to Josie's love in his last words:

> Forgive me, Josie. I do remember! I'm glad I remember! I'll never forget your love! *(He kisses her on the lips.)* Never! *(kissing her again)* Never, do you hear! I'll always love you, Josie. *(He kisses her again)* Good-bye—and God bless you! *[He leaves quickly without looking back.]* (4.944)

The very fact that Jim can say "God bless you!" without having to recant it and debunk "God" furnishes Josie with reason to believe that she has alleviated his despair.[16]

Although the play ends with Jim's departure, closure actually begins at the end of act 3, when Josie literally informs the audience that the "end" is approaching: "God forgive me, it's a fine *end* to all my scheming, to sit here with the dead hugged to my breast, and the silly mug of the moon grinning down, enjoying the joke!" (3.934, emphasis added). Her references to schemes and jokes recall the tomfoolery of act 1, thus initiating the return of the play to its frame. Since many of O'Neill's plays conclude with a circular return to the opening "frame" or situation *(The Emperor Jones, All God's Chillun Got Wings, Desire under the Elms, The Great God Brown, The Iceman Cometh)*, closure is obviously imminent. The true conflict of the play, the "romantic" confrontation between Jim and Josie, is over. As she sits in the moonlight holding him like a child to her breast in the pietà position, her "options appear to [have] diminish[ed]," a situation that renders closure increasingly inevitable.[17] After the powerfully moving third act, the viewer can expect little more.

With the arrival of dawn in act 4 the magic is ended, and O'Neill re-

DUE DATE SLIP

Patron: Santana T Aker
Patron Group: Student - Undergraduate

Due Date: 12/12/2007 11:59 PM

Title: Perverse mind : Eugene O'Neill's struggle with closure / Barbara Voglino.
Author: Voglino, Barbara, 1940-
Call Number: PS3529.N5 Z886 1999
Enumeration:
Chronology:
Copy: 1
Item Barcode: 32260008014856

turns his audience to the necessities of farm life. Phil appears and exclaims of Jim, who is still sleeping, "Be God, he looks dead!" (4.935). Confirming her father's allusion to the terminal condition of death, which appears approaching for her beloved and thereby intensifies the suggestion of closure,[18] Josie replies, "Why wouldn't he? He is" (4.935). The description of Jim as corpselike relates back to his appearance in the first act, when Josie described him as "dead man walking slow behind his own coffin" (1.874). Still another element carried over from the opening frame is Josie's send-off of Jim as a "child" she has nurtured, which recalls her tearful send-off of her brother in act 1. Completing the circular nature of the frame that encloses the play, in act 1 Jim approached the cottage; in act 4 he leaves by the same path. Also, both acts conclude with the Hogans sitting down to a meal, but with a significant difference. Act 1 ended with Josie bringing the malnourished Jim into their kitchen and encouraging him to eat lunch. In act 4 Josie does not suggest that Jim join them for breakfast. The dead do not require nourishment. No longer wishing to prolong the life of torment he so fervently desires to escape, she wishes him Godspeed in his journey to death.

The closure of *A Moon for the Misbegotten* is one of the finest in the canon. Although "open" to some degree (regarding Josie's future and the exact date of Jim's death), no ambiguity remains. All the relevant questions have been answered, "creat[ing] in the [viewer] the expectation of nothing."[19] Yet, paradoxically, suspense still exists in the form of a "hopeless hope"[20] almost to the very end. Even as Jim sleeps on her breast, hope swells unbidden in Josie: "Oh, Jim, Jim, maybe my love could still save you, if you could want it enough!" (3.934). At the same time, she cannot help realizing, "No. That can never be" (3.934). The audience, also, is reluctant to abandon hope. When Jim kisses Josie several times in parting, the viewer still halfhopes that her love will recall him to life. But "their night" was to be one night only (3.915), and with the dawn it is done. The tragic conclusion is entirely in keeping with Jim's irrevocably deteriorated condition, thus fulfilling the requirements of "honesty" and "appropriateness" that Marianna Torgovnick proclaims the true test for effective closure.[21] Jim Tyrone does not suddenly recover his lost vitality, as does Robert Mayo at the end of *Beyond the Horizon* (1918). Nor does he experience an unaccountable "leap of faith," as does John Loving in *Days without End* (1933). The violent deaths, either imminent or depicted, that conclude *Beyond the Horizon*, *The Straw* (1919), *Desire under the Elms* (1924), and *Dynamo* (1928), among other O'Neill plays, are unnecessary here. In the final lines of the play, Josie prays Jim will die in his sleep (4.946).

Phil Hogan's curse provides a suitable coda to the play's outcome:

HOGAN—May the blackest curse from the pit of hell—
JOSIE—*(with an anguished cry)* Don't father! I love him!
HOGAN—. . . . It was life I was cursing— *(with a trace of his natural manner)* And, be God, that's a waste of breath, if it does deserve it. . . .
(4.945)

Life is cruel because the only goals worth having, as O'Neill wrote in 1919, are unattainable to man: "[E]ach one of our lives is a hopeless hope—that failure to realize our dreams is the inexorable fate allotted to us."[22]

Although O'Neill's fatalistic philosophy does not appear to have evolved throughout his career to the same degree as his facility with closure, a somewhat more cheerful view of life emerges from O'Neill's last play through its emphasis upon such positive values as love, compassion, and self-sacrifice. The spectator leaves the drama still awed by the mythic magnificence of O'Neill's remarkable heroine. Furthermore, there is genuine friendship and laughter in the Hogan house not found elsewhere in the O'Neill canon (the inmates of Harry Hope's saloon in *The Iceman Cometh* are inebriated), with the exception of *Ah, Wilderness!* Moreover, the humorous banter between Josie and her father does not represent an attempt to escape life so much as a coping device: they may be defeated in their efforts, but they keep trying and are able to accept what life brings.

Ironically, there appears to be more survival value for the audience in this realistic closure, which does not attempt to resolve anything but merely presents life as O'Neill sees it, than in the closures of many of his earlier plays, which deliberately seek to solve the problems of mankind. O'Neill's ecstatically rendered but incredible "solutions" in such plays as *Beyond the Horizon* (1918), *The Fountain* (1922), *Welded* (1923), *Lazarus Laughed* (1926), and *Days without End* (1933) alienate the audience with their artificiality. In strong contrast, the closure of *A Moon for the Misbegotten* (1943) is not only believable but excruciatingly honest. Because the viewer is better able to identify with the characters and their actions, he is more likely to gain the valuable insight into human experience that has been cited as a benefit of dramatic literature.[23] The "failure to realize our dreams" may be "the inexorable fate allotted to us," but the way man reacts to this failure emerges as the important determinant of his true mettle in *Moon*. Josie, by no means a passive character like the denizens of Harry Hope's saloon *(The Iceman Cometh),* has truly exerted herself to save Jim. Having failed due to circumstances beyond her control, she does not succumb to despair, but rather finds solace in what remains—a warm relationship with her father and the mutual exercise of their keen wits. The courage demonstrated by Josie Hogan impresses the survival value of acceptance and resignation on the audience far more effectively than Lazarus laughing while his flesh burns *(Lazarus Laughed)* or John Loving's pompous "sermon" on acceptance in *Days without End* (3.2.158). O'Neill has learned to substitute character and action for high-sounding speeches in the closure of his plays.

Finally, it would appear obligatory to deal with O'Neill's last recorded word on *A Moon for the Misbegotten.* Although he had, with typical enthusiasm for the play in progress, expressed a "real affection" for the play while writing it,[24] in his inscription to Carlotta in 1952 he stated that he had "come to loathe" this play. Various explanations have been offered for O'Neill's change of attitude toward *Moon.* The Gelbs cite the mood of black despair that overcame O'Neill as a result of reliving his brother's last years in order to create this drama.[25] Travis Bogard enumerates the numerous personal difficulties—O'Neill's own illness and grave problems concerning his children—that afflicted him while writing this play.[26] Roger Brown suggests O'Neill may have disliked *Moon* either because the prayerful ending "did not express honestly his feelings for his brother," whom, Brown gives evidence, O'Neill appears to have disliked; or for "reasons intrinsic to the structure of the play,"[27] upon which Brown does not attempt to elaborate.

I am not convinced that personal problems affected O'Neill's attitude toward his work, since writing was the one refuge through which he managed to escape the numerous difficulties that besieged him. Furthermore, in answer to Brown's speculations, the structure of the play appears highly effective, if its successful closure may be considered an indication. Moreover, the brunt of evidence suggests O'Neill really loved his brother, who is presented with unmistakable affection in *A Moon for the Misbegotten.* Jamie's sense of humor, his sense of values, and capacity for understanding are painstakingly presented right along with the less desirable aspects of his character. In 1931 O'Neill told a schoolmate that he had been "terribly close" to his brother.[28] Even during the Guild rehearsals for the first production of *Moon,* O'Neill defended his brother's character. He complained that the actor playing Jim "was not making him enough of a gentleman."[29] If O'Neill avoided seeing his brother during his last years of life,[30] his reason appears to have been not so much dislike as the excruciating pain of knowing that he could not save his brother, and perhaps also the fear that through associating with Jamie he, too, might be lost (as he nearly was in his youth).

If I may hazard my own guess regarding the reason for O'Neill's expressed "loathing" for *Moon,* it has to do with its ending, which, despite its biographical veracity, was not the ending O'Neill, like Josie and her father, and like the audience, really wanted. I believe it was all O'Neill could do to refrain from falsifying reality by "saving" his brother through Josie's love. If he could actually have saved Jamie with his pen, he would no doubt have done so. But Jamie had long since gone to his rest. O'Neill was too late to change Jamie's closure, and his helplessness affected his feelings toward this play.

10

Conclusion

Various explanations have been offered for the exceptional difficulty Eugene O'Neill experienced with closure. C. W. E. Bigsby cites O'Neill's equation of life with "unending struggle" as the reason "so few of his plays end with any sense of real completion."[1] Gustav H. Blanke blames the circular structure of many of the plays for precluding the possibility of a satisfying ending.[2] A new explanation for O'Neill's difficulty with closure has emerged as a result of this study, which while not negating the merits of the preceding suggestions has the merit of elucidating some of his closural strategies—his fear of death.

Frank Kermode's assertion that people fear the End they imagine because "the End is a figure for their own deaths," as "perhaps, are all the ends in fiction,"[3] seems particularly applicable to Eugene O'Neill, who for all his superior intelligence and sensitivity retained some of the superstitious nature of his Irish heritage. O'Neill explicitly expressed his fear of "endings" as associated with death or disaster for their author through the semiautobiographical heroes of *Days without End* (1933) and *The Iceman Cometh* (1940). In *Days without End* John Loving, who is undergoing a crisis of faith (which some scholars[4] believe reflects O'Neill's condition at this time), is having difficulty ending the autobiographical novel he is writing (O'Neill wrote eight drafts of *Days without End* and agonized over the ending). To his alter ego, Loving, who has been urging him to conclude his story with the wife's death and the suicide of the hero, John responds shakily, "It is dangerous—to call things" (1.114). John fears "call[ing]" or decisively ending the lives of his characters as having possible prescriptive force regarding his own "end" and that of his wife. Similarly, in *The Iceman Cometh* (1940), O'Neill's next new play to be produced on Broadway after *Days without End*, Larry Slade, a sixty-year-old man (O'Neill was fifty-two when he wrote this play) of sensitivity and compassion, expounds upon the danger of "calling" one's end. While attempting to solve the mystery surrounding Hickey's changed personality, Larry realizes that the salesman has not told his usual anecdote about his wife sleeping with the iceman. Speculating that Hickey's often repeated "joke" may have become a self-fulfilling prophecy, Larry admonishes Hickey, "You should have remembered there's truth in the old superstition that you'd better look what you call because in the end it comes to you!" (2.644). Hickey retaliates by warning Larry about the ex-anarchist's own pose of waiting for death: "[Y]ou'd better watch out how you keep calling for that old Big Sleep! *(Larry starts and for a second looks superstitiously frightened. . . .)*" Larry's alarmed reaction suggests that, despite his bravado about that "old superstition," he (like O'Neill) has not fully escaped the specious beliefs of his ancestors.

The conclusions of both *Days without End* and *The Iceman Cometh* confirm their heroes' earlier-stated anxieties regarding the possibly self-fulfilling nature of "calling" ends. When John Loving *(Days without End)* finally decides upon death by pneumonia for the wife in his fiction, his own wife nearly dies of pneumonia. Similarly, at the end of *The Iceman Cometh* Larry Slade attains the very state he has "called" upon himself. Throughout the play he has deludedly professed to be waiting for death; as the play closes, his death wish becomes real. Even Hickey is affected, according to the most defensible interpretation of his ambiguous exit. After having explained his expression of hatred toward his wife as an act of insanity, he may be construed as having "called" derangement upon himself at the close of the play.

If O'Neill's fear of death was of a more inordinate variety than that implied by Kermode's generalization (people fear the End they imagine because "the End is a figure for [one's] own [death]"), the playwright's early brushes with death may have contributed to this anxiety. Ironically, as a youth O'Neill appears to have deliberately sought death through years of drinking and dissipation. He even attempted suicide in 1912. It was only after he finally contracted a potentially fatal case of tuberculosis that he realized he wanted to live. In a sudden about-face the still youthful O'Neill not only battled against the illness to win back his health, but even after he was pronounced cured continued to exercise elaborate precautions against a recurrence for many years. Driven by his newly discovered desire to create drama, he slept outdoors in frigid weather (as was recommended for tubercular patients). He also swam long distances in cold water to build up his strength. The devastating deaths of his father, mother, and brother in quick succession (1920–23) seem only to have augmented his determination to live. After his brother Jamie's death, the playwright is reported to have expressed concern about being the only "pure Irish" O'Neill of his branch left.[5] Now, in addition to his powerful goal to create drama as a motivation for survival, he seems also to have felt obligated to carry on the O'Neill line. Larry Slade's desperate prayer for life *(The Iceman Cometh)*, although uttered with attempted irony, seems an outpouring from O'Neill's own heart:

> Beloved Christ, let me live a little longer at any price! If it's only for a few days more, or a few hours even, have mercy, Almighty God, and let me still clutch greedily to my yellow heart this sweet treasure, this jewel beyond price, the dirty, stinking bit of withered old flesh which is my beautiful little life! (3.675)

O'Neill's obsession with life and consequently excessive fear of death appears to have contributed to his difficulty with closure. Because he unconsciously feared that the tragic ends he "called" for his characters (many of whom are veiled substitutes for himself, as John Loving's hero is for his author in *Days without End*) might have repercussions on his own life, he "choked" when it came to ending his plays. Like a nervous player of Russian roulette, too often he either misfires and misses his target (with an inappropriate ending), or he postpones pulling the potentially fatal trigger (by concluding with ambiguity or openness). By avoiding the anticipated ending through ineptness or postponement (a practice that O'Neill, dimly recognizing, attributed to his "perverse mind"),[6] he may unwittingly have been attempting to prolong his own life.

"Life doesn't end," he wrote in 1921 regarding the uncertain closure of *"Anna Christie."* "One experience is but the birth of another. And even death—."[7] But with the word "death" O'Neill stops abruptly. Death is the "experience" to end all experiences—the very finality he was seeking to avoid through his writing. Perhaps, he may have unconsciously reasoned, if he could keep writing—faster and faster in an unending cycle of creative output—one play giving "birth" to another, he would build up enough centrifugal force, or some such power, to defeat that "meaningless chance—electricity or something, which whirls us—on to Hercules" ([Loving] *Days without End* 3.158) and thereby remain within the circle of life.

O'Neill does not avoid the subject of death in his dramas. Most of his earlier plays, in fact, culminate in suicide, murder, or death by consumption. Too often, however, he hurries through the suicide or death (*Warnings* [1913], *Abortion* [1914], *Bread and Butter* [1914], and *Dynamo* [1928]), which usually occurs offstage, so quickly he may be suspected of fleeing the possibly fatal implications for himself. Another tack, perhaps unconsciously employed to divert harm from himself, is concluding with the death or suicide as imminent rather than a fait accompli (*The Dreamy Kid* [1918], *The*

Straw [1919], *Diff'rent* [1920], *Desire under the Elms* [1924], *A Moon for the Misbegotten* [1943]). A third means by which, as I have suggested, O'Neill avoids the confrontation with mortality he might incur through truly "ending" his plays is to leave many of the closures ambiguous (*Beyond the Horizon* [1918], *"Anna Christie"* [1920], *All God's Chillun Got Wings* [1923]). Still a fourth procedure which may be construed as a strategy to deflect harm from himself is his insistence upon ameliorating the characters of his personae at the close of his plays.

During a rehearsal (1946) for *The Iceman Cometh* O'Neill is reported by Croswell Bowen to have said, "In all my plays sin is punished and redemption takes place."[8] Even if O'Neill never uttered these words, they constitute an insightful gloss on the closures of all nine of his plays examined in this study. Moreover, if Bowen's account may be credited,[9] this remarkably revealing assertion ("in *all* my plays" [emphasis added]) indicates the obsessive nature of the effort to show redemption on the part of a writer who professed no religious faith. O'Neill's purpose in ameliorating his frequently autobiographical characters seems best explained as an attempt to safeguard himself. In *Beyond the Horizon* (1918), for example, he could not allow his much altered fictional counterpart, Robert Mayo, to simply die of consumption after wasting his life. Instead, O'Neill undermines the whole structure of the play, which revolves about the ironic contradiction of expectations, by trying to impose meaning upon Robert's death in Robert's concluding, poetically rendered speeches. However, the final sequence, which depicts the utter despair of Andrew and Ruth, suggests that O'Neill himself was unable to accept the artificial "redemption" he tried to impose upon Robert.

Undercutting or negating the anticipated ending in the manner of *Beyond the Horizon* is almost a trademark of O'Neill's earlier plays. In *"Anna Christie"* (1920) Chris's fatalistic allusions to the unpredictable sea, with which the play concludes, negate Anna's proposed happy ending, which generic expectations have induced viewers to expect. In the tonally unstable *Dynamo* (1928) the tragedy of the young lovers' deaths is undercut by the whimsical concluding sequence—Mrs. Fife pounding on the dynamo, calling it a "hateful old thing" (3.3.885). Even the more tonally consistent *Desire under the Elms* (1924), which depicts the devastating effects of greed, concludes with a theatricalized redemption of Abbie and Eben, a redemption itself somewhat undercut by the sheriff's concluding remark, which recalls the greed that precipitated the tragedy. In *Days without End* (1933) the entire premise of the play—John's power to "call" or create his own end through the novel he is writing—is obliterated by its miraculous conclusion. None of the several endings proposed by John for his hero was founded on a "leap of faith." Apparently fearful of concluding this highly autobiographical play with the hero's death, O'Neill projected his own wished-for ending upon John Loving.[10] That this less tragic, if badly contrived, ending failed to have prescriptive force for its creator, however, is evidenced by O'Neill's rueful admission that he had "unfortunately" not been able to return to Catholicism in the manner of his hero.[11]

After the failure of *Days without End* (1933) O'Neill stopped trying to impose artificial endings on his plays. The successful closure of *Mourning Becomes Electra* (1931) had opened up a new technique for him that was to prove an invaluable aid to closing the dramas of his late period—commencing with a preconceived ending. O'Neill had planned the "tragic end" of his "Yankee Electra"[12] before starting to write the trilogy. Beginning with an ending in mind, as opposed to a situation that could end innumerable ways (as in the much labored-over *"Anna Christie"* and *Days without End*), also contributed to the successful closures of at least two of O'Neill's finest plays. The endings of *Long Day's Journey into Night* (1941) and *A Moon for the Misbegotten* (1943) were deeply engraved in O'Neill's memory before he ever picked up a pencil. He was writing about members of his then-deceased family, whose "ends" he knew. Working backward from a given end appears to have relieved O'Neill from the "dangerous" responsibility of "calling ends" for his characters. All he had to do was develop them and let them play out their lives.

The closures of the late plays, many of which deal with people from O'Neill's own past, are truly excellent. Among the many ways his endings may be said to have evolved is the remarkable use of pantomime he demonstrates in the conclusions of such plays as *Mourning Becomes Electra* (1931), *The Iceman Cometh* (1940), and particularly *Long Day's Journey into Night* (1941). Still more important aspects of his improved closure, which merit further elaboration, include increased structural fulfillment, more believable reversals of character, a more purposeful use of ambiguity, and greater truthfulness or fidelity to life.

Regarding structural continuity, the theatricalized endings of many of the earlier plays frequently rely on violence and/or sudden redemption to render a closure inconsistent with the preceding text (*Beyond the Horizon* [1918], *Desire under the Elms* [1924], *Dynamo* [1928], and *Days without End* [1933]). In contrast, the later plays contain few surprises, since O'Neill prepares for his endings throughout the dramas. In *The Iceman Cometh* (1940), for example, the startling climax (Hickey's act 4 confession of the murder of his wife) is, in part, revealed by Hickey in acts 2 and 3. Larry's involvement with Parritt has been similarly anticipated from the beginning: Hickey keeps reminding Larry of his responsibility regarding the desperate young man who has come seeking his help. Also, significant textual details throughout the play assure the viewer that Larry is by no means so detached from mankind as he insists.

In *Long Day's Journey into Night* (1941), O'Neill's masterpiece and one of the most tragic plays to be penned by an American, nobody dies, and no true acts of violence are committed. The action—Mary's relapse into drugs and consequent deterioration—is inevitable from the outset. Similarly lacking in surprise is Josie's failure to save Jim in *A Moon for the Misbegotten* (1943). The hopelessness of Jim's condition is noted even before his first entrance when Josie describes him approaching her cottage as "a dead man walking slow behind his own coffin" (1.874). The late plays, then, do not require the heavy, often melodramatic plotting of the earlier plays. Closure comes about as a result of the fulfillment of the well-developed characters, who attain the fates toward which they have been progressing from the start.

When a dramatic reversal of character does occur in the late plays, such as the transformation of Larry Slade toward a more active involvement with Parritt in *The Iceman Cometh*, more adequate preparation renders the change believable. In the earlier plays the reversals of character that precipitate closure are often rendered incredible by inadequate preparation, lofty language, theatricality, and sudden changes in tone (*Beyond the Horizon* [1918], *Desire under the Elms* [1924], and *Days without End* [1933]). In *Desire under the Elms*, for example, Abbie murders her baby and changes very suddenly from a greedy, lascivious woman into one who desires to be punished for her crime. In strong contrast to Abbie's unsubstantiated transformation is the change in Lavinia (*Mourning Becomes Electra* [1931]) upon recognizing her guilt. Lavinia, like Abbie, wants to be castigated and, in fact, administers that punishment herself. However, whereas Abbie's desire for punishment violates the structure of the preceding play, which depicts the evils of greed and offers little indication of any moral awareness on her part, Lavinia's concluding act of incarcerating herself in the mansion seems the natural consequence of the passion for "justice" she has demonstrated throughout the trilogy. In act 1 of the first play, *The Homecoming*, she resolves to seek "justice" for her father's death by punishing his murderers; in act 4 of the final play, *The Haunted*, upon recognizing her guilt she turns that fastidious concern for "justice" upon herself.

Similarly well-motivated is the change in Larry Slade in *The Iceman Cometh* (1940). The viewer has been waiting for Larry, whose professed detachment from mankind is depicted as delusional, to recognize his involvement with Parritt, as the viewer has waited for Lavinia to discover her passion for Brant in *Mourning Becomes Electra*. Larry's acceptance of his responsibility toward Parritt thus becomes necessary to the completion of the drama. Still another very credible reversal of character occurs in *A Moon for the Misbegotten* (1943). Josie, upon recognizing the hopelessness of her efforts to win Jim for a lover, reverts to the hugeness of heart she has demonstrated throughout the play with her father and brothers. She plays "mother confessor" to Jim in the moonlight, attempting to lighten his burden of guilt in the short time remaining to him before death. Self-recognition or reversal of character in the late plays does not require the lofty language of the earlier plays. O'Neill has learned to convey meaning through action and character, rather than through words.

The use of ambiguity also becomes demonstrably more skillful in the closure of the late plays. In the early *Beyond the Horizon* (1918) the dying Robert Mayo's ambiguously rendered resumption of his quest is distracting, as is the negation of Anna's happy ending in the final sequence of *"Anna Christie"* (1920), which contemporary audiences apparently chose to ignore. Some undesirable ambiguity still lingers in the highly praised closure of *Mourning Becomes Electra* (1931). In this drama, which depicts complex psychological states with often undesirable explicitness, the omission of the extent of Lavinia's acknowledgment of her guilt emerges as a flaw. In *The Iceman Cometh* (1940), however, a play filled with mystery from the beginning, in which ambiguity or epistemological uncertainty itself may be considered the subject, the ambiguity enriches the play with multiple meanings. Similarly, in *Long Day's Journey into Night* (1941) ambiguity, in the form of the ambivalent relationships between the various Tyrones, enriches O'Neill's remarkable insight into these characters and enhances the shades of meaning to be gathered from the play. Comparably enriching is the ambivalence of Jim Tyrone's conflicting feelings toward Josie in *A Moon for the Misbegotten* (1943).

Finally, the most significant factor in the evolution of O'Neill's closures is their increasing fidelity to objective reality, or what the audience perceives as "life." Despite indications that O'Neill was a forerunner of the absurdists, most of his plays are written primarily in the realistic tradition. As a result, when his dramas conflict with the viewer's experience of life, as do the conclusions of many of the earlier plays, the viewer is discomfited by the unexpectedly discordant note. According to Vera M. Jiji's study of audiences' reactions to O'Neill's plays, spectators are most powerfully affected by those dramas that "reinforce" rather than conflict with their "objective sense of reality."[13]

Modern audiences have indicated an overwhelming preference for O'Neill's late plays (*A Touch of the Poet, The Iceman Cometh, Long Day's Journey into Night,* and *A Moon for the Misbegotten*) with their generally more open endings. One probable explanation is that "openness" confirms people's experience more truthfully in a society of dissolving values and increasingly blurred identities.[14] However, the actual evaluative criterion appears to be not "openness" per se, but fidelity to reality (in a realistic play), or Marianna Torgovnick's "honesty" and "appropriateness."[15] For example, the ending of *"Anna Christie"* (1920) is quite open, but the closure is flawed because it is not "appropriate" to the comedic style of the text. In contrast, the closure of *A Moon for the Misbegotten* (1943), although not particularly open[16] (the spectator sees Jim's coming death and Josie's survival almost as if they were depicted in the play), is excellent because it seems an honest and appropriate termination to Jim's debilitated condition as represented at the outset of the drama. The realistic artist, then, would appear to achieve his goal, not through the degree of "openness" in his work, as some artists have argued,[17] but by the extent to which he manages to affirm the viewer or reader's sense of "felt life."[18]

In conclusion, O'Neill's late plays, by dint of their more consistent realism and lack of artificiality as rendered possible through the improved closures, fulfill one of the most important functions of literature—moral direction. Able to identify with the lifelike characters and their credible situations, the viewer gains the "heightened insight into human experience"[19] that will help him to "endure and prevail."[20] O'Neill's earlier dramatic efforts to assist man in this regard are too obviously didactic to move audiences. For example, O'Neill's late-midperiod attempt to "broadcast" the survival value of stoic acceptance in John Loving's "on to Hercules" speech (*Days without End* 3.2.158 [1933]) emerges as a didactic intrusion upon the action of the play: the audience tends to ignore this pompous sermon. Similarly, the theatrical speeches about love in *Welded* (3.275–76 [1923]) strike the viewer as "rant."

In contrast to the foregoing heavy-handed efforts, the late plays do not "preach" a particular mode of conduct: they dramatize its value. *Long Day's Journey into Night* (1941), for example, illustrates the survival value of stoic acceptance far more effectively than John's "sermon" in *Days without End.* Edmund's laughter at his father's inability to overcome his acknowledged miserliness shows Edmund's acceptance of his father's weakness, thus demonstrating the young man's own potential for survival in an imperfect world. Similarly, in *A Moon for the Misbegotten* (1943) Josie's courage in facing the inevitable—her inability to "save" Jim and her effort to help him the only way that she can—demonstrates human love at its finest and the flexibility that will enable her to endure.

Another value that emerges from the late plays is the primary importance of human relationships. O'Neill's early heroes and heroines are remarkably self-centered. Reuben Light, who shoots his devoted girlfriend (*Dynamo* [1928]), Lavinia Mannon, who allows her mother and brother to commit suicide (*Mourning Becomes Electra* [1931]), and John Loving, who nearly destroys his caring wife by having a sexual encounter with her best friend (*Days without End* [1933]) are almost totally egocentric. Involvement with others becomes a much more significant factor in O'Neill's late work. The Tyrone men are all, to some extent, redeemed by their genuine concern for each other (*Long Day's Journey into Night* [1941]). Josie's unselfish devotion to Jim is the crux of *A Moon for the Misbegotten* (1943). Even in the one-act play, *Hughie* (1942), involvement with each other gives focus to the two characters' lives and saves at least one of them (the night clerk) from solipsism.

Hughie, O'Neill's next to last play, may be construed as predicting O'Neill's personal closure as well. The cast list describes Erie Smith as "*a teller of tales,*" an occupation that links him with O'Neill himself. Throughout the canon many of O'Neill's heroes have been artists of various sorts who, through their greater sensitivity and vision, have encountered difficulties surviving in the world. Robert Mayo is a would-be poet *(Beyond the Horizon)*, Orin Mannon writes a history of his family *(Mourning Becomes Electra)*, John Loving is a novelist *(Days without End)*, Simon Harford is a poet turned businessman *(A Touch of the Poet* and *More Stately Mansions)*, Larry Slade looking out the window at the end of *The Iceman Cometh* suggests the artist trying to make sense of life, and Edmund Tyrone is a budding poet/journalist *(Long Day's Journey into Night)*. In 1942 when O'Neill wrote *Hughie*, he had not had any new plays produced for nearly a decade. Like Erie Smith, who longs for an audience for his "tales" to replace that which he has lost in the former night clerk who died, O'Neill must have felt out of touch with the American public, whose laurels he had once reaped. Erie Smith's elation at finally securing a listener prefigures or "calls" O'Neill's own happy postmortem closure. Although he did not live to see *The Iceman Cometh* and *A Moon for the Misbegotten* fully appreciated, and although he suppressed production of *Long Day's Journey into Night* during his lifetime,[21] these three plays will long be remembered as his distinct contribution to American literature and the drama of the world.

Notes

PREFACE

1. Marianna Torgovnick, *Closure in the Novel* (Princeton: Princeton University Press, 1981), 6–7.
2. Eugene O'Neill, *Complete Plays*, ed. Travis Bogard, 3 vols. (New York: Library of America, 1988). All quotations from O'Neill's plays cited in this study refer to this edition and are incorporated in the text. With regard to the unfinished *More Stately Mansions*, Library of America presents the complete text of the revised typescript edited by Martha Gilman Bower and published by Oxford University Press (1988).
3. Travis Bogard, *Contour in Time: The Plays of Eugene O'Neill*, rev. ed. (New York: Oxford University Press, 1988), 326; Judith E. Barlow, *Final Acts: The Creation of Three Late O'Neill Plays* (Athens: University of Georgia Press, 1985), 34–35.

ACKNOWLEDGMENTS

1. *Selected Letters of Eugene O'Neill*, ed. Travis Bogard and Jackson R. Bryer (New Haven: Yale University Press, 1988); Louis Sheaffer, *O'Neill: Son and Artist* (Boston: Little, Brown, 1973; reprint, New York, Paragon House, 1990 [page references refer to the reprint edition]); idem, *O'Neill: Son and Playwright* (Boston: Little, Brown, 1968); Arthur Gelb and Barbara Gelb, *O'Neill* (New York: Harper & Row, 1973); Jordan Y. Miller, ed., *Eugene O'Neill and the American Critic: A Bibliographical Checklist*, rev. ed. (Hamden, Conn.: Archon-Shoestring Press, 1973).

CHAPTER 1. O'NEILL'S QUEST FOR CLOSURE

1. Eugene O'Neill, to Beatrice Ashe, 14 January 1915, in "Letters to Beatrice Ashe, 1914–1916," MS located in the Berg Collection of English and American Literature, The New York Public Library, Astor, Lenox and Tilden Foundations.
2. Henry J. Schmidt, *How Dramas End: Essays on the German Sturm und Drang, Buchner, Hauptmann, and Fleisser* (Ann Arbor: University of Michigan Press, 1992), 3–4.
3. Francis Fergusson, "Melodramatist" (1930); reprinted in *O'Neill and His Plays: Four Decades of Criticism*, ed. Oscar Cargill, N. Bryllion Fagin, and William J. Fisher (New York: New York University Press, 1961), 276.
4. Sheaffer, *Son and Playwright*, 121–22.

5. Barrett H. Clark, *Eugene O'Neill: The Man and His Plays*, rev. ed. (New York: Dover Publications, 1947), 81.

6. Hugo von Hofmannsthal, "Reflections on O'Neill" (1923); reprinted in *O'Neill and His Plays*, ed. Cargill, Fagin, and Fisher, 255.

7. The Wooster Group in New York City forestalls boredom by using experimental techniques to "[distract] attention from the play and the dialogue to the theatrical medium itself" in recent productions of *The Hairy Ape* (1997) and *The Emperor Jones* (1988). Robert Brustein, review of *The Emperor Jones*, by Eugene O'Neill, as performed by the Wooster Group at the Performing Garage, New York, *New Republic*, 27 April 1998, 30. See also Robert Brustein, review of *The Hairy Ape*, by Eugene O'Neill, as performed by the Wooster Group at the Selwyn Theater, New York, *New Republic*, 12 May 1997, 20.

8. Eugene O'Neill, "Memoranda on Masks" (1932); reprinted in *Playwrights on Playwriting: The Meaning and Making of Modern Drama from Ibsen to Ionesco*, ed. Toby Cole (New York: Hill and Wang, 1960), 71.

9. *Welded* is rarely produced. In reviewing what he refers to as an "unwarranted exhumation of . . . one of O'Neill's most dreadful plays [*Welded*]," Mel Gussow reports, "The actors deliver their lines in dead earnest, which occasionally provokes unintentional laughter from the audience." Mel Gussow, "In a Sea of Symbolism," review of *Welded*, by Eugene O'Neill, as performed at the Horace Mann Theater, Columbia University; reprinted in *New York Times Theater Reviews: 1981–1982* (New York: Times Books, 1984), 127.

10. Gustav H. Blanke, "Die Dramenschlusse bei O'Neill," in *Das Amerikanische Drama von den Anfangen bis zur Gegenwart*, ed. Hans Itschert (Darmstadt: Wissenschaftliche Buchgesellschaft, l972), 159; passage translated from the German by Barbara Voglino.

11. Edwin A. Engel, *The Haunted Heroes of Eugene O'Neill* (Cambridge: Harvard University Press, 1953), 94.

12. Gelb and Gelb, *O'Neill*, 517; Sheaffer, *Son and Artist*, 100–102.

13. Sheaffer, *Son and Artist*, 403–4, 410; Edward L. Shaughnessy, *Down the Nights and Down the Days: Eugene O'Neill's Catholic Sensibility* (Notre Dame, Ind.: University of Notre Dame Press, 1996), 2–3; and Gelb and Gelb, *O'Neill*, 762, 779 (citing Philip Moeller) interpret *Days without End* as an effort on O'Neill's part to alleviate anxiety regarding his lack of religious belief. Downplaying this interpretation is Doris Alexander's explanation of the play as one in a series of dramas about the divinity of marital love (Doris Alexander, *Eugene O'Neill's Creative Struggle: The Decisive Decade, 1924–1933* [University Park: Pennsylvania State University Press, 1992], 313–14).

14. Eugene O'Neill, to Sophus Keith Winther, 1 May 1934, in *Selected Letters*, ed. Bogard and Bryer, 433.

15. Joseph Conrad, "Henry James: An Appreciation (1905)," in *Joseph Conrad on Fiction*, ed. Walter F. Wright, Regents Critics Series, (Lincoln: University of Nebraska Press, 1964), 88; Murray Krieger, "An Apology for Poetics," in *American Criticism in the Poststructuralist Age*, ed. Ira Konigsberg, Michigan Studies in the Humanities (n.p.: University of Michigan, 1981), 96–97; Frank Kermode, *The Sense of an Ending: Studies in the Theory of Fiction* (New York: Oxford University Press, 1966), 7.

16. By most accounts (including that offered by O'Neill in the autobiographical *Long Day's Journey into Night*), Ella O'Neill's morphine addiction commenced following the birth of Eugene when she was given the drug to relieve pain. Doris Alexander's assertion that Ella was given morphine even before Eugene's birth (Doris Alexander, *The Tempering of Eugene O'Neill* [New York: Harcourt, Brace & World, 1962], 14) is refuted by Louis Sheaffer ("Correcting Some Errors in Annals of O'Neill, Part 1," *Eugene O'Neill Newsletter* 7, no. 3 [1983]: 16–17).

17. Virginia Floyd, *The Plays of Eugene O'Neill: A New Assessment* (New York: Frederick Ungar, 1985), 476; Gelb and Gelb, *O'Neill*, 11; Sheaffer, *Son and Playwright*, 55.

18. In contrast to the rather bleak pictures of Eugene's childhood that emerge from the Sheaffer and Gelb biographies, Doris Alexander recounts a relatively happy childhood for O'Neill (*Tempering of Eugene O'Neill*, 17).

19. According to the *Complete Plays* chronology, C. W. E. Bigsby (*A Critical Introduction to Twentieth-Century American Drama*, vol. 1, *1900–1940* [New York: Cambridge University Press, 1982], 41), and Louis Sheaffer (*Son and Playwright*, 89, and *Son and Artist*, 411), O'Neill was nearly fifteen when he learned about his mother's addiction as a result of her effort to drown herself in the Thames in the summer of 1903. The Gelbs, however, follow Carlotta O'Neill's account that her husband had returned unexpectedly from school one day to find his mother injecting herself with morphine in their New York apartment. They date O'Neill's discovery in the fall of 1900, several years earlier (*O'Neill*, 72). In "Correcting Some Errors, Part 1," 18, Sheaffer refutes Carlotta's account with impressive evidence that the rendition of Edmund's discovery in *Long Day's Journey into Night* is "closer to what actually happened."

20. Sheaffer, *Son and Playwright*, 87–89.

21. Sheaffer dates her recovery at 1914–15 (ibid., 280). Edward L. Shaughnessy ("Ella, James, and Jamie O'Neill," *Eugene O'Neill Review* 15, no. 2 [1991]: 14) settles on 1913–14 for Ella's cure.

22. Floyd, *New Assessment*, 479.

23. O'Neill, to Malcolm Mollan, December 1921, in *Selected Letters*, ed. Bogard and Bryer, 159.

24. Sheaffer, *Son and Playwright*, 396; idem, *Son and Artist*, 44, 190; Gelb and Gelb, *O'Neill*, 375.

25. This manuscript, which is located at Yale University, has been developed into play form by Donald Gallup and published (New York: Ticknor and Fields, 1982).

26. Gelb and Gelb, *O'Neill*, 456.

27. Ibid., 573; Sheaffer, *Son and Artist*, 179–80.

28. Gelb and Gelb, *O'Neill*, 311; Sheaffer, *Son and Playwright*, 396.

29. Robert Brustein, *The Theatre of Revolt* (Boston: Little, Brown, 1964), 22–23.

30. As cited by Mary B. Mullett, "The Extraordinary Story of Eugene O'Neill" (1922), in *Conversations with Eugene O'Neill*, ed. Mark W. Estrin (Jackson: University Press of Mississippi, 1990), 37.

31. Bigsby, *Critical Introduction*, 1:117.

32. Lyn Hejinian defines the "closed" text as one in which "all the elements of the work" are "directed toward a single reading" ("The Rejection of Closure," in *Writing/Talks*, ed. Bob Perelman [Carbondale: Southern Illinois University Press, 1985], 270).

33. Gerhart Hauptmann, as cited by Schmidt, *How Dramas End*, 9.

34. O'Neill, to Malcolm Mollan, December 1921 (regarding the ending of *"Anna Christie"*), in *Selected Letters*, ed. Bogard and Bryer, 159.

35. Hejinian, "Rejection of Closure," 273.

36. David H. Richter, "Closure and the Critics," *Modern Philology* 80, no. 3 (1983): 287.

37. Henry James, while acknowledging the impossibility of closure ("relations stop nowhere"), defined "the exquisite problem of the artist" as "eternally . . . to draw, by a geometry of his own, the circle within which they [the "relations" which "stop nowhere"] shall happily *appear* [*sic*] to do so" (preface to *Roderick Hudson* [London: Macmillan, 1921], x).

38. According to June Schlueter, dramatic closure is "a collaborate act" between the

author and his audience (*Dramatic Closure: Reading the End* [Madison, N.J.: Fairleigh Dickinson University Press, 1995], 27).

39. Mary Kay Zettl Myers, "Closure in the Twentieth-Century American Problem Play" (Ph.D. diss., University of Delaware, 1992; Ann Arbor, Mich.: UMI, 1993, AAG 9301793), 5.

40. Schlueter, *Dramatic Closure*, 60.

41. For a fuller discussion of the controversy, see chapter 3 on *"Anna Christie."*

42. Malcolm Mollan, "Making Plays with a Tragic End: An Intimate Interview with Eugene O'Neill, Who Tells Why He Does It" (1922), in *Conversations with Eugene O'Neill*, ed. Estrin, 15.

43. O'Neill, to George Jean Nathan, 1 February 1921, in *Selected Letters*, ed. Bogard and Bryer, 148.

CHAPTER 2. UNSETTLING AMBIGUITY IN *BEYOND THE HORIZON*

1. J. Y. Miller, ed., *Eugene O'Neill and the American Critic*, 252–57.

2. Vera M. Jiji, "Audience Response in the Theater: A Study of Dramatic Theory Tested against Reviewers' Responses to the Plays of Eugene O'Neill" (Ph.D. diss., New York University, 1971), 238.

3. Hofmannsthal, "Reflections on O'Neill," 255.

4. Alexander Woollcott, review of *Beyond the Horizon*, by Eugene O'Neill (1920); reprinted in Jordan Y. Miller, ed., *Playwright's Progress: O'Neill and the Critics* (Fairlawn, N.J.: Scott, Foresman, 1965), 19–20. Heywood Broun, review of *Beyond the Horizon*, by Eugene O'Neill (1920); reprinted in *Playwright's Progress*, ed. Miller, 17.

5. Hofmannsthal, "Reflections on O'Neill," 255. See chapter 1, page 16, for the more complete quotation.

6. Myers defines closure as "a process resting on audience perception of structure" ("Closure in the Twentieth-Century American Problem Play," 18).

7. H. G. Kemelman, "Eugene O'Neill and the Highbrow Melodrama" (1932); reprinted in *Playwright's Progress*, ed. J. Y. Miller, 103.

8. Barbara Herrnstein Smith, *Poetic Closure: A Study of How Poems End* (Chicago: University of Chicago Press, 1968), 34.

9. Schlueter, *Dramatic Closure*, 23.

10. O'Neill, to Beatrice Ashe, 14 January 1915, in "Letters to Beatrice Ashe, 1914–1916."

11. O'Neill, to Malcolm Mollan, December 1921, in *Selected Letters*, ed. Bogard and Bryer, 159.

12. See chapter 1, page 21.

13. Schlueter, *Dramatic Closure*, 23.

14. Stanley Fish, "How to Recognize a Poem When You See One," in *Is There a Text in This Class? The Authority of Interpretive Communities* (Cambridge: Harvard University Press, 1980), 326–27.

15. Wolfgang Iser, *The Implied Reader: Patterns of Communication in Prose Fiction from Bunyan to Beckett* (Baltimore: Johns Hopkins University Press, 1974), 275.

16. Schmidt, *How Dramas End*, 8.

17. Peter Brooks, *The Melodramatic Imagination: Balzac, Henry James, Melodrama, and the Mode of Excess* (New Haven: Yale University Press, 1976), 201.

18. T. S. Eliot, review of *All God's Chillun Got Wings*, by Eugene O'Neill (1923); reprinted in *O'Neill and His Plays*, ed. Cargill, Fagin, and Fisher, 169.

19. Arthur Hobson Quinn, *A History of the American Drama from the Civil War to the Present Day*, rev. ed. (New York: Appleton-Century-Crofts, 1936), 2:172–73.

20. Bogard, *Contour in Time*, 130. This interpretation appears in both the earlier (1972) and revised editions.

21. Floyd, *New Assessment*, 122.

22. Torgovnick, *Closure in the Novel*, 19.

23. Albert E. Kalson and Lisa M. Schwerdt, "Eternal Recurrence and the Shaping of O'Neill's Dramatic Structures," in *Eugene O'Neill in China: An International Centenary Celebration*, ed. Haiping Liu and Lowell Swortzell (New York: Greenwood Press, 1992), 79.

24. O'Neill, to Jessica Rippin, 17 May 1914, in *Selected Letters*, ed. Bogard and Bryer, 22–23.

25. O'Neill, to Beatrice Ashe, 11 December 1914, in "Letters to Beatrice Ashe, 1914–1916." O'Neill does not give a source for this quotation.

26. O'Neill, to the *New York Times*, 11 April 1920. As cited by Sheaffer, *Son and Playwright*, 417.

27. Sheaffer, *Son and Playwright*, 188.

28. William J. Scheick, "The Ending of O'Neill's *Beyond the Horizon*," *Modern Drama* 20, no. 3 (1977): 296–97.

29. Ibid., 295.

30. Mullett, "The Extraordinary Story of Eugene O'Neill," 37. See chapter 1, page 21, for the more complete quotation.

31. Terry Eagleton, *Literary Theory: An Introduction* (Minneapolis: University of Minnesota Press, 1983), 178.

32. As paraphrased by Karl Shapiro, *In Defense of Ignorance* (New York: Random House, 1952), 161. Shapiro does not give a source for his paraphrase of Williams.

33. Torgovnick, *Closure in the Novel*, 6.

CHAPTER 3. FEMINISM VERSUS FATALISM: UNCERTAINTY AS CLOSURE IN *"ANNA CHRISTIE"*

1. The ending of *"Anna Christie,"* as I shall proceed to demonstrate in this chapter, is not generally interpreted as "happy" by modern viewers. Travis Bogard offers the following explanation for the discrepancy in audience reactions since the play's debut: "There is perhaps some doubt which ending [that of *The Ole Davil* or of the script as printed] was used in the original production [of *"Anna Christie"*]. . . . Reviewers speak of the action ending in laughter, which is the ending of *The Ole Davil*, not *Anna Christie"* (*Contour in Time*, 162). More specific corroboration would be helpful. The numerous excerpts from reviews of the first production cited by Jordan Miller (*Eugene O'Neill and the American Critic*, ed. J. Y. Miller, 240–46), while frequently referring to the play's "happy ending," make no mention of laughter. Louis V. De Foe, in fact, hails *"Anna"* as "another grim O'Neill drama" (ibid., 241).

2. Louis V. De Foe, as cited by Bogard, *Contour in Time*, 163.

3. Sheaffer, *Son and Artist*, 67; *Eugene O'Neill and the American Critic*, ed. J. Y. Miller, 240–46.

4. O'Neill, as cited by Sheaffer, *Son and Artist*, 68.

5. O'Neill, to George Jean Nathan, 1 February 1921, in *Selected Letters*, ed. Bogard and Bryer, 148.

6. Leslie Eric Comens, foreword to *Chris Christophersen,* by Eugene O'Neill (New York: Random House, 1982), viii.

7. Sheaffer, *Son and Playwright,* 462.

8. O'Neill, to Beatrice Ashe, 14 January 1915, in "Letters to Beatrice Ashe, 1914–1916."

9. Bernard Beckerman, "Shakespeare Closing," *Kenyon Review* 7, no. 3 (1985): 80.

10. David F. Hult, preface to *Concepts of Closure,* ed. David F. Hult, Yale French Studies 67 (New Haven: Yale University Press, 1984), iv–v.

11. Krieger, "An Apology for Poetics," 96–97.

12. Gerhart Hauptmann, as cited by Schmidt, *How Dramas End,* 9. For the more complete quotation see chapter 1, page 22.

13. O'Neill, to Jonathan Cape, 15 May 1923, in *Selected Letters,* ed. Bogard and Bryer, 176.

14. John V. Antush, "Eugene O'Neill: Modern and Postmodern," *Eugene O'Neill Review* 13, no. 1 (1989): 21.

15. Henry James, preface to *The Portrait of a Lady,* from *The Notebooks* (1947), in *Perspectives on James's* The Portrait of a Lady: *A Collection of Critical Essays,* ed. William T. Stafford (New York: New York University Press, 1967), 4.

16. O'Neill, to Malcolm Mollan, December 1921, in *Selected Letters,* ed. Bogard and Bryer, 159.

17. Schlueter, *Dramatic Closure,* 20.

18. Clifford Leech, *O'Neill* (New York: Barnes & Noble, 1963), 31.

19. Bogard, *Contour in Time,* 157–58.

20. Ibid., 163.

21. The staging of the 1993 New York production appears to have conveyed the uncertainty O'Neill intended with fog billowing out over the thrust stage and the characters gazing in different directions. John Lahr describes the final misty tableau: ". . . Chris turns away from the new couple to look out to sea, Burke takes hold of Anna's wrist, but Anna is turned away from him, gazing upstage into the gray horizon" ("Selling the Sizzle," review of *"Anna Christie,"* by Eugene O'Neill, as performed at the Roundabout Theater, New York; reprinted in *New York Theatre Critics' Reviews: 1993,* ed. Norma Adler, Pat Willard, Joan Marlowe, and Betty Blake [New York: Critics' Theatre Reviews, 1993], 10–12).

22. Richter, "Closure and the Critics," 287.

23. Schlueter, *Dramatic Closure,* 23.

24. Iser, *Implied Reader,* 279.

25. Terence Hawkes, "Opening Closure," *Modern Drama* 24, no. 3 (1981): 355–56.

26. O'Neill, to George Jean Nathan, 1 February 1921, in *Selected Letters,* ed. Bogard and Bryer, 148.

27. Torgovnick, *Closure in the Novel,* 6.

28. Robert M. Adams, *Strains of Discord: Studies in Literary Openness* (Ithaca: Cornell University Press, 1958), 33.

29. O'Neill, to the *New York Times,* December 1921. As cited by Quinn, *History of the American Drama,* 177–78.

30. Ward Morehouse III attests to unexpected laughter during a performance of the 1993 New York production of *"Anna Christie"* ("*'Anna Christie'* Sends Off Sparks," review of *"Anna Christie,"* by Eugene O'Neill, as performed at the Roundabout Theater, New York; reprinted in *New York Theatre Critics' Reviews: 1993,* ed. Adler et al., 6–7).

31. As cited by Gelb and Gelb, *O'Neill,* 481.

32. O'Neill, to George Jean Nathan, 1 February 1921, in *Selected Letters*, ed. Bogard and Bryer, 148.
33. Schmidt, *How Dramas End*, 10.

CHAPTER 4. *"DEVOUT"* ADMIRERS OF THE SUNRISE:
THEATRICALITY IN *DESIRE UNDER THE ELMS*

1. As cited in *Eugene O'Neill and the American Critic*, ed. J. Y. Miller, 268–83.
2. Ibid., 271.
3. Sheaffer, *Son and Artist*, 158.
4. Frederic I. Carpenter, *Eugene O'Neill*, rev. ed., Twayne United States Authors Series 66 (Boston: Twayne-G. K. Hall, 1979), 104.
5. Sheaffer, *Son and Artist*, 158.
6. Ibid.
7. Gelb and Gelb, *O'Neill*, 570.
8. Ephraim's fantasy recalls O'Neill's own much later act of burning or otherwise destroying his many unfinished manuscripts. Ephraim, who was contemptuous of his sons because he was convinced they fell short of his own stature, appears to have distrusted their ability to carry on the farm he had successfully built. O'Neill's destruction of his manuscripts may have been similarly protective toward the fledgling products of his imagination, to which both he (Gelb and Gelb, *O'Neill*, 805) and Carlotta (Sheaffer, *Son and Artist*, 667) referred as children. ". . . I don't want anybody else finishing up a play of mine," O'Neill is reported to have told Carlotta in defense of the slaughter (Sheaffer, *Son and Artist*, 666).
9. Frederick Wilkins, "The Pressure of Puritanism in O'Neill's New England Plays," in *Eugene O'Neill: A World View*, ed. Virginia Floyd (New York: Frederick Ungar, 1979), 243.
10. Ibid., 240.
11. Ibid., 244.
12. Engel, *Haunted Heroes*, 132.
13. Ibid., 126–27.
14. Clark, *Eugene O'Neill*, 98–99.
15. Bigsby, *Critical Introduction*, 1:63.
16. Floyd, *New Assessment*, 284. Floyd does not give a reference for this quotation. Croswell Bowen maintains that O'Neill said this to his cast during a rehearsal for *The Iceman Cometh* in 1946 (*The Curse of the Misbegotten*, written with the aid of Shane O'Neill [New York: McGraw-Hill, 1959], 309).
17. Edgar F. Racey Jr., "Myth as Tragic Structure in *Desire under the Elms*," in *O'Neill: A Collection of Critical Essays*, ed. John Gassner, Twentieth Century Views S-TC-9 (Englewood Cliffs, N.J.: Prentice-Hall, 1964), 61.
18. Bogard, *Contour in Time*, 214.
19. H. G. Kemelman, "Eugene O'Neill and the Highbrow Melodrama" (1932); reprinted in *Playwright's Progress*, ed. J. Y. Miller, 104.
20. Richter, "Closure and the Critics," 287.
21. O'Neill's dramatization "The Ancient Mariner" was performed only twenty-nine times as part of a double bill with Molière's *George Dandin* in Provincetown (Sheaffer, *Son and Artist*, 137–38).
22. Engel, *Haunted Heroes*, 94. The relevant plays include *The Fountain* (1922), which concludes with Juan's joyful entrance into eternity through his reabsorption into the mate-

rial universe; *Welded* (1923), which ends in a crucifixional embrace; *The Great God Brown* (1925), which echoes T. S. Eliot's *The Waste Land* (1922) on the return of spring bearing life (4.2.532); *Lazarus Laughed* (1926), which concludes with Lazarus laughing as his flesh burns; and *Days without End* (1931), which ends with John Loving's rhapsodic declaration: "Life laughs with God's love again! Life laughs with love!" (4.2.180).

23. Engel, *Haunted Heroes*, 132.

24. Bigsby, *Critical Introduction*, 1:45; Ruby Cohn, "The Wet Sponge of Eugene O'Neill," in *Dialogue in American Drama* (Bloomington: Indiana University Press, 1971), 24.

25. Leech, *O'Neill*, 52.

26. Robert Bechtold Heilman, *The Iceman, the Arsonist, and the Troubled Agent* (Seattle: University of Washington Press, 1973), 83.

27. Gerhart Hauptmann, as cited by Schmidt, *How Dramas End*, 10.

28. Schlueter, *Dramatic Closure*, 31, 22.

29. Smith, *Poetic Closure*, 34.

30. Schlueter, *Dramatic Closure*, 23.

31. As cited by Sheaffer, *Son and Artist*, 159.

CHAPTER 5. TWO FAILED THESIS PLAYS:
DYNAMO AND *DAYS WITHOUT END*

1. O'Neill, to George Jean Nathan, 26 August 1928, in *Selected Letters*, ed. Bogard and Bryer, 311.

2. Hult, preface to *Concepts of Closure*, iv–v.

3. O'Neill, to George Jean Nathan, 19 March 1929, in Egil Törnqvist, *A Drama of Souls: Studies in O'Neill's Super-naturalistic Technique* (New Haven: Yale University Press, 1969), 73. This letter is not included in Bogard and Bryer's *Selected Letters*.

4. O'Neill, to Benjamin De Casseres, 15 September 1928, in *Selected Letters*, ed. Bogard and Bryer, 317.

5. Bogard, *Contour in Time*, 321.

6. O'Neill, to George Jean Nathan, 19 March 1929, in Törnqvist, *Drama of Souls*, 73.

7. O'Neill, to Benjamin De Casseres, 15 September 1928, in *Selected Letters*, ed. Bogard and Bryer, 317.

8. Armine Mortimer's assertion that there is always closure, whether imposed by interpretive reading or amply supplied by the text, despite its apparent validity with regard to works of genuine artistic merit, does not seem applicable to crude attempts to scale Parnassus like *Dynamo* (Armine Kotin Mortimer, *La Clôture Narrative* [Paris: José Corti, 1985], 221; passage translated from the French by Barbara Voglino).

9. Schmidt, *How Dramas End*, 3–4.

10. For O'Neill the traumatic event was the discovery of his mother's morphine addiction when she tried to drown herself in the Thames in the summer of 1903 (Sheaffer, *Son and Playwright*, 89). O'Neill had apparently begun doubting his faith earlier that year upon recognizing the inefficacy of his prayers to ameliorate his mother's erratic behavior (ibid., 87–88). For John Loving the event was the death of both his parents from pneumonia during his adolescence.

11. Father Baird describes John Loving's philosophical odyssey (1.122), and Shaughnessy (*Down the Nights and Down the Days*, 2) recounts O'Neill's.

12. Bogard, *Contour in Time*, 326.

13. Carpenter, *Eugene O'Neill*, 141.

14. In O'Neill's earliest sketch of the ending, Elsa died and John committed suicide before the statue of the Blessed Virgin (Bogard, *Contour in Time*, 25–26).

15. Philip Moeller reports on his conversation with O'Neill regarding *Days:* "He said the end of the play was undoubtedly a wish fulfillment on his part. He told me about the simple trusting happiness of some of his Catholic relatives. . . . He wants to go that way and find a happiness which apparently he hasn't got . . ." (as cited by Sheaffer, *Son and Artist*, 428–29).

16. Sheaffer, *Son and Artist*, 426; Alexander, *Eugene O'Neill's Creative Struggle*, 206.

17. Shaughnessy, *Down the Nights and Down the Days*, 2–3.

18. In "Memoranda on Masks," written for *American Spectator* in 1932, O'Neill called for a return of theater "to its highest and sole significant function as a Temple where the religion of a poetical interpretation and symbolical celebration of life is communicated to human beings, starved in spirit by their soul-stifling daily struggle to exist as masks among the masks of the living" (as cited by Sheaffer, *Son and Artist*, 403–4).

19. Carlotta O'Neill, to Saxe Commins, 5 July 1933, in Alexander, *Eugene O'Neill's Creative Struggle*, 313–14. The italics are Carlotta's. For a convincing refutation of Carlotta's interpretation of the play's ending, see Shaughnessy, *Down the Nights and Down the Days*, 141.

20. Alexander, *Eugene O'Neill's Creative Struggle*, 189–90. As a young man O'Neill had taken romantic love to be "the ultimate goal of all . . . striving. I become a part of God and He of me. For are you [Beatrice Ashe] not—my God?" (O'Neill, to Beatrice Ashe, 2 March 1915, in "Letters to Beatrice Ashe, 1914–1916").

21. Bogard, *Contour in Time*, 323.

22. O'Neill, to Sophus Keith Winther, 1 May 1934, in *Selected Letters*, ed. Bogard and Bryer, 433.

23. Doris V. Falk, *Eugene O'Neill and the Tragic Tension*, (New Brunswick, N.J.: Rutgers University Press, 1958), 146–48.

24. Schmidt, *How Dramas End*, 147.

25. Schlueter, *Dramatic Closure*, 31.

26. Falk, *O'Neill and the Tragic Tension*, 148; Sheaffer, *Son and Artist*, 412.

27. Falk, *O'Neill and the Tragic Tension*, 152.

28. Blanke, "Die Dramenschlusse bei O'Neill," 163; passage translated from the German by Barbara Voglino.

29. Lionel Trilling, "Eugene O'Neill," in *Modern Critical Views: Eugene O'Neill*, ed. Harold Bloom (New York: Chelsea House, 1987), 19–20.

30. Wayne C. Booth, "Are Narrative Choices Subject to Ethical Criticism?" in *Reading Narrative: Form, Ethics, Ideology*, ed. James Phelan (Columbus: Ohio State University Press, 1989), 67.

31. As paraphrased by Karl Shapiro, *In Defense of Ignorance*, 161. Shapiro does not give a source for his paraphrase of Williams.

32. Conrad, "Henry James: An Appreciation (1905)," 88.

33. John Keats, to George and Thomas Keats, 21 December 1817, in *English Romantic Poetry and Prose*, ed. Russell Noys (New York: Oxford University Press, 1956), 1211.

CHAPTER 6. SUCCESS AT LAST:
CLOSURE IN *MOURNING BECOMES ELECTRA*

1. Joseph Wood Krutch, *The American Drama since 1918*, rev. ed. (New York: George Braziller, 1957), 120; Roger Asselineau, *"Mourning Becomes Electra* as Tragedy," *Modern Drama* 1, no. 3 (1958): 149; and Leech, *O'Neill*, 89.

2. Bigsby, *Critical Introduction*, 1:84.

3. Ibid., 86.

4. Engel, *Haunted Heroes*, 259.

5. Jean Chothia, *Forging a Language: A Study of the Plays of Eugene O'Neill* (New York: Cambridge University Press, 1979), 108.

6. Floyd, *New Assessment*, 403.

7. Chothia, *Forging a Language*, 108.

8. Wilkins, "The Pressure of Puritanism," 239–44.

9. Gelb and Gelb, *O'Neill*, 721–22; Törnqvist, *Drama of Souls*, 18.

10. Smith, *Poetic Closure*, 34.

11. Chester Clayton Long, *The Role of Nemesis in the Structure of Selected Plays by Eugene O'Neill* (The Hague: Mouton, 1968), 222.

12. Maya Koreneva, "One Hundred Percent American Tragedy: A Soviet View" (n.d.), in *Eugene O'Neill: A World View*, ed. Floyd, 167.

13. Ibid.

14. As a very young man (1914) O'Neill had defined "be[ing] true to one-self [*sic*] and one's highest hope" as the ultimate "good" (O'Neill, to Jessica Rippin, 17 May 1914, in *Selected Letters*, ed. Bogard and Bryer, 22–23).

15. Ugo Betti, "Religion and the Theatre," from *Corruption in the Palace of Justice* (1949), trans. Gino Rizzo and William Meriwether, in *The New Theatre of Europe*, ed. Robert W. Corrigan (New York: Delta-Dell, 1962), 332.

16. T. S. Eliot, *The Cocktail Party* (act 2), in *The Complete Poems and Plays: 1909–1950* (New York: Harcourt, Brace, 1952), 366.

17. Chothia, *Forging a Language*, 109–10.

18. Asselineau, "*Mourning Becomes Electra* as Tragedy," 148.

19. O'Neill, to Brooks Atkinson, 19 June 1931, in *Selected Letters*, ed. Bogard and Bryer, 390. The italics are O'Neill's.

20. Schlueter, *Dramatic Closure*, 51.

21. Törnqvist, *Drama of Souls*, 246.

22. D. V. K. Raghavacharyulu, *Eugene O'Neill: A Study* (Bombay: G. R. Bhatkal, Popular Prakashan, 1965), 105.

23. Doris Alexander recounts O'Neill's admiration for the conclusion of *Oedipus Rex*, in which Sophocles, rather than killing his hero, blinds him, thus setting him apart from the world (*Eugene O'Neill's Creative Struggle*, 166).

24. George Pierce Baker, with whom the young O'Neill studied playwriting for six months at the beginning of his career, recommends the use of pantomime and quiet speech to follow strong emotional scenes in his manual for playwrights (*Dramatic Technique* [New York: Houghton Mifflin, 1919], 222, 378).

CHAPTER 7. KALEIDOSCOPIC CLOSURE: MULTIFACETED
MEANING IN *THE ICEMAN COMETH*

1. John Henry Raleigh, introduction to *Twentieth Century Interpretations of* The Iceman Cometh: *A Collection of Critical Essays*, ed. John Henry Raleigh (Englewood Cliffs, N.J.: Prentice-Hall, 1968), 17.

2. O'Neill, to Lawrence Langner, 11 August 1940, in *Selected Letters*, ed. Bogard and Bryer, 511.

3. O'Neill, to Lawrence Langner, 17 July 1940, in *Selected Letters*, ed. Bogard and Bryer, 510.

4. Sheaffer, *Son and Artist*, 550.

5. *Eugene O'Neill and the American Critic*, ed. J. Y. Miller, 342–49.

6. The opening night performance suffered considerably from the loss of voice experienced by James Barton, who played Hickey. Barton appears to have incurred some blame for entertaining visitors during the dinner-length intermission instead of resting his voice (Sheaffer, *Son and Artist*, 582).

7. Ibid., 584–85.

8. Ibid., 583.

9. Gelb and Gelb, *O'Neill*, 877.

10. Kermode, *Sense of an Ending*, 46–50.

11. T. S. Eliot, *Murder in the Cathedral* (act 2), in *Complete Poems and Plays*, 209. Eliot uses this line again in *Four Quartets* ("Burnt Norton").

12. Barlow, *Final Acts*, 34–35.

13. Brustein, *Theatre of Revolt*, 346; J. Dennis Rich, "Exile without Remedy: The Late Plays of Eugene O'Neill" (1976), in *Eugene O'Neill: A World View*, ed. Floyd, 266; Normand Berlin, "Endings" (1982), in *Eugene O'Neill's* The Iceman Cometh, ed. Harold Bloom (New York: Chelsea House, 1987), 99; and Gelb and Gelb, *O'Neill* (1987), 832.

14. Barlow, *Final Acts*, 34–35.

15. Thomas P. Adler, "A Cabin in the Woods, a Summerhouse in a Garden: Closure and Enclosure in O'Neill's *More Stately Mansions*," *Eugene O'Neill Newsletter* 9, no. 2 (1985): 27.

16. Reviewer Benedict Nightingale describes a "long, long silence not specified by O'Neill's always garrulous stage directions" that precedes Hickey's admission of insanity in this production. Nightingale's interpretation (that Hickey is "summoning up the pity and fellow-feeling to make a moral U-turn") was most likely influenced by acting and directorial choices ("In London, Three Revelations of Cosmic Despair," review of *The Iceman Cometh*, by Eugene O'Neill, as performed at the Almeida Theater, London, in the *New York Times*, 19 May 1998.

17. Brustein, *Theatre of Revolt*, 347.

18. *The World Book Encyclopedia*, 1976 ed., s. v. "insanity." State laws vary considerably regarding the criteria for judging a person who has committed a crime insane.

19. E. James Zeiger reviews a 1992 Denver production in which the actor (Richard Lyon) played Hickey as insane and therefore not responsible for his actions. "The result," notes Zeiger, "was a curiously dry-eyed experience," since the audience was unable to identify with Hickey (review of *The Iceman Cometh*, by Eugene O'Neill, as performed at the Germinal Stage, Denver, in *Eugene O'Neill Review* 16, no. 1 (1992): 111–15.

20. Hult, preface to *Concepts of Closure*, iv–v.

21. Peter Brooks, *Reading for the Plot: Design and Intention in Narrative* (New York: Alfred A. Knopf, 1984), 23.

22. Myers, "Closure in the Twentieth-Century American Problem Play," 18. See chapter 2, note 6 for Myers' more complete definition of closure.

23. Smith, *Poetic Closure*, 34.

24. Schlueter, *Dramatic Closure*, 23.

25. John Gerlach, *Toward the End: Closure and Structure in the American Short Story* (University: University of Alabama Press, 1985), 9.

26. Schmidt, *How Dramas End*, 12.

27. Smith, *Poetic Closure*, 34.

28. Torgovnick, *Closure in the Novel*, 6–7.

29. T. S. Eliot, "What the Thunder Said," from *The Waste Land* (lines 338–45), in *Complete Poems and Plays*.

30. Samuel Beckett, *Waiting for Godot*, act 2 (New York: Grove Press, 1954), 46.

31. Bigsby, *Critical Introduction*, 1:88.

32. All references to *The Waste Land* by T. S. Eliot are from "What the Thunder Said," lines 402–33 (*Complete Poems and Plays*).

33. *Republic* 7.519–20 in *The Collected Dialogues of Plato*, ed. Edith Hamilton and Huntington Cairns, Bollingen Series 71 (Princeton: Princeton University Press, 1963).

34. In December 1939, when O'Neill was completing *Iceman*, Germany had already devastated Poland and was preparing to begin its blitzkrieg against much of Europe the following spring. The United States, as in World War I, was once again attempting to remain neutral.

35. During a rehearsal for the London production of *Godot*, Beckett is reported to have told one of his actors that he was not boring his audience enough (John Fletcher, *Samuel Beckett's Art* [London: Chatto & Windus, 1971], 67).

36. Sheaffer, *Son and Artist*, 572. The emphasis is O'Neill's.

37. John Orr, *Tragic Drama and Modern Society: Studies in the Social and Literary Theory of Drama from 1870 to the Present* (London: Macmillan, 1983), 189–90.

38. Kermode, *Sense of an Ending*, 47.

39. Chothia, *Forging a Language*, 126.

40. Floyd, *New Assessment*, 531.

41. O'Neill, to Dudley Nichols, 16 December 1942, in *Selected Letters*, ed. Bogard and Bryer, 537.

42. O'Neill, to Kenneth MacGowan, 30 December 1940, in Barlow, *Final Acts*, 27. This letter is not included in Bogard and Bryer's *Selected Letters*.

43. O'Neill, to Beatrice Ashe, 14 January 1915, in "Letters to Beatrice Ashe, 1914–1916."

44. O'Neill, to Malcolm Mollan, December 1921, in *Selected Letters*, ed. Bogard and Bryer, 159.

45. As cited by Mullett, "The Extraordinary Story of Eugene O'Neill," 37. See chapter 1, page 21, for the more complete quotation.

46. Fish, "How to Recognize a Poem," 326–27.

47. O'Neill, to Lawrence Langner, 17 July 1940, in *Selected Letters*, ed. Bogard and Bryer, 510.

48. Richter, "Closure and the Critics," 287.

49. O'Neill, to Norman Holmes Pearson, 18 June 1942, in *Selected Letters*, ed. Bogard and Bryer, 530. The emphasis is O'Neill's.

CHAPTER 8. *LONG DAY'S JOURNEY INTO NIGHT*: THE QUESTION OF BLAME

1. Joseph Golden, "O'Neill and the Passing of Pleasure," in *The Death of Tinker Bell: The American Theatre in the Twentieth-Century* (Syracuse, N.Y.: Syracuse University Press, 1967), 44.

2. Koreneva, "One Hundred Percent American Tragedy," 170.

3. Edwin Engel, "O'Neill 1960," *Modern Drama* 3, no. 3 (1960): 221.

4. O'Neill, to Sean O'Casey, 5 August 1943, in *Selected Letters*, ed. Bogard and Bryer, 546.

5. Floyd, *New Assessment*, 46; Carpenter, *Eugene O'Neill*, 155.

6. Brustein, *Theatre of Revolt*, 350.

7. Normand Berlin, "The Beckettian O'Neill," *Modern Drama* 31, no. 1 (1988): 33–34.

8. Judith Barlow's examination of the successive drafts of *Long Day's Journey* appears to confirm O'Neill's intention to postpone Mary's initial morphine injection until after the first act (*Final Acts*, 78–79).

9. J. Yellowlees Douglas, "'How Do I Stop This Thing?': Closure and Indeterminacy in Interactive Narratives," in *Hyper/Text/Theory*, ed. George P. Landow (Baltimore: Johns Hopkins University Press, 1994), 162.

10. Ibid., 185.

11. Fish, "How to Recognize a Poem," 327. Fish is referring to poetry, but his definition seems applicable to any literary work that requires analysis.

12. Schlueter, *Dramatic Closure*, 30.

13. Kermode defines *kairos* as time "charged with . . . meaning derived from its relation [to the beginning and] to the end (*Sense of an Ending*, 47).

14. Ibid., 50.

15. Törnqvist, *Drama of Souls*, 23.

16. The 1986 Broadway production permitted the quarreling and blaming "sub-text to dominate the actual words" (Clive Barnes, "'Day's Journey' to Glory: B'way at Its Greatest," review of *Long Day's Journey into Night*, by Eugene O'Neill, as performed at the Broadhurst Theater, New York [1986]; reprinted in *New York Theater Critics' Reviews: 1986*, ed. Joan Marlowe and Betty Blake [New York: Critics' Theatre Reviews, 1986], 304). The result of Jonathan Miller's directorial choice was a rushing and overlapping of speeches that was emotionally effective but often unintelligible.

17. Alvin Kernan, *Character and Conflict: An Introduction to Drama*, 2d ed. (New York: Harcourt, Brace & World, 1969), 7.

18. Barbara Voglino, "'Games' the Tyrones Play," *Eugene O'Neill Review* 16, no. 1 (1992): 100.

19. Louis Sheaffer ("Correcting Some Errors, Part 1," 16) sets Jamie's age at six at the time of his infant brother's death.

20. Sheaffer, *Son and Playwright*, 73.

21. For an account of Jamie O'Neill's academic progress, including his expulsion from Fordham University in his senior year, see Shaughnessy, "Ella, James, and Jamie O'Neill," 50–59.

22. The state hospital at Shelton, Connecticut. James O'Neill Sr. may have considered sending Eugene there because the brother of one of his prosperous acquaintants was being treated at this facility (Sheaffer, *Son and Playwright*, 242).

23. O'Neill appears to have exaggerated his father's parsimony (probably for dramatic purposes) in this play. Sheaffer notes that O'Neill's father "could be generous with his family, for he saw to it that Ella always had fine clothes, he gave her costly pieces of jewelry, and he certainly never stinted on his sons' education" (*Son and Playwright*, 22).

24. In real life Eugene O'Neill did, in fact, initially enter the state hospital, but left after only two days. Subsequently, James O'Neill Sr. allowed Eugene to be treated at Gaylord Farm Sanatorium, where he was eventually cured (Sheaffer, *Son and Playwright*, 242–45).

25. Voglino, "'Games' the Tyrones Play," 98–100. Much of this paragraph is derived from the indicated pages of the "'Games'" article.

26. Sheaffer (*Son and Playwright*, 19) refers to Ella's "unhappiness" and "chronically low spirits" before conceiving Eugene. The Gelbs (*O'Neill*, 9, 54) appear to confirm this. Doris Alexander recounts a triple trauma as having devastated Ella prior to the birth of Eugene in October 1888: the death of her infant, the death of her mother, and surgery for breast cancer in the spring of 1887 (*Tempering of Eugene O'Neill*, 14). Sheaffer, however, refutes Alexander's assertion that Ella had a mastectomy as a young wife. He cites two extant doctors' reports that confirm that Ella underwent "breast amputation" in 1918, several years before her death in 1922 ("Correcting Some Errors, Part 1," 16–17).

27. Sheaffer asserts that the morphine not only freed Ella from pain but "from any feelings of loneliness and anxiety, and made life endurable" (*Son and Playwright*, 22). "According to medical evidence," the Gelbs note, "it is unusual for a person to become addicted to morphine unless she actively wishes to sustain the sense of unreality that it provides" (*O'Neill*, 59).

28. *The World Book Encyclopedia*, 1976 ed., s. v. "Drug Addiction, Treatment of."

29. According to Sheaffer, Tyrone's description of his father's death by poisoning, which both rumor and Edmund contend was not accidental (4.807), is biographically accurate regarding the death of Eugene O'Neill's paternal grandfather ("Correcting Some Errors, Part 1," 14).

30. Kermode, *Sense of an Ending*, 46.

31. Ibid., 54–55.

32. Barlow, *Final Acts*, 106–7; Long, *Role of Nemesis*, 217; and William Jennings Adams, "The Dramatic Structure of the Plays of Eugene O'Neill" (Ph.D. diss., Stanford University, 1956), 393.

33. Clive Barnes pays tribute to O'Neill's impartiality: "O'Neill never makes judgments in his plays—he is almost Shakespearean in his ambivalence to character" (review of *A Moon for the Misbegotten*, by Eugene O'Neill, as performed at the Morosco Theater, New York [1973]; reprinted in *New York Times Theater Reviews: 1973–1974* [New York: *New York Times* and Arno Press, 1975], 162).

34. O'Neill, to George Jean Nathan, 15 June 1940, in *Selected Letters*, ed. Bogard and Bryer, 506–7.

35. Barlow, *Final Acts*, 82–83.

36. Chothia, *Forging a Language*, 183.

37. "Ends have become difficult to achieve," concludes Peter Brooks. Traditional endings, he continues, have to a large extent been replaced with permanent deferral, game playing, or the stasis of irresolution (*Reading for the Plot*, 313–14).

38. See Smith, *Poetic Closure*, 102.

39. Barlow, *Final Acts*, 80–81.

40. See chapter 1, note 21, on Ella O'Neill's recovery from her addiction to morphine.

41. Chothia, *Forging a Language*, 182–83.

42. Jack Lemmon's portrayal of James Tyrone Sr. in the 1986 Broadway production emphasized the comically endearing aspects of Tyrone's character, which have often been overlooked.

43. Berlin, "The Beckettian O'Neill," 33–34.

44. Schmidt, "How Dramas End," 20–21.

45. Bigsby, *Critical Introduction*, 1:99.

46. Heilman, *The Iceman, the Arsonist, and the Troubled Agent*, 108.

47. Laurin Roland Porter, *The Banished Prince: Time, Memory and Ritual in the Late Plays of Eugene O'Neill*, Theater and Dramatic Studies 54 (Ann Arbor, Mich.: UMI Research Press, 1988), 89–91.

48. In real life, it should be remembered, the O'Neills fared somewhat better. Ella recovered from her addiction a few years later, and Eugene, with his father's help, recovered from tuberculosis and began writing plays.

49. Steven F. Bloom, "Empty Bottles, Empty Dreams: O'Neill's Use of Drinking and Alcoholism in *Long Day's Journey into Night*," in *Critical Essays on Eugene O'Neill*, ed. James J. Martine (Boston: G. K. Hall, 1984), 175–76.

50. Beckett, *Waiting for Godot*, act 1, 38.

51. Berlin, "The Beckettian O'Neill," 33.

52. Much of this paragraph is derived from Voglino, "'Games' the Tyrones Play," 102.

53. Albert Camus, *The Myth of Sisyphus and Other Essays*, trans. Justin O'Brien (New York: Vintage-Random House, 1955), 23.

54. Martin Esslin, *The Theatre of the Absurd*, rev. ed. (Garden City, N.Y.: Doubleday Anchor, 1969), 377.

CHAPTER 9. "HOPELESS HOPE": SUSPENSE IN *A MOON FOR THE MISBEGOTTEN*

1. Mary McCarthy, no title (1956), reprinted in *O'Neill and His Plays*, ed. Cargill, Fagin, and Fisher, 209–10; Falk, *O'Neill and the Tragic Tension*, 171–72.

2. Clive Barnes, review of *A Moon for the Misbegotten*, 162. See chapter 8, note 33.

3. Walter Kerr, "It's a Rich Play, Richly Performed," review of *A Moon for the Misbegotten*, by Eugene O'Neill, as performed at the Morosco Theater, New York; reprinted in *New York Times Theater Reviews: 1973–1974*, 170–71.

4. John Henry Raleigh, *The Plays of Eugene O'Neill* (Carbondale: Southern Illinois University Press, 1965), 242; Raghavacharyulu, *Eugene O'Neill: A Study*, 153; Timo Tiusanen, *O'Neill's Scenic Images* (Princeton: Princeton University Press, 1968), 311; Sheaffer, *Son and Artist*, 530; and Gelb and Gelb, *O'Neill*, 849.

5. Carpenter, *Eugene O'Neill*, 148.

6. Sheaffer, *Son and Artist*, 530.

7. Tiusanen, *O'Neill's Scenic Images*, 312–13.

8. Carpenter, *Eugene O'Neill*, 162–63.

9. Bogard, *Contour in Time*, 452; Suzanne Flèche-Salgues, "Trois Pièces Récentes d'Eugene O'Neill," *Études Anglaises* 10 (October–December 1957): 418–20.

10. Sheaffer, *Son and Artist*, 530.

11. *Moon* is not truly one of "the posthumous plays" like *Long Day's Journey into Night* and *Hughie*, which were performed in front of audiences only after O'Neill's death. Although *Moon* did not reach Broadway until 1957, several years after O'Neill's death in 1953, it was produced during his lifetime in Columbus, Ohio (1947), where it was unfavorably reviewed; in Pittsburgh, where it was attacked for "vulgarity" and "corn"; in Detroit, where it was briefly closed for "obscenity"; and in St. Louis, where it closed after one week (Sheaffer, *Son and Artist*, 595–96).

12. Allan Lewis, *American Plays and Playwrights of the Contemporary Theatre* (New York: Crown, 1965), 29.

13. Nicola Chiaromonte, "Eugene O'Neill," *Sewanee Review* 68 (Summer 1960): 499.

14. According to Edward L. Shaughnessy the virgin/whore complex is common among Irish-Catholic husbands and sons. Shaughnessy attributes this phenomenon to the bride's postnuptial practice of dedicating herself to the Blessed Virgin, a ritual dedication that, he

conjectures, makes her "in a sense untouchable or, if taken in love, somehow violated" (*Eugene O'Neill in Ireland: The Critical Reception*, Contributions in Drama and Theatre Studies 25 [New York: Greenwood Press, 1988], 12).

15. Porter, *Banished Prince*, 95.

16. James R. Scrimgeour, "From Loving to Misbegotten: Despair in the Drama of Eugene O'Neill," *Modern Drama* 20, no. 1 (1977): 52.

17. Schlueter, *Dramatic Closure*, 22.

18. Smith, *Poetic Closure*, 102.

19. Ibid., 34.

20. O'Neill, to John Peter Toohey, press agent for producer George C. Tyler, 5 November 1919, regarding O'Neill's hopes for *The Straw*; in *Selected Letters*, ed. Bogard and Bryer, 96. See the following paragraph for the more complete quotation.

21. Torgovnick, *Closure in the Novel*, 6.

22. O'Neill, to John Peter Toohey, press agent for producer George C. Tyler, November 1919, regarding O'Neill's hopes for *The Straw*; in *Selected Letters*, ed. Bogard and Bryer, 96.

23. Iser, *Implied Reader*, 290; Torgovnick, *Closure in the Novel*, 5; Schlueter, *Dramatic Closure*, 52–53; and Bernard Beckerman, *Dynamics of Drama: Theory and Method of Analysis* (New York: Alfred A. Knopf, 1970), 153–54.

24. Roger Brown, "Causality in O'Neill's Late Masterpieces," in *Eugene O'Neill's Century: Centennial Views on America's Foremost Tragic Dramatist*, ed. Richard F. Moorton (New York: Greenwood Press, 1991), 45.

25. Gelb and Gelb, *O'Neill*, 848–49.

26. Bogard, *Contour in Time*, 452–53.

27. Brown, "Causality in O'Neill's Late Masterpieces," 46.

28. Sheaffer, *Son and Artist*, 88.

29. Ibid., 594.

30. Sheaffer explains O'Neill's failure to visit the New Jersey sanitarium in which Jamie had been placed before his death as due to frustration and helplessness: "He [O'Neill] knew Jamie had set out to destroy himself, he was convinced there was nothing he could do about it (but he sent a specialist to Paterson several times to try and help), and he preferred to avoid a reunion that could only be painful on both sides" (*Son and Artist*, 116). Regarding O'Neill's failure to attend his brother's funeral or interment, Sheaffer indicates that O'Neill, recovering from a recent alcoholic binge, was too ill and heartsick to go (*Son and Artist*, 117).

CHAPTER 10. CONCLUSION

1. Bigsby, *Critical Introduction*, 1:117.

2. Blanke, "Die Dramenschlusse bei O'Neill," 154–55; passage translated from the German by Barbara Voglino.

3. Kermode, *Sense of an Ending*, 7.

4. See chapter 1, note 13. See also chapter 5 on *Days without End*.

5. Gelb and Gelb, *O'Neill*, 533; Sheaffer, *Son and Artist*, 117.

6. O'Neill, to Beatrice Ashe, 14 January 1915, in "Letters to Beatrice Ashe, 1914–1916."

7. O'Neill, to Malcolm Mollan, December 1921, in *Selected Letters*, ed. Bogard and Bryer, 159.

8. Bowen, *Curse of the Misbegotten*, 309.

9. Virginia Floyd uses this quotation in *New Assessment*, 284.

10. O'Neill, to Sophus Keith Winther, 1 May 1934, in *Selected Letters*, ed. Bogard and Bryer, 433. See also chapter 5, note 15.

11. Carpenter, *Eugene O'Neill*, 141. When O'Neill was on his deathbed in Boston, a Catholic priest attempted to see him in order to administer the sacrament of Extreme Unction. Carlotta refused to allow the priest to see her dying husband (Sheaffer, *Son and Artist*, 669), whom she buried apart from the O'Neill family with great secrecy (Sheaffer, *Son and Artist*, 672–73).

12. As cited by Chothia, *Forging a Language*, 108.

13. Jiji, "Audience Response in the Theater," 379.

14. According to Barbara Herrnstein Smith, we live in a suspicious age in which "the only resolution may be in the affirmation of irresolution, and conclusiveness may be seen as not only less honest but *less stable* than inconclusiveness" (*Poetic Closure*, 240–41).

15. Torgovnick, *Closure in the Novel*, 6.

16. For discussions on the relativity of the terms "open" and "closed," see R. M. Adams, *Strains of Discord*, 201; J. Hillis Miller, "The Problematic of Ending in Narrative," *Nineteenth-Century Fiction* 33, no. 1 (1978): 7; Joseph Allen Boone, *Tradition Counter Tradition: Love and the Form of Fiction* (1982), Women in Culture and Society Series (Chicago: University of Chicago Press, 1987), 146; and Booth, "Are Narrative Choices Subject to Ethical Criticism?," 65.

17. For views opposed to the ethical evaluation of the term "openness," see Booth ("Are Narrative Choices Subject to Ethical Criticism?," 75) and Gerlach (*Toward the End*, 8).

18. Jiji, "Audience Response in the Theater," 379.

19. Beckerman, *Dynamics of Drama*, 153–54.

20. William Faulkner, Nobel Prize Address (1952), in *Essays, Speeches and Public Letters*, ed. James B. Meriwether (New York: Random House, 1965), 120.

21. Carlotta released *Long Day's Journey* for publication and production several years after O'Neill's death, contending that the suicide of O'Neill's elder son, Eugene Jr., who she said had urged the restriction, made withholding the play from the public no longer necessary. According to Sheaffer, however, Carlotta betrayed O'Neill's wishes by releasing the play. In a letter to Bennet Cerf in 1951, almost a year after Eugene Jr.'s death, O'Neill wrote with regard to *Long Day's Journey*, "That, as you know is to be published twenty-five years after my death—but never produced as a play" (Louis Sheaffer, "Correcting Some Errors in Annals of O'Neill, Part 2," *Eugene O'Neill Newsletter* 8, no. 1 [1984]: 21).

Works Cited

Adams, Robert M. *Strains of Discord: Studies in Literary Openness*. Ithaca: Cornell University Press, 1958.

Adams, William Jennings. "The Dramatic Structure of the Plays of Eugene O'Neill." Ph.D. diss., Stanford University, 1956.

Adler, Thomas P. "A Cabin in the Woods, a Summerhouse in a Garden: Closure and Enclosure in O'Neill's *More Stately Mansions*." *Eugene O'Neill Newsletter* 9, no. 2 (1985): 23–27.

Alexander, Doris. *Eugene O'Neill's Creative Struggle: The Decisive Decade, 1924–1933*. University Park: Pennsylvania State University Press, 1992.

———. *The Tempering of Eugene O'Neill*. New York: Harcourt, Brace & World, 1962.

Antush, John V. "Eugene O'Neill: Modern and Postmodern." *Eugene O'Neill Review* 13, no. 1 (1989): 14–26.

Asselineau, Roger. "*Mourning Becomes Electra* as Tragedy." *Modern Drama* 1, no. 3 (1958): 143–50.

Baker, George Pierce. *Dramatic Technique*. New York: Houghton Mifflin, 1919.

Barlow, Judith E. *Final Acts: The Creation of Three Late O'Neill Plays*. Athens: University of Georgia Press, 1985.

Barnes, Clive. "'Day's Journey' to Glory: B'way at Its Greatest." Review of *Long Day's Journey into Night*, by Eugene O'Neill, as performed at the Broadhurst Theater, New York. Reprinted in *New York Theater Critics' Reviews: 1986*, edited by Joan Marlowe and Betty Blake, 304. New York: Critics' Theatre Reviews, 1986. First published in *New York Post*, 29 April 1986.

———. Review of *A Moon for the Misbegotten*, by Eugene O'Neill, as performed at the Morosco Theater, New York. Reprinted in *New York Times Theater Reviews: 1973–1974*, 162. New York: *New York Times* and Arno Press, 1975. First published in *New York Times*, 31 December 1973.

Beckerman, Bernard. *Dynamics of Drama: Theory and Method of Analysis*. New York: Alfred A. Knopf, 1970.

———. "Shakespeare Closing." *Kenyon Review* 7, no. 3 (1985): 79–95.

Beckett, Samuel. *Waiting for Godot*. New York: Grove Press, 1954.

Berlin, Normand. "The Beckettian O'Neill." *Modern Drama* 31, no. 1 (1988): 28–34.

———. "Endings." In *Eugene O'Neill's* The Iceman Cometh, edited by Harold Bloom, 95–106. New York: Chelsea House, 1987.

Betti, Ugo. "Religion and the Theatre." From *Corruption in the Palace of Justice*. 1949. Translated by Gino Rizzo and William Meriwether. In *The New Theatre of Europe*, edited by Robert W. Corrigan, 322–32. New York: Delta-Dell, 1962.

153

Bigsby, C. W. E. *A Critical Introduction to Twentieth-Century American Drama*. Vol. 1, *1900–1940*. New York: Cambridge University Press, 1982.

Blanke, Gustav H. "Die Dramenschlusse bei O'Neill." In *Das Amerikanische Drama von den Anfangen bis zur Gegenwart*, edited by Hans Itschert, 155–67. Darmstadt: Wissenschaftliche Buchgesellschaft, 1972.

Bloom, Steven F. "Empty Bottles, Empty Dreams: O'Neill's Use of Drinking and Alcoholism in *Long Day's Journey into Night*." In *Critical Essays on Eugene O'Neill*, edited by James J. Martine, 159–77. Boston: G. K. Hall, 1984.

Bogard, Travis. *Contour in Time: The Plays of Eugene O'Neill*. Rev. ed. New York: Oxford University Press, 1988.

Boone, Joseph Allen. *Tradition Counter Tradition: Love and the Form of Fiction*. Women in Culture and Society Series. Chicago: University of Chicago Press, 1987.

Booth, Wayne C. "Are Narrative Choices Subject to Ethical Criticism?" In *Reading Narrative: Form, Ethics, Ideology*, edited by James Phelan, 57–79. Columbus: Ohio State University Press, 1989.

Bowen, Croswell. *The Curse of the Misbegotten*. Written with the aid of Shane O'Neill. New York: McGraw-Hill, 1959.

Brooks, Peter. *The Melodramatic Imagination: Balzac, Henry James, Melodrama, and the Mode of Excess*. New Haven: Yale University Press, 1976.

———. *Reading for the Plot: Design and Intention in Narrative*. New York: Alfred A. Knopf, 1984.

Broun, Heywood. Review of *Beyond the Horizon*, by Eugene O'Neill. 1920. Reprinted in *Playwright's Progress: O'Neill and the Critics*, edited by Jordan Y. Miller, 17–18. Fairlawn, N.J.: Scott, Foresman, 1965.

Brown, Roger. "Causality in O'Neill's Late Masterpieces." In *Eugene O'Neill's Century: Centennial Views on America's Foremost Tragic Dramatist*, edited by Richard F. Moorton, 41–54. New York: Greenwood Press, 1991.

Brustein, Robert. Review of *The Emperor Jones*, by Eugene O'Neill, as performed by the Wooster Group at the Performing Garage, New York. *New Republic*, 27 April 1998, 28–30.

———. Review of *The Hairy Ape*, by Eugene O'Neill, as performed by the Wooster Group at the Selwyn Theater, New York. *New Republic*, 12 May 1997, 19–21.

———. *The Theatre of Revolt*. Boston: Little, Brown, 1964.

Camus, Albert. *The Myth of Sisyphus and Other Essays*. Translated from the French by Justin O'Brien. New York: Vintage-Random House, 1955.

Cargill, Oscar; N. Bryllion Fagin; and William J. Fisher, ed. *O'Neill and His Plays: Four Decades of Criticism*. New York: New York University Press, 1961.

Carpenter, Frederic I. *Eugene O'Neill*. Rev. ed. Twayne United States Authors Series 66. Boston: Twayne-G. K. Hall, 1979.

Chiaromonte, Nicola. "Eugene O'Neill." *Sewanee Review* 68 (Summer 1960): 494–501.

Chothia, Jean. *Forging a Language: A Study of the Plays of Eugene O'Neill*. New York: Cambridge University Press, 1979.

Clark, Barrett H. *Eugene O'Neill: The Man and His Plays*. Rev. ed. New York: Dover Publications, 1947.

Cohn, Ruby. "The Wet Sponge of Eugene O'Neill." In *Dialogue in American Drama*, 8–67. Bloomington: Indiana University Press, 1971.

Comens, Leslie Eric. Foreword to *Chris Christophersen*, by Eugene O'Neill. New York: Random House, 1982.

Conrad, Joseph. "Henry James: An Appreciation (1905)." In *Joseph Conrad on Fiction*, edited by Walter F. Wright, 82–88. Regents Critics Series. Lincoln: University of Nebraska Press, 1964.

Douglas, J. Yellowlees. "'How Do I Stop This Thing?': Closure and Indeterminacy in Interactive Narratives." In *Hyper/Text/Theory*, edited by George P. Landow, 159–88. Baltimore: Johns Hopkins University Press, 1994.

Eagleton, Terry. *Literary Theory: An Introduction*. Minneapolis: University of Minnesota Press, 1983.

Eliot, T. S. *The Complete Poems and Plays: 1909–1950*. New York: Harcourt, Brace, 1952.

———. Review of *All God's Chillun Got Wings*, by Eugene O'Neill. Reprinted in *O'Neill and His Plays: Four Decades of Criticism*, edited by Oscar Cargill, N. Bryllion Fagin, and William J. Fisher, 168–69. New York: New York University Press, 1961. First published in *Criterion*, 1926.

Engel, Edwin A. *The Haunted Heroes of Eugene O'Neill*. Cambridge: Harvard University Press, 1953.

———. "O'Neill 1960." *Modern Drama* 3, no. 3 (1960): 219–23.

Esslin, Martin. *The Theatre of the Absurd*. Rev. ed. Garden City, N.Y.: Doubleday Anchor, 1969.

Estrin, Mark W., editor. *Conversations with Eugene O'Neill*. Jackson: University Press of Mississippi, 1990.

Falk, Doris V. *Eugene O'Neill and the Tragic Tension*. New Brunswick, N.J.: Rutgers University Press, 1958.

Faulkner, William. Nobel Prize Address (1952). In *Essays, Speeches and Public Letters*, edited by James B. Meriwether, 120. New York: Random House, 1965.

Fergusson, Francis. "Melodramatist." Reprinted in *O'Neill and His Plays: Four Decades of Criticism*, edited by Oscar Cargill, N. Bryllion Fagin, and William J. Fisher, 271–82. New York: New York University Press, 1961. First published as "Eugene O'Neill," *Hound and Horn*, January 1930.

Fish, Stanley. "How to Recognize a Poem When You See One." In *Is There a Text in This Class? The Authority of Interpretive Communities*, 322–38. Cambridge: Harvard University Press, 1980.

Flèche-Salgues, Suzanne. "Trois Pièces Récentes d'Eugene O'Neill." *Études Anglaises* 10 (October–December 1957): 410–20.

Fletcher, John. *Samuel Beckett's Art*. London: Chatto & Windus, 1971.

Floyd, Virginia. *The Plays of Eugene O'Neill: A New Assessment*. New York: Frederick Ungar, 1985.

———, ed. *Eugene O'Neill: A World View*. New York: Frederick Ungar, 1979.

Gelb, Arthur, and Barbara Gelb. *O'Neill*. 1962. New York: Harper & Row, 1973.

Gerlach, John. *Toward the End: Closure and Structure in the American Short Story*. University: University of Alabama Press, 1985.

Golden, Joseph. "O'Neill and the Passing of Pleasure." In *The Death of Tinker Bell: The American Theatre in the Twentieth-Century*, 30–51. Syracuse, N.Y.: Syracuse University Press, 1967.

Gussow, Mel. "In a Sea of Symbolism." Review of *Welded*, by Eugene O'Neill, as performed at the Horace Mann Theater, Columbia University. Reprinted in *New York Times Theater Reviews: 1981–1982*, 127. New York: Times Books, 1984. First published in the *New York Times*, 19 June 1981.

Hawkes, Terence. "Opening Closure." *Modern Drama* 24, no. 3 (1981): 353–56.

Heilman, Robert Bechtold. *The Iceman, the Arsonist, and the Troubled Agent.* Seattle: University of Washington Press, 1973.

Hejinian, Lyn. "The Rejection of Closure." In *Writing/Talks*, edited by Bob Perelman, 270–91. Carbondale: Southern Illinois University Press, 1985.

Hofmannsthal, Hugo von. "Reflections on O'Neill." Reprinted in *O'Neill and His Plays: Four Decades of Criticism*, edited by Oscar Cargill, N. Bryllion Fagin, and William J. Fisher, 249–55. New York: New York University Press, 1961. First published in the *Freeman*, 21 March 1923.

Hult, David F. Preface to *Concepts of Closure*, edited by David F. Hult. Yale French Studies 67. New Haven: Yale University Press, 1984.

Iser, Wolfgang. *The Implied Reader: Patterns of Communication in Prose Fiction from Bunyan to Beckett.* Baltimore: Johns Hopkins University Press, 1974.

James, Henry. Preface to *The Portrait of a Lady*. From *The Notebooks* (1947). In *Perspectives on James's* The Portrait of a Lady: *A Collection of Critical Essays*, edited by William T. Stafford, 1–5. New York: New York University Press, 1967.

———. Preface to *Roderick Hudson*. London: Macmillan, 1921.

Jiji, Vera M . "Audience Response in the Theater: A Study of Dramatic Theory Tested against Reviewers' Responses to the Plays of Eugene O'Neill." Ph.D. diss., New York University, 1971.

Kalson, Albert E., and Lisa M. Schwerdt. "Eternal Recurrence and the Shaping of O'Neill's Dramatic Structures." In *Eugene O'Neill in China: An International Centenary Celebration*, edited by Haiping Liu and Lowell Swortzell, 71–88. New York: Greenwood Press, 1992.

Keats, John. Letter to George and Thomas Keats (21 December 1817). In *English Romantic Poetry and Prose*, edited by Russell Noys, 1211. New York: Oxford University Press, 1956.

Kemelman, H. G. "Eugene O'Neill and the Highbrow Melodrama" (1932). Reprinted in *Playwright's Progress: O'Neill and the Critics*, edited by Jordan Y. Miller, 94–105. Fairlawn, N.J.: Scott, Foresman, 1965.

Kermode, Frank. *The Sense of an Ending: Studies in the Theory of Fiction.* New York: Oxford University Press, 1966.

Kernan, Alvin B. *Character and Conflict: An Introduction to Drama.* 2d ed. New York: Harcourt, Brace & World, 1969.

Kerr, Walter. "It's a Rich Play, Richly Performed." Review of *A Moon for the Misbegotten*, by Eugene O'Neill, as performed at the Morosco Theater, New York. Reprinted in *New York Times Theater Reviews: 1973–1974*, 170–71. New York: *New York Times* and Arno Press, 1975. First published in the *New York Times*, 13 January 1974.

Koreneva, Maya. "One Hundred Percent American Tragedy: A Soviet View" (n.d.). In *Eugene O'Neill: A World View*, edited by Virginia Floyd, 145–71. New York: Frederick Ungar, 1979.

Krieger, Murray. "An Apology for Poetics." In *American Criticism in the Poststructuralist Age*, edited by Ira Konigsberg, 87–101. Michigan Studies in the Humanities. Ann Arbor: University of Michigan, 1981.

Krutch, Joseph Wood. *The American Drama since 1918*. Rev. ed. New York: George Braziller, 1957.

Lahr, John. "Selling the Sizzle." Review of *"Anna Christie,"* by Eugene O'Neill, as performed at the Roundabout Theater, New York. Reprinted in *New York Theatre Critics' Reviews: 1993*, edited by Norma Adler, Pat Willard, Joan Marlowe, and Betty Blake, 10–12. New York: Critics' Theatre Reviews, 1993. First published in *New Yorker*, 1 February 1993.

Leech, Clifford. *O'Neill*. New York: Barnes & Noble, 1963.

Lewis, Allan. *American Plays and Playwrights of the Contemporary Theatre*. New York: Crown, 1965.

Long, Chester Clayton. *The Role of Nemesis in the Structure of Selected Plays by Eugene O'Neill*. The Hague: Mouton, 1968.

McCarthy, Mary. (No title.) Reprinted in *O'Neill and His Plays: Four Decades of Criticism*, edited by Oscar Cargill, N. Bryllion Fagin, and William J. Fisher, 209–10. New York: New York University Press, 1961. First published in *Sights and Spectacles*, 1956.

Miller, J. Hillis. "The Problematic of Ending in Narrative." *Nineteenth-Century Fiction* 33, no. 1 (1978): 3–7.

Miller, Jordan Y., ed. *Eugene O'Neill and the American Critic: A Bibliographical Checklist*. Rev. ed. Hamden, Conn.: Archon-Shoe String Press, 1973.

———. *Playwright's Progress: O'Neill and the Critics*. Fairlawn, N.J.: Scott, Foresman, 1965.

Mollan, Malcolm. "Making Plays with a Tragic End: An Intimate Interview with Eugene O'Neill, Who Tells Why He Does It" (1922). In *Conversations with Eugene O'Neill*, edited by Mark W. Estrin, 13–20. Jackson: University Press of Mississippi, 1990.

Morehouse, Ward, III. "'Anna Christie' Sends Off Sparks." Review of *"Anna Christie,"* by Eugene O'Neill, as performed at the Roundabout Theater, New York. Reprinted in *New York Theatre Critics' Reviews: 1993*, edited by Norma Adler, Pat Willard, Joan Marlowe, and Betty Blake, 6–7. New York: Critics' Theatre Reviews, 1993. First published in *Christian Science Monitor*, 21 January 1993.

Mortimer, Armine Kotin. *La Clôture Narrative*. Paris: José Corti, 1985.

Mullett, Mary B. "The Extraordinary Story of Eugene O'Neill" (1922). In *Conversations with Eugene O'Neill*, edited by Mark W. Estrin, 26–37. Jackson: University Press of Mississippi, 1990.

Myers, Mary Kay Zettl. "Closure in the Twentieth-Century American Problem Play." Ph.D. diss., University of Delaware, 1992. Ann Arbor: UMI, 1993. AAG9301793.

Nightingale, Benedict. "In London, Three Revelations of Cosmic Despair." Review of *The Iceman Cometh*, by Eugene O'Neill, as performed at the Almeida Theater, London. *New York Times*, 19 May 1998.

O'Neill, Eugene. *Complete Plays*. Edited by Travis Bogard. 3 vols. New York: Library of America, 1988.

———. "Letters to Beatrice Ashe, 1914–1916." MS located in the Berg Collection of English and American Literature. The New York Public Library. Astor, Lenox and Tilden Foundations.

———. "Memoranda on Masks." In *Playwrights on Playwriting: The Meaning and Making of Modern Drama from Ibsen to Ionesco*, edited by Toby Cole, 65–71. New York: Hill and Wang, 1960. First published in *American Spectator*, 1 November 1932.

———. *Selected Letters of Eugene O'Neill*. Edited by Travis Bogard and Jackson R. Bryer. New Haven: Yale University Press, 1988.

Orr, John. *Tragic Drama and Modern Society: Studies in the Social and Literary Theory of Drama from 1870 to the Present.* London: Macmillan Press, 1983.

Plato. *Republic.* In *The Collected Dialogues of Plato,* edited by Edith Hamilton and Huntington Cairns. Bollingen Series 71. Princeton: Princeton University Press, 1963.

Porter, Laurin Roland. *The Banished Prince: Time, Memory and Ritual in the Late Plays of Eugene O'Neill.* Theater and Dramatic Studies 54. Ann Arbor: UMI Research Press, 1988.

Quinn, Arthur Hobson. *A History of the American Drama from the Civil War to the Present Day.* Rev. ed. 2 vols. New York: Appleton-Century-Crofts, 1936.

Racey, Edgar F., Jr. "Myth as Tragic Structure in *Desire under the Elms.*" In *O'Neill: A Collection of Critical Essays,* edited by John Gassner, 57–61. Twentieth Century Views S-TC-9. Englewood Cliffs, N.J.: Prentice-Hall, 1964.

Raghavacharyulu, D. V. K. *Eugene O'Neill: A Study.* Bombay: G. R. Bhatkal, Popular Prakashan, 1965.

Raleigh, John Henry. *The Plays of Eugene O'Neill.* Carbondale: Southern Illinois University Press, 1965.

————, ed. *Twentieth Century Interpretations of* The Iceman Cometh: *A Collection of Critical Essays.* Englewood Cliffs, N.J.: Prentice-Hall, 1968.

Rich, J. Dennis. "Exile without Remedy: The Late Plays of Eugene O'Neill." In *Eugene O'Neill: A World View,* edited by Virginia Floyd, 257–78. New York: Frederick Ungar, 1979.

Richter, David H. "Closure and the Critics." *Modern Philology* 80, no. 3 (1983): 287–92.

Scheick, William J. "The Ending of O'Neill's *Beyond the Horizon.*" *Modern Drama* 20, no. 3 (1977): 293–99.

Schlueter, June. *Dramatic Closure: Reading the End.* Madison, N.J.: Fairleigh Dickinson University Press, 1995.

Schmidt, Henry J. *How Dramas End: Essays on the German Sturm und Drang, Buchner, Hauptmann, and Fleisser.* Ann Arbor: University of Michigan Press, 1992.

Scrimgeour, James R. "From Loving to Misbegotten: Despair in the Drama of Eugene O'Neill." *Modern Drama* 20, no. 1 (1977): 37–53.

Shapiro, Karl. *In Defense of Ignorance.* New York: Random House, 1952.

Shaughnessy, Edward L. *Down the Nights and Down the Days: Eugene O'Neill's Catholic Sensibility.* Notre Dame, Ind.: University of Notre Dame Press, 1996.

————. "Ella, James, and Jamie O'Neill." *The Eugene O'Neill Review* 15, no. 2 (1991): 5–92.

————. *Eugene O'Neill in Ireland: The Critical Reception.* Contributions in Drama and Theatre Studies 25. New York: Greenwood Press, 1988.

Sheaffer, Louis. "Correcting Some Errors in Annals of O'Neill, Part 1." *Eugene O'Neill Newsletter* 7, no. 3 (1983): 13–25.

————. "Correcting Some Errors in Annals of O'Neill, Part 2." *Eugene O'Neill Newsletter* 8, no. 1 (1984): 16–22.

————. *O'Neill: Son and Artist.* Boston: Little, Brown, 1973. Reprint, New York: Paragon House, 1990.

————. *O'Neill: Son and Playwright.* Boston: Little, Brown, 1968.

Smith, Barbara Herrnstein. *Poetic Closure: A Study of How Poems End.* Chicago: University of Chicago Press, 1968.

Tiusanen, Timo. *O'Neill's Scenic Images.* Princeton: Princeton University Press, 1968.

Torgovnick, Marianna. *Closure in the Novel.* Princeton: Princeton University Press, 1981.

Törnqvist, Egil. *A Drama of Souls: Studies in O'Neill's Super-naturalistic Technique.* New Haven: Yale University Press, 1969.

Trilling, Lionel. "Eugene O'Neill." In *Modern Critical Views: Eugene O'Neill,* edited by Harold Bloom, 13–20. New York: Chelsea House, 1987.

Voglino, Barbara. "'Games' the Tyrones Play." *The Eugene O'Neill Review* 16, no. 1 (1992): 91–103.

Wilkins, Frederick. "The Pressure of Puritanism in O'Neill's New England Plays." In *Eugene O'Neill: A World View,* edited by Virginia Floyd, 237–44. New York: Frederick Ungar, 1979.

Woollcott, Alexander. Review of *Beyond the Horizon,* by Eugene O'Neill (1920). Reprinted in *Playwright's Progress: O'Neill and the Critics,* edited by Jordan Y. Miller, 19–20. Fairlawn, N.J.: Scott, Foresman, 1965.

Zeiger, E. James. Review of *The Iceman Cometh,* by Eugene O'Neill, as performed at the Germinal Stage, Denver. *The Eugene O'Neill Review* 16, no. 1 (1992): 111–15.

Index

Usage Guide: Parenthetical inclusions of the words "quoted," "paraphrased," "reference," or "citing . . ." after a page number indicate that the author's name does not appear on that page. The reader should check the notes (also listed) applicable to that page for the correct reference.

162 Index